Our Father, who art in bed

Grateful acknowledgement is made to Peter Owen Ltd, London, for permission to reprint excerpts from Siddhartha by Hermann Hesse.

ISBN: 1-4196-7662-8
ISBN-13: 978-1419676628

A NAIVE AND
SENTIMENTAL DUBLINER
IN THE LEGION OF CHRIST

OUR FATHER, WHO ART IN BED

J. PAUL LENNON, IRISH
CO-FOUNDER
OF THIS MEXICAN ORDER

2008

Our Father, who art in bed

CONTENTS

ACKNOWLEDGMENTS

During the writing I came to fully realize how much I love my deceased parents, Jack Lennon and Christine O'Connor, and my sisters Patty, Mary, Carmel and Christine with their families who welcomed me with open arms after many years of estrangement caused by my membership in the Legion of Christ.

I am also very indebted to Jose Barba, Juan-Jose Vaca, Arturo Jurado, Alejandro Espinosa, Saúl Barrales, and other survivors of sexual abuse by Marcial Maciel who provided information and support.

I will always fondly remember my old Legion confreres, the wonderful people of the Quintana Roo Mission in Mexico, and even my students in Mexico City who, for the most part, turned their backs on me after I left the Legion and dared criticize Father Maciel.

Thanks to those who touched me and were touched by me during my Legionary life and priestly ministry, and to

REGAIN friends and supporters who enriched me over the past fifteen years; to

My fellow-travelers, believers and non-believers, to

My colleagues at the International Cultic Studies Association, and to

Diana M., my clinical supervisor, and the team at the Child and Family Services Division, DHS.

My close Spanish and English-speaking friends have accompanied me during the past twenty years with the warmth of their friendship and hospitality: Roberto & Romelia, Alberto & Judith, Gustavo & Maria Luisa, Esmeralda & Eugene, and Sally, Theo & Sybil.

Gracias a la familia Conde-Medina de Chetumal y Mérida.

Special brotherly thanks to Glenn and Kevin. Thanks to Gerry Renner, RIP, and Jason Berry for advice, to Diana Friedman and Mike Livingston for their generous editorial help during the final stretch, and to Alberto for his expertise with the photos.

To beloved Ireland that bore me,
To Mexico that made me, and
To the Land of the Free that welcomed me.

St. Nicholas of Myra, Dublin, August 15, 1939

To My Dear Friend, Father Peter Cronin, R.I.P.,
And All Other Legion Of Christ And Regnum Christi
Survivors Who Truthfully Tell Their Tale

FOREWORD

Frank McCourt, move over! If you could make millions out of telling your tale of a miserable Irish Catholic childhood, why shouldn't I be able to make at least a few hundred out of my exciting Irish Catholic story with the Legion of Christ Mexican religious order? You were born in the USA and spent your miserable childhood in Ireland. I was born in Dublin, had no miserable childhood, but then spent most of my early adult life being miserable in Spain, Italy and Mexico. It all started off very nice but by the time it was over I was on the verge of a nervous breakdown, and feeling very sorry for myself.

That was in 1984 when I got out. Since I left Mexico and came to the USA in 1985, life has improved; from being a plain nervous wreck I became a nervous wreck in recovery. With no intention here of vying with memoirs that may be more literary and amusing, I will tell the simple and serious saga of a naïve and sentimental Dublin Catholic boy and his Passion for, Death with and Resurrection after the Legion of Christ.

This story is indisputably unique: I have always been burdened by that serious character defect, castigated by Novice Instructor, Father Arumí, in the Explanation of Rules as a no-no for any Legionary aspirant: *el individualismo*, individualism. But it is also universal, one with which many Legionaries can identify, and in which they will find themselves reflected. Those who did not reach premature ordination in the Legion may sigh: “there but for the grace of God go I”. On the other hand, I have no regrets about my twenty-three years in the Legion: somehow, I did it my way.

1
RECRUITING

Goodbye (*The White Horse Inn*)

Words & Music by Ralph Benatsky

My heart is broken, but what care I? Such pride inside me has woken; I shall do my best not to cry, by and by,
When the final farewells must be spoken.
I'll join the legion, that's what I'll do, and in some far distant region,
Where human hearts are staunch and true; I shall start my life anew.
Goodbye, it's time I sought a foreign clime,
Where I may find there are hearts more kind than I leave behind.
And so I go to fight the savage foe,
Although I know that I'll be sometimes missed by the girls I've kissed. [. . .]
I'll do or die, or know the reason why when told,
Of boldly opposed last stands for the fatherland.

Goodbye. Goodbye. I wish you all a last "Goodbye".
Goodbye. Goodbye. I wish you all a last "Goodbye"

Remembered by the writer in the stirring rendition of Irish tenor Joseph McLaughlin, also known as Josef Locke.

BUNDORAN BY THE SEA

A free trip to Bundoran in County Donegal changed my life forever. On July 1, 1961, as the beige VW van swung into Bundrowes House gravel driveway, my heretofore unremarkable life took a dramatic turn. In that glorious setting of sheer cliffs, wide beaches, salt breezes, and soft hills I would begin the first lap of my vacation-cum-vocation with then unknown Mexican Order, the Legion of Christ. Little did I suspect that as the van crunched to a halt my life was pulling away on a vertiginous tour full of pleasant, and unpleasant, surprises.

Beaming bright and warm on that Saturday afternoon, the sun spot-lighted a bunch of shirts, ties, and jackets tumbling carefree onto the gravel. About a dozen Dubliners and Limerick men had been packed into the van, with names like Donal, Brian, Adrian, Dermot, Brendan, Colm, Páraic, Fintan, Damien, and Liam, all fine specimens of Irish late teens. There must have been at least one more vehicle, as over twenty recruits eventually lined up to be snapped against the backdrop of our temporary abode, Bundrowes House, a once fashionable Georgian mansion. Its name, from the Gaelic, "the mouth of the Drowes," describes how the residence was built at the river estuary as it flows into Donegal Bay. To this day the river is renowned for its salmon and sea trout. On that idyllic first day we were not aware that Father Maciel, the founder of this young Mexican religious order new to Ireland, had decided to make this picturesque spot his fishing grounds for vocations to the Catholic priesthood. Although the charismatic Maciel had originally targeted the teeming banks of Dublin Bay, Archbishop John Charles McQuaid had been unyielding. The Legion would be allowed to recruit competitively in the diocese of Dublin but not set up house there. So the resourceful young founder would bring recruits from Dublin and other parts of Ireland to summer camp in beautiful Bundoran.

Most of the gullible young salmon eagerly leaping upstream had recently passed their Leaving Certificate Exam "with honors"—naturally, for to even think of becoming a priest required being endowed with more than average intelligence. Earning academic honors is not the same as being smart.

In the Ireland of the late '50s and early '60s, with a Catholic Church that was alive, strong and vibrant in home, school and society, entering a seminary or a convent seemed a very viable and acceptable career choice—one of the best available to a generation of limited options. A rapier thrust from hard-nosed psychologist, Mona Shevlin, would many years later puncture my presumptuous bubble at the Catholic University of America: "Was the seminary a door to higher studies?"

Thousands of youth were being forced to flee the country for England, the USA, and Australia in search of employment. Entry-level positions in technical, commercial, accounting, book-keeping or bureaucracy of some kinds were available to low-income youth. But college or university was not a viable choice for the majority of high-school graduates in the Ireland of the early 1960s. Achievement-based university scholarships were for the gifted. In that situation, a "vocation" as an overseas missionary opened the door to pursue higher studies free of charge, avoid the monotony of family life, and escape the cultural and geographical confines of our tiny, backward, and at times bigoted country.

Seven out of twenty-eight graduates of my St. Vincent's Christian Brothers High School were to enter seminary that year. The three of us who joined the Legion felt we had made the best choice. Single-handedly, charismatic Father James Coindreau sold us on how attractive it would be to join his new and modern religious order. The lyrics of "I'll join the Legion" faithfully reflected our indomitable do or die spirit as we sped towards Bundoran. Some months previously the "Texan Padre" had come to our school inviting us to try out as the first Irish candidates of this exotic order called the Legion of Christ. He apologized for not bringing his guitar to serenade the class with the "Ay, ay, ay, ay" of *Cielito Lindo.* A blocky five-foot-eight, always ramrod straight and full of positive energy, the handsome suntanned recruiter hailed from San Antonio, Texas or Monterrey, Mexico, as the audience required. Jimmy with the sleek black hair must have already kissed the Blarney *Piedra* back home. His enthusiasm was contagious, igniting our idealism, generosity and trust. At the time we said "yes" he was the only Legion member we had ever met, and we took his word the Legion was the place to be: a Mexican order for Mexico and Latin America in response to Pope John XXIII's plea for missionary priests seemed so much better than any of the Irish-born or more established institutions.

Warm fantasies of Spain, Rome, Mexico and Latin America were soon fueling the imagination of one who had left Ireland only once before for murky Liverpool via the Port of Holyhead on the Isle of Anglesey in North Wales. Lacking experience, exposure and alternative enticements, without second thoughts, I chose the Legion try-out. The fact that the venture was sponsored by the Catholic Church assuaged the cautious and insecure aspects of my nature while simultaneously attracting the unconventional adventurer hidden inside that short working-class teenager. I hoped to be successful and do a lot of good. The Legion adventure in Latin America would also satisfy other—then unconscious—deeply hidden drives: I would always be needed; I would always be loved; I would never be rejected.

In the van that day, as we sped toward Bundoran, we had been singing the popular songs of the time: Elvis, Ricky Nelson, Roy Orbison, Connie Francis, The Everly Brothers, Paul Anka, and an assortment of Irish standbys and Scottish favorites like "Keep right on to the end of the road". "I'll join the Legion" from *The White Horse Inn*, very popular at the time, was also lustily rendered. Pearse Allen adapted the lyrics of "It's a long way to Tipperary" and wanted it to be our anthem as future novices.

We were not fans of mushy Mel Torme's "In our mountain greenery" or sensuous Peggy Lee's "You give me fever!", and maybe even jaunty Guy Mitchell with his "She wears red feathers and a hula-hula skirt" was off limits. Frankie Lane's Jezebel told us just how dangerous girls could be and maybe we would have to renounce Johnny Ray's "Walkin' my baby back home" over meadows and fields "in a white sport coat and a pink carnation".

Celts sing in love and war. I sang along and was quite lively and gregarious the day we drove to Bundoran, coming out of my shy shell. I do not know whether I sang because I was happy or because I was trying to be happy. Father James created an atmosphere of heady excitement and euphoria. Underneath, my heart was heavy; the butterflies in my stomach lively, and the lump stuck in my throat hard and sour as a lemon drop when I took leave of parents and sisters. It meant leaving behind the warmth of next-door neighbors Mr. and Mrs. McCann and their bunch of good-natured children, Mr. and Mrs. McEvoy with Paddy, Val and Linda, Mrs. Slattery across the back garden who always referred to her husband as "John, God love him," Mrs. Freeman, whose husband, Tucker, was permanently in blackface because he worked shoveling coal on the docks; and kind Mrs. Dineen, the country lady with hens in the back yard on the corner of Faussagh Avenue and Broombridge Road.

Life was never boring in Cabra West, the Dublin Corporation housing scheme designed in the 1940s to lure inner-city families out of tenements such as Lower Kevin St. where my mother was born. My parents were very proud of the semi-detached two-story house allotted to them. Daddy's salary at Alex Thom & Son, Printers, Ltd, of just over £5.00 a week, judiciously administered by my mother, covered the rent and utilities, and left enough over for food, clothing and the occasional treat.

I lived on Fassaugh Avenue, the main road, and the number 22 bus terminal was just outside my door. This was bane and boom—we lacked privacy by always having people ten yards from our front door queuing up for the bus outside, but we could peek at them with their foibles from behind lace curtains.—A little unselfconscious 5-year-old, I would straddle the wall as if on horseback and people-watch. "Mad Joe," a deranged young man harassing the women at the bus stop, would simultaneously fascinate and frighten me. I was not sure what he meant by shouting "rubber hump!"—But it sounded like something vulgar. People would smile, say nothing, and turn away.

"Bang-Bang from Inchicore," another mentally ill man, would jump onto the double-decker open platform, hold onto the pole of the moving vehicle, pull an imaginary pistol out of his imaginary holster and "shoot" bystanders on the sidewalk. Many would duck and run for cover to humor him. These were the people of Dublin: sharp-tongued, compassionate and fun-loving.

Another great advantage of my house was the vacant lot just across the road on the corner of Rathoat: "gypsies" (in reality, Irish itinerants) set up their caravans there a few times a year. While ponies grazed peacefully on the grass, their ragged children played and scared us away. On other occasions small fairs would set up shop with amusements to entertain the neighborhood families.

As I grew into late childhood and was able to withdraw from Mammy's close supervision, I played soccer and "rounders"—a mix of cricket and baseball—on Broomer, a side road, and got chased by the coppers. I often ignored my mother's pleas: "Paul, come in, you're not supposed to be playing on the street!" She was always concerned about me associating with those "rough" boys, but I was happy with them. Others might have considered them "gurriers," but they were my friends. Together with Jackie Walsh, tan-skinned Jamesie Gilligan, and the Guineys I would defy the authorities, jumping over the low walls running through the front gardens and in around the houses into the back yards when the local "rozzer" came prowling on his bike. We were proud to include one Protestant in our gang, Alfie, a real nice guy.

Chrissie, Paul, Jack, Mary, Christine & Carmel

Some of the other kids were more physically daring than me. They would *scut* the buses that took off from outside my house: while the bus conductor was busying himself collecting the fares and ringing them up on his little ticket machine, one or two boys would latch onto the back of the moving bus. Keeping their feet off the ground, they would hang onto the rear fender with their hands and arms to feel the thrill of speed. Then the other kids would shout "look behind and lash the whip!" to alert the conductor. At this he would peer around the entrance to see whether there was anyone *scutting*. He would shout at the *bowsies* to let go. If they didn't, he would take off the leather strap that passed over his shoulders holding the ticket machine. He would try to dislodge the *scutter* with a swing of the belt, with more or less intention to do bodily harm, according to his personality. Pretty risky business, and one of the reasons my neighborhood was called the Wild West. But that was tame compared to the joy-riding that became popular in the 1970s when young people stole cars and raced the police squads up and down Faussagh Avenue. With that and an outbreak of petty burglary, my mother left the family home and moved to Ennis, County Clare, with my sister Christine and her husband, Christy. On July 1st, 1961, without second thoughts I left behind those familiar and beloved streets of my childhood.

For a shy person, revealing such a personal decision as a vocation trial was not easy; nor was saying good-bye. I remember telling my high school teacher on the last day of class that I was considering a seminary. Brother Earnest Carew, Ernie, always fair and respectful to students, looked at me with a smile and ground out in his habitual way from behind clenched teeth: "Well, well, well, Mr. Lennon, you certainly kept that one up your sleeve." He wished me well.

The reaction I got from my soccer coach, Seán Goggins, was less encouraging. He had known me for many years and must never have noticed my inclination for the religious life...He had watched me train in the rain and mud, mix and joke with team mates, and play on Sunday mornings with so much passion.

He only knew my smart-alecky outward shell of toughness and glib remarks One evening, as we were leaving the training pitch in Santry on our bicycles, a couple of girls walked by. My tongue got ahead of my brain and, "Hey, young ones, do yis want a lift on me crossbar?" somehow slipped out. Immediately I felt hot crimson fire sear my cheeks and neck, as I turned to see the shocked look on Seán's face. Now he was disconcerted when I told him I was going away. "You certainly had me fooled." I felt I owed it to him to tell him but I did not tell any of my football pals, anyone from the tennis club or my school chums, fearing they would not understand, or call me a sissy.

But perhaps Seán was right. I did not have the clerical look about me; that sanctimonious, holier-than-thou, butter-wouldn't-melt-in-your-mouth look. I have never been solemn, at least not consciously or as a pose. People who take themselves too seriously or parade around with an air of supercilious superiority are almost certain to become the butt of a Dubliner's wit. "Who the hell does he think he is?" There is something instinctual in us that wants to take the proud and the vain down a peg. So I was not "priest material" in the conventional sense of the term.

The day before leaving home, I had carefully packed my dusty brown cardboard suit case. Mammy, from her meager finances, and following Fr. James' instructions, had bought me enough clothes to "go away": six pairs of underwear and socks smelling nice and new. Sewn to each item was a personal name tag, from Arnott's, the fancy store on Henry St.

As I sucked the briny sea air deep into my lungs that fateful late July 1 afternoon, I noticed with disappointment we were not the absolutely first candidates to this new order. Half a dozen other young "Postulants" in frayed black cassocks, recruited earlier during the school term, were standing in the driveway ready to greet us. While appreciating the reception, I felt neither overly impressed nor totally displaced by these earlier recruits. To us Dubliners they were "culchies," provincials, who were not up to our Dublin, "jackeen," standards. I wonder now how *they* felt that first day when we new guys crashed the founders' exclusive party! I do know that they warmly, if awkwardly, received each one of us with a Mexican hug, the Legionary "abrazo," which was to be part of our new life. That first time was really uncomfortable. Some of us would not have known how to embrace a woman, never mind a man. But I liked the novelty and wanted to learn Mexican customs.

> Old photos and footage I recently discovered in Jason Berry's documentary on *Vows of Silence* reveal a slightly earlier Legion foray into Ireland during that 1960-61 school term. They portray Frs. Maciel, Félix Alarcón and Neftalí Sanchez in a group with the pre-pioneers. One blurry take shows the neophytes receiving the religious habit from the founder, and therefore beginning their Novitiate months before our arrival! This ceremony, of course, would have been held clandestinely, or at least privately, as it had not been officially sanctioned by Catholic authorities. As the Archbishop of Dublin, Monsignor John Charles McQuaid, had not permitted the Legion to open a house in his diocese, the Legion was only allowed to open a summer vacation center on an experimental basis in faraway Donegal. In order for our first group to legitimately begin Novitiate we would have

> to travel to Salamanca, Spain, where in 1961 the Legion had their one and only sanctioned Novitiate. In July 1961 I was ignorant of the fact that the older brothers already had discreetly taken the habit, and so my illusion of being one of the very first Irish Legionaries remained intact.

We had not the slightest idea of what we were getting into. I must admit in hindsight that on entering the Legion I knew next to nothing about the Religious Life and the Practice of the Vows. I had not realized that would be part of the Legion packet. My goal was to be a Missionary priest in Latin America. During the next couple of years I would accept the demanding rules of Legion Consecrated Religious Life as a toll to be paid on the road to becoming a priest. At the beginning I had not even seriously considered the heavy responsibilities of the priesthood and celibacy as I flung myself impetuously into the breach.

A strong and generous spirit throbbed forcefully in our innocent young temples. Everything was new and different and exciting. We immediately attempted to adjust and bond. During the following days I got on well with the other fellows. I knew how to please everyone and was always ready with a smile or a joke. It was good to feel liked and accepted by everyone.

There were some artistic elements among us, boys who painted landscapes and portraits: Damien, Adrian and Jude, I can remember. Jude, a handsome sandy-head with a Kirk Douglas Van Gogh cleft-chin, was as gentle as a kitten and wouldn't hurt a fly. He used to get on my nerves sometimes though; if I bumped into him at games he would apologize, whether it was his fault or not. He was always walking around with a Spanish dictionary in his hand, a real "swot." Such was his flair for languages. Still a Legionary today, he became a Scripture scholar. Sad to say, I lost track of the other two artistes.

Declan was the most popular. Standing 6' 3" in his stocking feet he was outgoing and good-natured. Father James liked to say he plucked Declan out of rock 'n' roll to follow Christ. Actually, he did play in a band and could belt out Jerry Lee Lewis's "Great Balls of Fire" or Floyd Kramer's "On the Rebound" pretty well. With himself, Pearse and company we had great sing-alongs during our time at Bundrowes. Dec always encouraged me to have a go at those Dean Martin songs. He thought I sounded like Deano. I had wanted to be Johnny Mathis or Perry Como. But I was to surrender all that to be one of the first Irish founding members of the Legion of Christ. Our generation did not have a problem with delayed gratification—inspired as we were by Harry Lauder's popular Scottish song:

Keep right on to the end of the road
Keep right on to the end
Tho' the way be long, let your heart be strong
Keep right on to the end
Tho' you're tired and weary still journey on,
Till you come to your happy abode
Where all you love, you've been dreaming of
Will be there, at the end of the road

***

Postulancy & Padres

After a few weeks we joyfully welcomed new reinforcements from Rome. One was recently ordained Father Neftalí Sánchez Tinoco. We were impressed to learn that he was one of the very first Mexican 10-year-olds Father Maciel recruited for his junior seminary during the order's early foundation period in the 1940s. Three other new staff members also arrived at Bundrowes. We began addressing them as *Padre*; however, they, like our recruiter, were not ordained priests or even deacons, but rather theology students. I liked having these "assistants" with us during our daily activities, including playing basketball and soccer, lending a certain *gravitas* to our high jinks: "Fathers" Ramiro Fernandez, huge by Mexican standards—a wall on the soccer field—who always seemed child-like in his demeanor; Angel Sáez, a dark-haired Spaniard with thick horn-rimmed glasses, with the most intellectual look of the three; and Francisco (Orozco) Yépez, the most playful and endearing one.

Despite my holy side I played soccer like a demon to beat Padre Yépez, scaled mountains like a goat to beat Ramiro, and did not mind getting on Angel's nerves because he took himself so seriously. One day as I was helping Padre Angel sweep up the dust I kept dragging the dustpan away from his brush so the remaining dust slipping under the pan could be picked up. He misunderstood and got angry because he thought I was toying with him. "You are like a man in a circus," he blurted petulantly; I supposed he meant a clown. I felt put down and angered by his outburst but said nothing. I had been well trained by the Irish Christian brothers to keep my mouth shut. At least to some extent.

Physical punishment, as in "biffing," was routine with the brothers. Most had a leather strap they kept under their cassock. It was standard size and must have been sold at the Irish Christian Brothers' outfitters; they came in a choice of colors, black and brown. This light official weapon was not enough for the real sadists—they preferred a long strip of thick rubber linoleum, a quarter or half an inch thick, which could really bite into the flesh of the palm leaving you bruised and swollen. To shouts of "You will do your homework" or, in my case, "You will not answer back"-the livid-faced brother, jowls trembling, would take a little bounce on his toes to lend more impetus to his wallop. Compared to this, Angel was easy to take—not to say it didn't hurt.

Bedtime was fun time. We were supposed to keep silence—remote preparation for the monastic great—silence from after last prayers until after breakfast the next morning. This is where our assistants came in. Ramiro, the impassive Mexican from a small town in the state of Michoacán with an unpronounceable name, Tangancícuaro, would watch over us at lights-out trying to keep us from devilment. He was so large and silent he looked like a totem pole topped by a lizard head with protruding eyes. Though paler than Father Neftalí, he had the stealthy Indian way about him: at any time, he could pop up unexpectedly and stand staring at you with those round unblinking eyes. His claim to fame and admiration was that Father Maciel had recruited him for the Legion when he was only nine. Some of those first Legionaries came from large families of 12 or 15. I surmised that maybe their parents would not miss one from the bunch.

On many afternoons, we played soccer and swam at isolated and pristine Mullaghmore, not far from the house. Those of us who were good soccer players could show off our skills and vie with the Padres and the Assistants who were quite good. Another great attraction for energetic and competitive young colts was the nearby hills. Climbing up the steep boggy sides we tested our stamina against nature, the foreigners, and each other. At 5' 3" and about 130 pounds, my wiry determination won me many a race to the top, proudly beating even Father James and the other padres.

A kind older—aged about 20—Irish student acted as my "angel" guide during Postulancy. Brother James Whiston, hailing from County Dublin, came to Bundrowes months before our big batch arrived in July. Wearing worn buttonless black cassocks held around the waist with a simple black sash, he and the other "older brothers" took their Postulancy very earnestly, as if they were already Novices. I remember that Pearse Allen, Michael Caheny (from Co. Sligo), Francis Coleman, Declan French (from Co. Waterford), Sean Keane (from Co. Westmeath), and Maurice Oliver McGowan from just a few farms down the road in County Leitrim, also belonged to that group. We liked and respected the young and quietly driven Oliver, who was always "very edifying" in his conduct. Soon renamed "Maurice" by Father Maciel, he would be the very first Irish Legionary ordained a priest.

During the months prior to the trip I had been writing to Father James Coindreau in Bundoran. Now as Bro. Whiston and I became acquainted, he confessed that he had written the personal letters I received from "Father James." This implied he had read my letters to the Padre, which I had assumed were confidential. Though hurt and disconcerted, I did not dwell on this, or resent it, since my beginner's acceptance of the Legion was unqualified and boundless. James Whiston took me under his wing and gave me some advice: "Everyone will treat you well here if you just keep quiet and stay out of mischief." He remarked that I wasn't as serious as I sounded in my letters. I decided to try to behave more seriously.

The novelty of the fast nonstop pace of daily life, full of hikes to the sea, mountain climbing, swimming, soccer and basketball, Spanish classes and chores, was thoroughly enjoyable. Father James began our days with First Prayers and Morning Meditation and ended them with Examination of Conscience and "Points for Meditation" at Last Prayers. How amused we were by Father James' pronunciation of "Jesus hanging 'nak't' on the cross." For me it added to the Legion's attractive "foreignness"

***

First pieces of advice

As the first crop from our country to join this Mexican order, we felt most privileged to be the "cofounders", close collaborators and contemporaries of the God-chosen founder. I was also intrigued by the foreign dimension, since the leaders came from another continent with different language and customs. I made allowances from the start for the fact that they did not speak our language fluently. Thus, when anything they said struck me as odd, or maybe even clumsy or hurtful, I was willing to give them the benefit of the doubt.

Our life was changing. It had started out like a vacation but unconsciously we were slowly but surely being transformed into aspirants to the religious life. As such we would not frequent the city of Bundoran, too worldly, and much less its popular and overcrowded beach which I have yet to visit.

The first orientation I received from my recruiter—who was now acting as my "formator"—was "not to be too familiar towards the other brothers." We were strolling together along the breezy Atlantic cliffs, seagulls screeching and wheeling, and the rollers thundering far below to our left. I should start calling them "Brother Joseph," "Brother Michael," instead of "Joe" or "Mike," and not slap them on the back or shoulder or bump them in camaraderie.

On another occasion Father Neftalí questioned me about a small flat brush I used for my crew cut. It had the word "vanity" on its side. "Does that mean that you are vain?" he asked. Always shy and self-conscious, I became confused, quietly swallowing my embarrassment. Maybe he was trying to engage this introvert in small talk. But he was way off the mark. My deeper flaws lay elsewhere, not in vanity or ambition: I needed to be liked, accepted and appreciated. I was possessed by a desire to please, to help, to serve, generously, without measuring the cost. These double-edged swords, seen by the 17-year-old me and the Legion as virtues, were to fuel my vocation.

***

Meeting "Our Father" Maciel

> The honorary title of "Our Father," from the Spanish *Nuestro Padre,* used by members when addressing or referring to our founder, Father Maciel, has, strictly speaking, no blasphemous connotation, as some critics allege. In Spanish it is not confused with the first two words of the "Our Father," or Lord's Prayer, because the Legion usage reverses the order of the words: the prayer begins in Spanish with the words "Padre Nuestro." Nevertheless, the name does signify special respect, affection and veneration. It is the title Jesuits use for their founder, St. Ignatius of Loyola. Members of Opus Dei are known to refer to their founder, Monsignor Escrivá de Balaguer, as *El Padre,* "The Father." Catholics use the term "Holy Father" and "The Holy Father" when addressing or referring to the Pope. We can conclude that the title *Nuestro Padre*, while in no way blasphemous, does attribute a distinctive and elevated status to Father Maciel.

From first contact with the Legionaries, we heard of the great priest who founded the order in Mexico in 1941 while still a 20-year-old seminarian. With the magical name of

Nuestro Padre, Father Maciel was presented to us as a living saint. I was familiar with a saintly Dublin workingman, Matt Talbot, just a generation before me, a recovering alcoholic who used to wear chains to mortify his flesh. I wondered what this living Mexican saint would look like.

A visit from the founder of the order, whom we too could call *Nuestro Padre,* answered my question, further reinforcing our feeling of being special. On our way up the road from the dilapidated building where the washbasins were housed, we met. I can still see him gliding, trunk erect, towards us as we strolled back to Bundrowes House one lovely summer afternoon.

There in the middle of the road we shook hands with this strange priest while James Coindreau translated and introduced us. He had an encouraging word for each one and was told something glowing about each prospect. Jimmy told him that I was one of the most intelligent students in Ireland, which I thought was an exaggeration. But anyway, they were foreigners and Jimmy was probably trying to sell the boss on the good recruiting work he had done. Father Maciel spent a short while with us. I was awed by the man, the founder, the saint; though slightly wary, reticent as I was towards authority figures. Maciel, a sallow-skinned Mexican from the western state of Michoacán, stood a bony 5' 11". With thin receding light-brown hair, an aquiline nose, long strong carefully manicured fingers, a masculine tone of voice, wearing a well-tailored double-breasted black clerical suit, sporting immaculate cuffs and cufflinks; the fashionable thin black-rimmed spectacle frames gave him a French or Italian look. The lean stranger greeted each one of us graciously; there was some kind of searching, piercing look in his pale blue eyes.

Paul, Irish language trip to Connemara, 1956

Attending Legionaries shrouded *Nuestro Padre* in an aura of religious reverence and respect. I perceived him as a commanding, self-assured man, a leader. I can't remember how many days Father Maciel spent with us "Postulants" or where he stayed; presumably at a comfortable hotel in Bundoran town. He certainly did not sleep in one of our cold and damp beds. But his status was so elevated that no questioning or curiosity crossed my mind. He was above holy nuns—who never used the bathroom—and above ordinary parochial priests. I did not need to know practical details about almost Christ-like Father Maciel.

One July day at dusk, on the beautiful sand dunes at Mullaghmore, Our Father spent some time with us to get to know his Legion recruits better. Someone mentioned that I liked to sing, and following an old Irish tradition, I was asked to perform my party piece. A big Johnny Mathis fan—at home I practiced ad nauseam, if you ask my sisters—I obliged the assembly with my rendition of "A certain smile, a certain face, can lead an unsuspecting heart on a merry chase". Such was my naïve and sentimental disposition. I felt a bit squeamish wondering about Nuestro Padre's reaction to the romantic lyrics translated by Father James. Maybe Jimmy fudged. For my part, I had no idea that, ironically, the lyrics could be applied to me.

> I was what they call in Ireland a "behind the door singer." From early childhood family gatherings were held at Granda Lennon's house in Connolly Gardens, Inchicore. A somewhat foreboding presence, the patriarch sat in his armchair with his back to the chimney, legs crossed, stroking the Yorkshire terriers' arse with his laced boot, puffing on his clay pipe and expectorating into the

spittoon. Each grandchild was expected to perform a party piece. Cousin Edmund recited his elocution. My sister Patty danced. I sang "How can you buy Killarney", a song I had learned from my cousin Harry, a good crooner, footballer, and my Baptismal godfather. Six-foot Harry was one of my first heroes. Aunt Maisie, or Minnie, Sheeran, Uncle Henry's wife, once told my mother that I should have my voice trained. That has always stuck in my memory. It fell on deaf ears. Maybe my mother felt that it was beyond our means, and so she chose the two-for-the-price-of-one deal for my sister and me with the Cora Kelly School of Irish Dancing.

I was so bashful that when performing my party piece I had to stand behind the half-open door to hide my face from the family assembled in the dining room. One evening when I was about five, I was feeling so particularly shy I could not sing. Despite much cajoling and begging by parents and aunts I was unable to perform even behind the door. Finally, Granda Lennon got so infuriated he leaped out of his armchair and gave me a violent kick in the arse with his big black leather boot. I turned red as a beet and began to sob. I imagine my mother or Aunt Annie must have comforted me.

Looking back I am sad my father did not stand up for me. He did not say to his father, Murtagh: "Lay off my son, you auld billy-goat! If you ever touch him again you will have to answer to me; for even though I am small I will stuff your clay pipe down your fecking throat!" And to me he would have said: "Come along, son; we're not coming back here again until that old blackguard apologizes to us." But he did not do or say anything. He was the youngest and smallest of the sons. Maybe he was afraid.

Oblivious to that childhood episode and to my father's omission I never knew I missed, I sat in the enveloping dusk on the dunes at Mullaghmore with the other recruits. As we looked out to sea that evening, my desire to please Nuestro Padre was so intense I picked up the courage and sang for him without shielding my face.

Another evening, against the backdrop of a large orange sun setting over glorious Donegal Bay, Father Maciel held court in main room at Bundrowes House. Nuestro Padre used this session of "Questions"—he thought the term cool, though he rarely answered questions—to explain the history of the Legion to us, the need for vocations, and Pope John XXIII's plea for priests in Latin America. "Any Questions?" In awe, most of the group remained silent. Being seventeen and eager to become a missionary as soon as possible—I had heard it took 15 years to be a Jesuit—I wanted to know how long it would take me to be ordained a Legionary. My "fatal attraction" for questions led me to inquire along those lines. "About seven years" was *Nuestro Padre*'s convincing reply through the interpreter. *Nuestro Padre* gave me the answer I wanted to hear.

***

Father Yépez

Everyone's favorite assistant was Francisco Orozco Yépez; Father *Yépez*—for some reason, against the custom, they used his maternal cognomen—the most Mexican, spontaneous and laid back, was very funny. He made the most wonderful whoppers learning English idioms, and then laughed at his own mistakes. "Brothers, how is my English? Very good? Yes? Sooner and later it will be better! No?" He was the skinny, high-forehead type Mexican, wiry and perpetually smiling. I suppose that Father Yépez' innocent kindness had a lot to do with our staying on. During the hikes he would tell us about that far-off wonderland, Mexico, in his broken English. "Eeeen México, very many—how you say?—drunkmans." This struck a familiar chord with the Irish while at the same time conjuring up images of peasants, shaded by ungainly sombreros, sleeping under cactus plants with half-empty tequila bottles dangling from their fingers; just what I needed. As we hiked along and chatted, I did my best imitation of the cowardly Irish drunk full of bravado: "Who said I'm flutered? Is he a man or a mouse? I'll hamstring him, I will. Let me at him! (aside)Hold me back!" Father Yépez was thrilled and laughed infectiously. He possessed the most charming childlike smile and the most contagious giggle I have ever known. We loved him dearly and he helped us through those first couple of months as we distanced from family and friends, followed a regimented schedule, and let go of our carefree youth.

One story was told of him arriving at Dublin Airport and asking for a taxi to take him to Bundoran (over a hundred miles away). He meant to ask for a "very inexpensive" (Sp.*'muy barato'*) ride but got his English adjectives mixed up and told the taxi rank he wanted a "very expensive" (Sp. *'muy caro'*) taxi. They were surprised that a Catholic priest should want to travel in luxury, but one driver did oblige and made a fortune.

Maybe this anecdote was embellished by Nuestro Padre to get a kick out of Father Yépez's apparent naïveté. Beloved by the Irish for his spontaneity and good nature, soon after ordination—in his thirties—around 1965, he replaced Father James as recruiter. Some Irish bishops had asked the Legion to relieve "the American salesman" of his recruiting duties. A few years later Father Yépez became the first Legionary priest to die in an accident. It happened near the town of Rapallo in northern Italy, under obscure circumstances. It was a great loss to all who knew him.

Father Neftalí, then a newly-ordained LC priest, athletic and skilled at soccer and basketball, was much admired and loved by our group; another hero. On one excursion he further enhanced his rating, displaying superior strength by lifting an iron hundredweight Father James couldn't handle. Because Father Neftalí Sánchez Tinoco, one of the Mexican founding children recruited by Father Maciel, was the first Legionary priest available, we began to go to him for confession. Up to then we had been traveling to the local community of Franciscan friars in Bundoran for confession. As a fervent practicing Catholic for years I had been going to confession once every week or two and going to Mass and receiving Holy Communion every day. So this was nothing new.

***

Feeling Special

In a few weeks, thanks to Father James' pep talks, I was further enthralled by the knowledge that I been chosen—by God—as one of the first Irish Legionaries. Indeed, feeling privileged and special was the big hook for me and, I would venture to say, for most of my companions. Another part of feeling special was going to "spiritual direction." Father James explained that it was customary in the Legion not only to go to frequent confession but to, in his words, "pass to spiritual direction" with the priest. I had never experienced spiritual direction before but he explained that it was just a chat with the Padre. Trying out this new experience was not too bad because Father Neftalí was kind and refined, and his Omar Sharif looks helped. I was not sure what to talk about, but I went to see him anyway. After a visit or two he revealed to me that *Nuestro Padre* had noticed my "qualities" and that he would like me to consider leaving at short notice, in a few weeks time, to start my Holy Novitiate in Salamanca, Spain. Although this meant a big upgrade in my commitment, and sudden separation from family, friends and country, it also made me feel very special: I would now be among the first eight Irish members in history to enter a Legion Novitiate. I was being chosen from the total of about 30, including those "Brothers" in cassock who had been there before our large group arrived; I was one of only three new boys who would join with five of the old brothers. I felt very important and gratified to be a Legion "co-founder".

2
REMINISCING
98 Faussagh Ave., Cabra West, Dublin, Ireland

In the shade of the house, in the sunshine on the river bank by the boats, in the shade of the sallow wood and the fig tree, Siddhartha, the handsome Brahmin's son, grew up with his friend Govinda...There was happiness in his father's heart because of his son who was intelligent and thirsty for knowledge; he saw him growing up to be a learned man, a priest, a prince among Brahmins.

There was pride in his mother's breast when she say him walking, sitting down and rising; Siddhartha—strong, handsome, supple-limbed, greeting her with complete grace. ...That was how everybody loved Siddhartha. He delighted and made everybody happy.

Siddhartha by Herman Hesse[1]

JOYS

Chrissie, my mother, the youngest of ten, was expected to be there for her parents in old age. She was always a loving caregiver to older relatives and neighbors in need, and remained the heart and lungs of the O'Connor extended family into her seventies. For most of her life she was unpretentious, selfless and practical in her love, remembering everyone's birthday and wedding anniversary, and visiting them in their homes. I was often in tow; thence, perhaps, my compassion and helpful nature. Granda and Granny O'Connor spent their last years in our home in Cabra West and died in their beds there; she first, then he, around their eightieth year. I remember standing in the room appalled at the ugliness of death which had taken their souls away, and watching Mammy industriously washing their corpses, unwilting in her love as she laid them out for burial. She dressed her father in a special brown habit because he was a member of the Third Order of St. Francis, a popular Catholic sodality.

Granda Paddy O'Connor was one of the joys of my infancy. From the time we moved into Faussagh Avenue, me a toddler, little Granda was there with his sunny disposition. I like to think that I take after him, and I would like to be as healthy and lucid into my later years. Mammy, in her own mischievous and irreverent way, once told us children that in his youth, her father was musically inclined: as a snare drummer in the British Army Marching Band, playing "tap-her-on-the-diddy." A great childhood thrill for me was going to one of his old haunts, having my hair cut with him at Tommy White's barbershop. After days of expectation little Paul would take his granda's hand, step onto the #22 bus, and begin the long trip into town. Arriving at the bus center on O'Connell Street, we took the tram across the bridge, traveling on the top deck up Camden Street, close to Jacob's Biscuit Factory where my mother had worked when she was single.

"Tommy, this is my grandson", Granda would proudly announce, showing me off. One of the marvels of Tommy White's that offset the ordeal of getting a haircut was the canaries. Pairs of yellow canaries sang merrily in cages. They fascinated me. Tommy, a nice, friendly and chatty white-haired man, would bring out the plank that went across the arms of the barber's chair to bring me up to level. While waiting my turn, with Tommy saying "Next for a haircut and a shave!," I would observe and listen to the laconic Dublin banter: "Did ye hear about yor man's accident in the Phoenix Part dee other nite? Wha' happened? He hit a sheep's head with his front wheel and went over the shaggin' handlebars. Ended up in Jervis Street," the hospital. My parents and adult relatives would get a kick out of asking me later: "Paul, what did you see at the barber's shop?" "One man cutting another man's hair." I could never figure out what amused them about my reply. That happens to me to this day when I say something innocently amusing off the cuff.

After the haircut came a moment of bliss. We would saunter down the street to Caffola's exotic "oitalian place," where the people looked really dark and foreign, to get a rich creamy vanilla ice cream cone. That was an ethnically diverse part of the city. The owners of Jacob's biscuit factor, a stone's throw away, were Jews. My mother said they always treated little hard-working Chrissie O'Connor well. She was full of stories about growing up in the tenements down on Kevin Street, close to Jewish families; the women would pay the Catholic kids to light the fire or the gas stove for them as sun set on the Saturday, as they could not perform such menial activities on the Sabbath.

From those happy times I remember a wonderful anecdote Mammy told us kids about one of her older sisters. Sally O'Connor, even shorter than mammy, was full of mischief.

> In the early 1900s Dublin was a city of trams and bowler hats, and Sally loved to ride the tram at the very back of the top deck. As the tram slowed for her stop Sally would make her way down the aisle hitting the hard hats on either side with all her might, sending them down and over the serious gentlemen's eyes, while she bolted down the stairs and jumped off.
>
> Free-spirited Aunt Sally broke strong social and Catholic taboos of the time by running away to England to marry Jim Conway, a Free Thinker and a conscientious objector to World War II. The story of Sally and Jim, in my mother's voice, took on a kind of Romeo and Juliet quality for me. It also showed that my mother was able to break with tradition, keep her affection for Sally, and maintain contact with her, when other family members shunned her. Her choice of mate was outrageous by the standards of that time: he was English, a non-Catholic, and a non-believer. Sally had the good taste and fortune to settle in Bath, Somerset, UK, and raise a family there with the love of her life. I am sorry I never met her or her beloved Jim.

The child is father of the man. How did that little happy boy ever join such an austere outfit as the Legion of Christ twelve years later? Now, 45 years down the pike I ask myself how it all could have happened. How could I have ever embarked on that perilous voyage? What was in my background, upbringing, in my make up that laid the groundwork for such foolhardiness? My life before the Legion keeps intruding on the narrative. I can only reminisce and try to understand my boyhood and youth by dialoguing with myself, by walking through the years and observing that naïve and sentimental lover.

***

Am I your boy, Mammy?

"A little bit about you.
You were born (on November 16, 1943)
At 1:30 pm, just after lunch.
Agnes took me to the Hospital.
It was a very easy birth, 7 ½ lbs.
From the start you used to keep saying:
'Am I your boy, mammy?'
I think I spoiled you a bit.
You were always a good boy.
You never gave your Daddy or me any trouble."
(From a letter of Chrissie Lennon to Paul circa 1989)

Sister Patty still gives me a hard time about my over-attachment to mother. I really wanted to please Mammy. Maybe she, for her part, pushed some of my insecurity buttons and liked to be so desperately needed. As a toddler I would follow close to her skirts as she cleaned up the kitchen and swept the floor, repeatedly asking "Am I your boy, Mammy?" Psychologists tell us that first interactions and the budding relationship between mother and child have a lasting influence. Could it be that "love as longing" was imprinted on Paul's infant soul?

Paul's First Communion, Patty's Confirmation, 1950

Later I must have been stuck for a long time in the "Why?" stage of my childhood. I'd need to consult Piaget or Erikson to figure out the precise ramifications. Anyway, "Why?" was important to me. And still is. Before, during and after obeying, I would want to know "Why?" Would that make me ineligible, or at least unsuitable, for the Legion later on? "Why, Daddy?," and daddy would reply "Because"; and then I would go "Why the because, Daddy?" And he would say "Because the because"; I would continue, "And why the because the because?"

Heaven was Saturday mornings, when Daddy could sleep in and get his breakfast in bed. According to some unspoken ritual Patty and I took turns creeping into bed in the morning beside him. Reading the funny pages of the Irish Press out loud from top to bottom, he chuckled more than I did at Dagwood and Mutt and Jeff. As he smoked his Woodbine, I was fascinated by the way he could expertly catch the ashes in the hollow beneath his Adam's apple. Saturday was also soccer day, followed by a visit to dad's sister for tea. Up at Aunt Annie's in Inchicore they used to call me "Pee Wee Lennon" when I played soccer and walked rings around much bigger kids, protected by my older friend Brian, the fellow with the startlingly deep blue eyes.

> Forty-five years later, as I remember noticing Father Maciel's eyes the first day we met, eye color takes me on a reverie. Daddy's eyes were slate gray, mammy's nut brown. Elder sister Patty's are hazel, mine brown-green. Patty was assertive to the point of being bossy and we would scrap as children. I also know that when we went on the bus down to Phibsboro on Sundays to the "four-penny rush" she was the one who stood up to the bullies who tried to skip ahead. It was a free for all when the line

> started moving into the theater because we all wanted to get the best seats. I loved going with my sister to see the trailers, the "follyin' upper" (serial) and the "big picture." Me, I was always inwardly gentle, warm and affectionate, though I lacked self-awareness, and was too busy trying to fit in. Wit and humor shielded my sensitivity on most occasions. Introverts are the eternally and universally unknown and misunderstood—even to themselves. I do know that when my two tough sisters picked on the soft ones at home I would protect the weak.

In an environment of relative scarcity, I was treated better, perhaps, than my sisters. Choices were a luxury and all were expected to "take what you're getting". On the other hand, besides room, board, clothing, education, nurturing, and supervision, treats were consistently available: sports equipment for me, Irish dancing lessons for Patty, and season tickets to the Theatre Royal.

> When I was about ten, it was the men's turn, and I went to the Theatre Royal with my dad "of a Sunday night". Our seats were up in the gods. Way below on the stage a raffle was held. The occupant of the lucky seat number would go on stage and take a quiz. When my number was called I felt a sour taste in my mouth. I made my way down to the stage, dazed and sweating bullets. Once up there the footlights blinded me and I became even more immobilized. The compere was kind but not enough to assuage my extreme discomfort. Flustered, I could hardly answer any questions correctly and did not win any of the big prizes. But I did get a nice radio as a consolation prize. Daddy congratulated me. The stout ladies with the thick make-up in our row where thrilled for me. I was

the talk of the family for a week. The radio was good and graced my bedroom for a long time.

Dancing lessons was Mammy's idea, maybe a bit of middle-class ambition. It was a good pastime for Patty. When I was about seven, Mammy decided she could get two for the price of one and off I went to Cora Caldwell's school of Irish dancing on Eden Quay by the River Liffey. Dancing in a kilt during grade school made me even more self-conscious as I considered this a sissy activity; but I went along with it; it wasn't all that bad, mitigated by the pleasant melodies and tempos, the rhythmic movements, and traveling to compete at different "Feis", Irish culture festivals, around the Dublin area. After entering puberty, though, I said "no more", and that was that. Soccer would become my main passion, followed by tennis, ping-pong and other sports.

***

Of Pain & Cabbage

Jack and Chrissie were excellent providers, devoted to each other and to the children. Despite modest means, the family never lacked for any essentials. Mammy, the responsible caretaker, could conjure up the best Dublin dishes from her meager supplies and leftovers. Time cannot erase the sweet smell and flavor of Mammy's pancakes, made from scratch, topped with butter and a twist of lemon, on Shrove Tuesday. One of the few things I can prepare. There was always the smell of something hearty in the kitchen, such as coddle, pig's feet, roast heart and potatoes, bacon and cabbage, fried black and white pudding, rashers and eggs, fish and chips, as well as the traditional Irish stew. Most family members preferred white to black pudding and I was always embarrassed when sent to the butcher's instructed to say: "half a pound of pudding, please, more white than black."

In early childhood I must have developed that excruciating self-consciousness, probably stemming from being short. Chrissie, apprehensive, brought me to the doctor when she felt I was not growing enough. She would laugh about it years later—how the doctor had asked her how tall her husband was, like, "What did you expect, lady?"

At age five I began sun-lamp treatment which apparently meant being exposed to ultra violet rays in a dark room for a couple of hours every week. I must have been going through some stage of psychosexual development at that time because I remember being vaguely uncomfortable with the fact that a fully developed attractive woman was part of the small group of artificial sun bathers in the pen. All wore special dark goggles which made everything even more ominous. I became a blusher.

Mother's worry, because she was a worry-wart, had her lay out the welcome mat to the visiting nurses who came through the neighborhood. Mammy and I got attached to a lovely young Nurse Shields. Mammy picked up on the benefit of vegetables—I always suffered from what was then diagnosed as conjunctivitis, actually blepharitis, and the vitamin C in vegetables was supposed to be the cure for that. Unfortunately, vegetable meant that my early childhood was blighted by cabbage. The smell revolted me and the taste made me vomit. Mammy wanted me to eat my cabbage. But not matter how much I forced myself I just couldn't stomach it. Why do parents make their kids suffer like this? She was stubborn and she thought I was being stubborn. Maybe children just become stubborn as a survival mechanism. Alice Miller, in *For Your Own Good*[2], decries poisoned parenting. Could this kind of hidden cruelty have laid the groundwork for Legion training 15 years later in Salamanca and Rome? There the cabbage was different but the mantra, Father *knows best*, was similar.

***

Sports Fan

I liked watching upper-middle-class rugby and went to the occasional international at Lansdowne Rd. with dad, although my size and social class precluded me from playing. Daddy exposed me to a lot of sports. He brought me occasionally to see the international amateur boxing contests at the National Stadium on the South Circular Road, and there was Olympic wrestling and judo. On one occasion we went up to Belfast to see a boxing match in the Queen's Hall between a Northern Ireland boxer and a Scotsman. The roar of the crowd was so loud and frightening that I could understand why the Scotsman would lay down after a couple of rounds. Daddy loved cycling and for years I was a fan of the famous Irish professional cyclist Shay Elliot who made a lot of money riding "on the Continent". But because of Cousin Harry and dad's own passion, soccer became my deepest and longest lasting passion.

Playing working-class Anglo soccer in the school yard meant ignoring the Gaelic Athletic Association's "ban" on "foreign" games, harshly enforced on occasions at St. Vincent's Irish Christian Brothers'. The saying went they were so mean they were put out of the Gestapo for cruelty but got into the Christian Brothers with flying colors. Not endowed with the Lennon's long legs but rather with the O'Connor's stockier frame—prompting sharp-witted Uncle Henry Lennon to remark I should be a jockey—soccer was my passion from infancy. Many a foggy Saturday afternoon Daddy would take the tot on the cross-bar seat of his bicycle to watch Cousin Harry who played "center-half," first for Bohemians at Dalymount Park in Phibsboro, and later for St. James Gate, the Guinness Brewery team, in Crumlin. Murtagh—his proper name after paternal grandfather Lennon—a strapping six-footer, tackled gingerly, and was often encouraged by hoarse shouts of "Get stuck in, Lennon!" from the faithful. Periodically the home side was incited to overrun the enemy with the battle cry: "In around the house, lads!" When a player fell to the ground, a typical Dublin wag might holler: "Kick him, he's breathing!

***

Hero Worship

Here appears a central characteristic that would later influence my involvement with the Legion: my capacity and desire to imitate and emulate heroes.

My childhood soccer idol was not the famous English Stanley Matthews but Tom Finney, a precursor to Pele, Maradona, Zico, and Ronaldinho. A short, crinkly haired member of Preston North End in Lancashire and an England "international," Finney was a good example of skill, hard work, and sportsmanship. Like me, he was a leftie. For a period, I *was* Tom Finney. I wanted boots like Tom Finney and had to tie them exactly like him, and dribble like him, and shoot like him with the outside of the boot.

Paul with Botanic soccer team, age 15

I followed his games, read all about him in soccer magazines and in the papers. I read his autobiography and followed his tips to become a great player. I applied his rigorous fitness program of daily gymnastic movements and breathing. Tom taught me that a good soccer player needed good lungs. Every morning, I would follow his instructions before the open bedroom window: standing on my toes, raising the arms above the head to gulp in as much fresh air as possible and then slowly coming down and folding the arms gently by the side.

Besides school and homework, soccer practice and training filled most of my free time. During high school years twice a week I would pedal to the soccer fields in Santry, braving all weather conditions. The budding soccer stars would change in a small wooden shed and then begin their laps around the pitch, jogging, then sprinting to trainer Sean Goggins' whistle. Sunday morning was game time. Any "knock" sustained in the fray would be cured instantly with a rub and a whiff of Sloan's pungent liniment or a dousing with the magical cold sponge.

My parents were renting a room on Botanic Rd. in middle-class Glasnevin and so I was baptized at St. Columba's parish church, Iona Rd. But I grew up from early childhood in Cabra West. The Dominican Sisters on Rathoat Rd. were my preschool teachers. First love at the age of five was Sister Mary Athanasius, a young nun with dark brows, a mole on her cheek, and a soft voice, her face boxed into a black veil and her body hidden in a spotless cream habit—nuns didn't go to the bathroom. After "High Babies" Chrissie wanted me to study at the Irish Christian Brothers Primary School in more "comfortable" Glasnevin. She achieved this through her brother, Jimmy O'Connor, another of my childhood heroes. Young Jimmy had taken part in the Irish

Civil War in 1922 and subsequently landed a position in De Valera's government as a "senior executive officer" in the Civil Service. He thus climbed directly into Dublin middle class, becoming the O'Connor family's most successful member. After marrying an educated woman—she had the brains but not the heart to understand him—he bought a house and settled in upscale Clontarf. Dark-skinned wavy-haired Jimmy drove a Rover and sent his children to the exclusive "all-Irish" Coláiste Mhuire School.

Jimmy always associated our house number, 98, with 1798, the year of one of many failed Irish uprisings against the English. He would often recite—impressing us children with his grasp of Irish history and literature—the first strophe of the nationalist poem in honor of Wolfe Tone:

> Who fears to speak of "Ninety-eight"?
> Who blushes at the name?
> When cowards mock the patriot's fate
> Who hangs his head for shame?
> He's all a knave or half a slave
> who slights his country thus,
> but a *true* man, like you, man,
> Will fill your glass with us.

Typically, Irish irony would have it that the author, Anglo-Irish John Kells Ingram, was never overtly nationalistic; indeed he became a strong unionist in later years.

Holding the briar firmly between his square front teeth, eyes squinting through a haze of aromatic smoke, Jimmy would also regale his sister's family with stories of "The Troubles," when intrepid Republican insurgents would outwit the cruel and blundering British "Black and Tans."

Out for a spin in his car, along the way, he would correct

his protégé's strong local accent: "Uncle Jimmy, look, ders a keuw." "No, Paul, 'There's a cow'". Nevertheless, I greatly admired Uncle Jimmy and from him got my love of learning and my will to improve and progress. Uncle Jimmy "put a word in" with one of the teachers, a Mr. Mc Ketrick, and I was admitted.

***

School

I was a happy child when I began first year at St. Vincent's at age seven and a half. "The Mighty Atom" was my moniker when I stormed around the elementary school playground with chums Tommy "Shocker" Gallagher, Mattie Donohue with the quaint County Louth northern accent, and Tommy Kiernan & Co, hiding my shyness under a cloak of bravado.

I liked to study and consistently got good marks, often winning the six-penny prize that Mr. McKetrick gave to the winner of the mental arithmetic quiz in 1A on Friday afternoons. Vinniers was one of the best Irish Christian Brothers Schools in Dublin. Socially it was step below the private secondary "colleges" of Terenure, Blackrock, Castleknock, Belvedere and Clongowes Wood (the latter two Jesuit) and Church of Ireland St Columba's, but it held its own with O'Connell's and "Synger," Synge Street CBS in academics and sports. At the posh colleges they played the English upper-class sports of rugby and cricket; the Irish Christian Brothers would have none of that and imposed Irish games such as "hurling" and Irish football, adhering rigidly to the rules of the Gaelic Athletic Association.

Elementary school education, although private, was free. However, to be able to continue secondary schooling at St. Vincent's I had to win a scholarship. My family could not afford the tuition. Negligible by present day standards—about fifty dollars a year—it was beyond the means of a family of seven living off the wages of a printer's assistant. At Alex Tom and Co. Ltd., Jack spent a lot of time and overtime cleaning "glue pots" and oiling the machines. Dublin Corporation offered scholarships to low-income students who demonstrated motivation and capability with good grades. A citywide competitive exam every year awarded about one hundred scholarships. The Christian Brothers assisted by creating a special Scholarship Class after the fifth grade to prepare. That year, one hundred ten scholarships were available. I placed 91st, and my buddy, John Devlin, 99th. Other low-income friends won a place too, and together all happily began secondary education at St. Vincent's in the autumn of 1956.

During secondary school every day, immediately after the midday break at 12:30, I would go with my friend, Rory, through the sawdust floor of Botanic House pub, say hello to his parents, Christy the manager and his mum, Nan, and then we'd climb to the dusty spare room to practice "heading,", using the side of the forehead to hit a small ball against the wall, taking turns with your competitor to see who could keep it up longer. Often Nan would regale the sweating players with a cool glass of rich milk and a piece of cake. At 1 pm I would hop on the back seat of Dad's motorbike as he left Alex Thom & Co. Ltd Printers across the street so we could go home for lunch together.

Daddy explained to me that his company made all kinds of cardboard boxes, such as for cigarettes, corn flakes and even boxes for chocolates—my mother's favorite was Black Magic and I think those dark chocolates were an integral part of my parents' courtship in the late 1930s. Anyway, my Da showed me how to take a cereal box apart and find the corners that were hidden in the finished product. On those little folded squares you could see the various colors and designs the printer had used to create the finished pictures and the tests that were run on the printing machines. He would often tell me about the different kind of machines he was handling, a lot of foreign stuff such as Miele and other German and Swiss typographic and cutting machines. When a new machine came into the factory it came with technicians from these European countries. Never being exposed to foreigners, dad found them fascinating, perhaps fueling my wonder at the otherness of people.

***

Holidays

Early childhood vacations at Bray, Country Wicklow, were arranged by my dad's extended family. Fondest early memories go back to glorious stays at the big rented house on the hill where uncles, aunts, and cousins of all ages rotated and intermingled. At about age five my curious mind questioned Cousin Mattie Lennon about linking arms with his girlfriend: "Why are you linking her?" He excused himself: "It's not my fault. I just bend my arm like this and she puts her arm through!" That made sense.

An exciting array of jugglers, clowns, carousels, candy floss, and improvised stages enlivened the promenade at Bray. Sister Patty, three years my senior, competed in the Irish dancing competitions and once won an incredible seven shillings and six-pence for first place in the reel. A couple of years later, in 1952, at age nine, I won a first prize for dancing the solo hornpipe at Bray's Feis Cualainn—a treasured silver medal engraved with a dash of gold Celtic ship.

Patty, Paul, Mammy holding baby Mary, with Uncle Johnny Dempsey and his car at the beach, 1947

During the elementary school summers good money management paid for frequent CIE public bus trips to nearby popular Sandymount and Dollymount strands. Aunt Sarah Lennon's husband, Philip Howard, who worked at the Whitethorn Laundry, was always available to take the family for a jaunt in his Ford-T to beautiful Powerscourt Villa and other sights. This childless couple was very kind to my siblings and me. They had a soft spot for my sister Mary who needed special care. I sensed they wanted to adopt her but my mother quickly quenched that desire. I fondly remember visiting the Howards in Ringsend close to the Dodder. Uncle Philip, the Lennon family clown and trickster, with a big mug of tea in his fist, devoured industrial quantities of ham and cheese sandwiches smothered in a substance with which I was heretofore unfamiliar: strong smelling greasy mustard. Philip was the one who abused my fascination with the large seagulls that perched on the walls alongside the river across the street from his front door. If I could put a pinch of salt on a gull's tail, he assured me, I would be able to capture it. I must have spent many patient hours on that quest.

Uncle Johnny Dempsey, Teresa Lennon's husband, drove the family to all the southern beaches reachable in a day trip in his Morris: rough Killiney, wonderful Bray, and rocky Greystones, even as far as Brittas Bay with its scallop shells. I often felt my life was imperiled by his poor eyesight and dreadful driving skills. But once on the wide sandy beaches, gulping the cool, fresh air into my lungs, and inhaling the salty smell of seaweed, I would forget the scare and go hunting for cockles and crabs.

There were also fishing days, sitting on the pier at Dun Laoghaire or Howth with my dad, learning the silent language of men. The messy work of threading bleeding ragworm onto the hook, setting up the line with its lead weight and casting out were just what a kid my age needed; and then, finger on line, waiting patiently for the mackerel, rockfish, whiting, pollack or plaice to bite; one had to be particularly attentive to the latter's nibble. Mammy never said no to the fishy cargo the tired fishermen dumped into the sink in the evening.

At 15, my parents' thrifty savings rented a little bungalow at sandy and windblown Rush to the north. The last couple of summers before joining the Legion were spent there, relaxing, playing and swimming. I was going through my track and field stage, and every morning jogged briskly along the beach in imitation of diminutive Australian long distance runner Albert Thomas—another idol, of course.

***

Not entirely without blemish

In general I was a well-behaved boy. Occasionally I would get into some kind of mischief, but nothing serious. At about age ten I took a dare from my buddies: there was a rather plain-looking young man in the neighborhood with a large, flat and round face. I was to slag him by calling him "Moon face." One night, walking home from the shops down the road, I saw my chance. After he passed by and was at a safe distance, I shouted "Moon face" after him and started running. But he ran faster and caught up with me. "What were you saying, you little bowsie?" he shouted at terrified little Paul while he clobbered me with the tails of his large crombie. I was scared to death and lucky to be rescued by a passerby who scolded Moon face, "Let the little boy go, you bloody big bully!"

One of my lesser moments as a young gentleman came around age twelve. It was rainy winter and it involved umbrellas. Two sisters were annoying me because they were "after" me—they had some kind of a silly preteen crush. Anyway, one evening their harassment reached the limit and I engaged them in a battle of the brollies. In the ensuing combat I must have given one of them a pretty decent belt and she went home crying. I was in my bed that night when the front door knocker sounded. I could hear my mother go down to open. The girls' mother was there to complain about her daughters being attacked by a ruffian. From the cowering comfort of my bed I heard Mammy say: "How dare you! My son Paul would never do a thing like that!" and slammed the door in her face.

***

Singing in my room

A source of youthful joy was singing. My family was not musical but my mother had a good singing voice, and my dad, though he did not have a note in his head, did his best to "tickle the ivories" on the upright piano. Patty and I did the Irish dancing, and the reels, jigs, hornpipes and some set pieces have lodged in my heart forever. My sister Mary and I are the singers.

Growing up I was exposed to a variety of songs. Both parents liked the great Irish tenor John McCormick and his lesser successors such as Josef Locke and Brendan O'Dowda. Walton's Saturday radio program exposed my generation to traditional Irish dance music and songs. Even though I considered that stuff corny as a teen, it became part of my cultural heritage. I loved the human singing voice, both male and female, and could always catch a note off key. Sinatra seemed to be off key all that time; at least that is what I thought until in later years I came to admire his peculiar style. Before the Rock'n'Roll revolution I listened to my share of Bing Crosby, Perry Como, and movies and stage musicals starring the likes of Gordon McCrea. "Some Enchanted Evening" I could handle, while stretching with "Ole Man River." Aunt Maisie thought I had a good voice as did other members of the Lennon family. At age thirteen, on the train to Connemara, as I sang with my companions, an attractive young woman in a nearby carriage told me what a lovely voice I had; quite a compliment for a 13-year-old. When the Legion came along in 1961 I was in my Johnny Mathis period. It was hard being in the Legion and not being able to sing or hum; humming being a peculiarly Celtic thing, as Enya has demonstrated. In Salamanca I joined the choir, enjoying the antics of the choirmaster, Prof. Bernal, who would screech when trying to demonstrate the high notes for tenors and counter tenors. He tested me—my first formal voice test at seventeen—and told me to go with the bass baritones, which is probably what crooners are. From then on I sang in the community choir, assimilating some technique and enjoying the Medieval, Spanish, Italian and Mexican repertoires. It offered a break from the monotony of training. To the Legion I also owe exposure to Gregorian chant and an appreciation for classical music. But I was not allowed to ever sing or hum spontaneously in my cell, room, on the corridors, or in the gardens. All would be regimented.

***

Primed

Looking back to young Paul in 1961, I see a short, shy, sheltered, sentimental, freckle-faced, crew-cut, and wide-eyed 17-year-old: a little guy with a big voice and sizeable nose; idealistic and quietly intense, strong and healthy, simultaneously studious and sports-crazy. He possessed a great sense of humor and fun and was not aware of an acerbic wit that sometimes got him into trouble, or gave others the wrong impression. He inherited that from his mother.

Religious and ambitious Chrissie O'Connor had brought him up as a fervent Catholic and made him an alter boy at the Church of the Precious Blood after Confirmation at age eleven. Amid the smell of incense and Easter lilies, and the chant of *Tantum Ergo*, he occasionally thought of being a priest. At 17, however, life consisted of friends, soccer, school, pop singers, 45rpm records, ice cream parlors, and movies. Future plans meant high school, "Leaving Cert" graduation, and getting a comfortable job, perhaps as a Junior Executive Officer in the Civil Service following Uncle Jimmy's footsteps; this possibility had the added advantage of leaving plenty of time for sports.

What about girls? Yes, they were nice. His buddy, Rory, encouraged him, bashful adolescent, first to join Ierne tennis club in Drumcondra, and later Charleville off Botanic Road, an opportunity to play tennis, meet girls, and go to Saturday night "hops." During "Inter Cert," middle school, he had a secret crush on the blond girl at Ierne. He played mixed doubles with her. She was shy, too, with a winning smile. Her name was nothing as American as Buddy Holly's "Peggy Sue" but something closer to the girl in *The Wizard of Oz*. During senior year he was starting to feel attracted to the girl with long thin Rock 'n' Roll dancing legs, without ever getting up the courage to ask her out. Another enjoyable pastime crammed into his frantic teen schedule nearing the Leaving Cert Exam was with Raymund Cumiskey jamming on the piano at home, and practicing for a Dee Wop talent contest with school friends, Martin and John. Oh, yes, the four also belonged to the Legion of Mary!

Young Paul was a joiner, a kind of reluctant joiner, influenced by the friendly invitation he did not want to reject: well, he really did not have a choice with the Irish dancing classes his mother enrolled him in. He joined the Irish language association "Gael-Linn" through the influence of school mate, Sean Kelly, about the age of twelve. He joined Botanic soccer teams through the influence of Sean Goggin's brother in his early teens. Another friend, Michael Keenan's, insistence had him join the Legion of Mary, a Catholic group that prayed the Rosary and visited the sick. Once he joined he would pretty much hang in there no matter what. Call it perseverance, fear of saying "no", of displeasing friends, of being rejected, or too much trouble to leave. He tended to conform, initially, agree, accept; later when he felt more secure he might have second thoughts, begin to doubt, to question. Not a risk-taker, in the conventional sense of the term, not a self-starter, fearing failure or making mistakes.

So Paul thrived in an atmosphere of kindness, encouragement and trust. Harshness did not suit him. He avoided, ignored, and walled himself away from it. The Christian Brother's school was a harsh environment. He stayed away from the toughest teachers and gravitated towards the kind. In the Wild West schoolyard he was protected from bullies by his group of pals. And when he had to, he fought. Anger protected him from anyone who went too far; for though he was small, he could fight furiously if pushed. But in general he preferred to gain acceptance by being friendly and agreeable, one of the brightest in the class, and good at sports. He was versatile and well-rounded.

His literary appetite was whetted by the occasional foray with best friend Rory Feeney to "Phizzer" Library. Besides the lives of famous English soccer players, he ventured into Fran Striker's *Lone Ranger* and Rex Dixon's *Pocomoto* books. He eagerly pounced on such fanciful multicultural nuggets.

> "The boy who comes to be called Pocomoto is the sole survivor of a wagon train massacre by hostile Indians. Two old prospectors called Hap and Seb find him hidden amongst a clump of trees crying out for food. They called him 'Poco' because that is the Spanish for small and he was just a baby when found. A clump of trees is called a 'motte' and so, first of all, be became Poco Motte which Seb says means a 'little lost fella found among the trees'. Over time Poco Motte gets changed into Pocomoto. The two old-timers with the help of an occasional frontier woman bring up the boy according to the rules of life that they have lived by. Most of their time is spent in desert camps well away from civilization and Pocomoto grows up to be a strong, self-reliant and honest young boy."

Maybe those Old West cowboy stories prepared the way for the arrival of Texan recruiter, Legionary James Coindreau, during Paul's high school senior year. He presented to Paul a hero above all heroes, Jesus Christ, worthy of admiration and imitation, and a life-project whereby Paul would always be needed, would always feel loved, and would never face rejection.

3
RESPONDING
TO THE CALL

Siddhartha had begun to feel the seeds of discontent within him. He had begun to feel that the love of his father and mother, and also the love of his friend, Govinda, would not always make him happy, give him peace, satisfy and suffice him. He had begun to suspect that his worthy father and his other teachers, the wise Brahmins, had already passed on to him the bulk and best of their wisdom, that they had already poured the sum total of their knowledge into his waiting vessel; and the vessel was not full, his intellect was not satisfied, his soul was not at peace, his heart was not still.

Siddhartha[3]

THE CALL

Final year of high school was punctuated by job recruiters visiting the classroom. In the Catholic Ireland of the early sixties the majority were Catholic priests, mostly missionaries. There was some interest in joining the Irish Air Force because it was known that trained pilots might get a commercial job with Aer Lingus. But I was too short to be a pilot. I must not have paid much attention to clerical or government jobs. I was impressed by the presentation and presence of a Dominican recruiter and told him I might be interested. I had a soft spot for them since my preschool crush on Sister Athanasius. I might have said yes to the Carmelites, too, because I had gone to the Men's Monthly Sodality at St Teresa's in Clarendon Street with my dad and listened to Father Hugh's moving sermons. The working men sang, holding their beat-up caps to the pew with one hand and bowing their knee at the Name:

> "Sweet Heart of Jesus, fount of love and mercy,
> Today we come, Thy Blessings to implore.
> Oh touch our hearts, so cold and so ungrateful,
> And make them Lord, Thine own for evermore.
> Sweet Heart of Jesus, we implore,
> Oh, make us love Thee, more and more."

Confirmation, March 22, 1954

I was typically brought up with a great respect for the clergy—respect tinged with fear. The higher the rank, the greater the fear, not just craven fear, but a kind of reverential fear, a strange feeling related to "Fear of the Lord," one of the Gifts of the Holy Spirit, inculcated from early childhood. Mammy brought me down to the church soon after my Confirmation to become an altar boy. As an altar boy at Precious Blood Parish, I met different kinds of priests, and some inspired more respect than others.

Good-natured Father O' Farrell, in the constant company of his Irish red setters, drove around with a bunch of kids in his beat up VW Beetle. Everybody in Cabra West looked forward to the ten o'clock Children's Sunday Mass. Father Farrell used the sermon to narrate the life of a popular saint in serial form "The Story of Dominic Savio!" Young and old enjoyed his dramatizations declaimed in his best Dublin accent and full of familiar street slang. Everyone hung on his final phrase every week: "And what will happen next in the life of...?"

So scrupulously devout, Father Farrell got very nervous during Mass, especially at the consecration of the host and chalice. I should know. I often assisted him in one of the Precious Blood side chapels at seven on a weekday morning. Afraid of his stutter he concentrated tensely as he pronounced the sacred words in Latin: "*Hoc est enim corpus meum*," enunciated in a painfully slow and halting way because Father was scared he might mispronounce the words, and so the bread would not be transformed into the Body of Christ. God, that would be terrible! Then he would not be sure whether he was distributing the Body of Christ or a piece of host. Just after I had empathized with him in that agonizing enunciation, he would slowly elevate the host over his head. I had to ring the bell, not too loud, not too soft, and not too long. Altar boys get a special kick out of ringing the bell and have to be prevented from over-indulging. Well, if by any chance I went beyond the five- second peal, or whatever limit Father Farrell had in his head, in the midst of his mystical rapture, he would lash out backwards with his heel and hit me a nasty clip on the bell-hand. Sometimes the bells would fall out of my hand and go clanging down the altar steps.

Father "Flash" Cavanaugh—he could say Mass in fifteen minutes flat and was the favorite of the less fervent men-preferred hanging around with the teenage girls. But he had also demonstrated his manhood by confronting a belligerent group of the boyos playing cards for money on church grounds: they stopped or they would have to contend with his fists. Another priest, a young curate from the North, was uppity, conscious of his superior class compared to the blue-collar kids. I got so nervous serving Mass for him that I bungled my Latins and he made me take the classes all over again.

I did fear the pastor, parish priest Canon Valentine Burke, kind of, maybe because my mother would sic him on me whenever I misbehaved. But I also remember greeting him when I passed him by on the footpath—"God Bless you, Father"—and his kind nod with a tip of his hat, "God Bless you, my son," made me feel good. He was a kind and mild-mannered man with a keening voice. The smart-mouthed faithful nicknamed him "Toucher Burke". Every Sunday morning from the pulpit he would request, "touch", for money for the church building society. His sermon usually ended something like: "My Dear Brethren, the parish's debt now stands at thirty-nine thousand pounds, eleven shillings and five-pence. Please give generously. God will repay you." No wonder I felt no inclination toward the diocesan priesthood…Neither accounting nor fundraising was my calling.

Early 1961 saw a vocational recruiter with an unusual

accent, calling himself Father James Coindreau, addressing my all-boys' senior high school class. He distributed file cards and I filled one out expressing my interest in his order. I already knew I did not want to be a "Brother", like my physically abusive teachers, or a diocesan priest, i.e. boring, and none of the other orders—with the exception of the Dominicans and Divine Word Missionaries—had stirred my interest. The Legion's expensive glossy brochure reeking of color ink, contained statistics underlined the dearth of priest in Latin American compared to the glut in Ireland. It featured His Holiness Pope John XXIII making a plea for vocations to Latin America. The attractive brochure, together with the "Mexican cowboy's" charismatic personality and pep talk, won me over.

Why did I say "yes"? Echoes of *The Lone Ranger*, *Pocomoto and the Pony Express* calling to me from down Mexico Way? Or my failure as the doo-wop back up singer? My unfilled dreams as a soccer star? A big component was unbridled idealism and generosity.

Once or twice monthly after that Father James and I exchanged personal letters and he encouraged me to consider joining other boys for fun vacations during the summer to "try out" with the Legion. When I got a letter from a Dominican padre in early summer it was too late. Father James had beaten him to the punch. Embarrassed, I had to write the Dominican no, thanks. He nobly replied along the lines of "I respect your decision and wish you good luck."

On the spring day Father James came to the school to interview the applicants, I was excited for myself and pleasantly surprised when two other boys showed up: old pal John Devlin, from St. Jarlath Road, Cabra, with whom I walked to school every morning during elementary years, and another acquaintance, Thomas Moylan from class 6B. Head Brother

"Butch" Feeney, six-foot-four of muscle and red skin with the edges of his prominent ears blighted, did not beat about the bush: "Have you thought about joining an Irish group instead of a foreign outfit like this that nobody knows?" A bigoted remark, but he may have had a point. Undeterred, the three idealists nervously awaited their personal interviews with Father Coindreau in an unfamiliar room at St. Vincent's. My companions and I were under the spell.

Recently, I realized that in comparison to my wonder about why I was so fortunate to be invited, Father James had sized me up in a more pragmatic and unflattering way. From a recent e-mail message:

> It seems like yesterday that I met that short, long-nosed Dubliner at St. Vincent's Glasnevin. I still remember his loving mother and his frail father. The Christian Brothers' principal told me Paul was the smartest in the class. I promise not to tell John Devlin and Thomas Moylan his classmates, in case they thought they were smarter.

John Devlin and Thomas Moylan continue as Legionary priests today.

***

Daddy

It seems that, like many Legionaries, Father James judged the book by its cover. He did not know that despite his frailty and his limp Jackie Lennon was very involved socially at work, and called "skipper" by all the fellows. He was so concerned about others and so good at organizing groups and clubs: the snooker and darts competitions, the department soccer team where I saw him bravely hurl yourself at the feet of the opposing strikers, and the loan fund which he collected every

Friday payday to help his companions save for the rainy day. How beloved and respected was he at the job!

Little Jack Lennon, with that Dublin square head of brushed-back mousey-brown hair à la Samuel Beckett, was noncommittal when approached by me that day in the early summer of 1961. I went out to meet him on hearing his Excelsior pull up at the gate. I helped him heave the motorbike out of the curb, through the side door and up the passage to the right of our semi-detached Dublin Corporation dwelling. He always seemed so fragile, and the bike, though small, too heavy for him to handle. I was afraid it might swing over and crush his bad leg. As I came up behind him pushing and lifting the back wheel of his Excelsior 125cc over the step, I sprung it on him: "Daddy, there was a priest in to see us a while ago and he asked us would we like to try out our vocation. And I said I wouldn't mind." He recovered fast enough, his slate-gray eyes looking gently at me as he uttered nonchalantly, "Whatever you want, son."

Small, quiet and kind, Jack Lennon probably did not know what to say, because he was not good at articulating feelings or broaching sensitive subjects. And if he did know what to say, he kept mum. The Lennons, dog fanciers, were always snapping at each other. They easily went into a huff, and you had to tread lightly when there was a "nark on" between members. Aunt Annie, the old maid, was the saintly placator. As the youngest son of a large, litigious, and tightly-knit clan, Jack was undemonstrative, usually limiting displays of emotion to the pleasure of reading the funny stories in the Sunday newspaper, and chuckling at some silly joke. But I remember once seeing him dance with Mammy in the dining room, maybe on their wedding anniversary; and as a 15-year-old, I felt embarrassed and happy at the same time. I never forget how gentle he was when he'd come up to my icy bedroom during the cold winter nights to tuck me in, reciting "as snug as a bug in a rug." And I recall the way he broke down when Mammy told him the news about his brother Henry's death. He just started to heave and sob like a little boy and went upstairs to his room. To grieve alone, I suppose. I now can cry openly, without shame. But it took me a long time to be able to do so. My Stoic upbringing both at home and at the hands of the Irish Christian Brothers instilled into me that only "sissies" cry in front of others. When I told him I was going away, Daddy put up a brave front, just as I would later when I arrived one afternoon at that strange house, close to the beautiful Bay of Donegal.

***

Mammy

Jack's wife, Chrissie, my Ma, a vivacious and lively dark-wavy-haired well built under-five-footer, more assertive and expressive than her husband, possessed a Dubliner's humor and sharp wit. A repository of Dublin slang and sayings—enriched by her own parents' contribution—she would always find the right one for the right occasion. On an unattractive acquaintance: "She was as ugly as a dishful of mortal sins"; on being left behind, "And me, sitting here like a pilgarlick while you're all going out gallivantin'"; big-mouthed, "a mouth like a Malahide cod"; cumbersome shoes, "the hobnail boots that Martha wore". On someone who was "as ignorant as a cise bróg," reverting to the Gaelic for "a basket of boots;" Seeing a skinny tight-rumped female pass by, "two eggs in a handkerchief"; and, finally, seeing teens dating, "and them not done shittin' yella yet!"

Chrissie was the forceful parent in most things. We did not want to displease Mammy, knowing from an early age that if we did not behave ourselves properly she would get into a huff. At all cost children had to be "good"—even if it meant getting the "good" into you, by scolding, emotional rejection, or "taking the strap," or having Daddy give us a good spanking with his printer's assistant's calloused hands when he came home from work at half past five. My sisters and I have commented in later years just how halfheartedly he dispensed that punishment.

A devout Catholic, Mammy went to Mass every Sunday and received Holy Communion. She said her prayers every day and taught us how to pray. In May she had us on our knees in the living room saying the Rosary in family; according to the teaching of Father Peyton, "The Family that prays together stays together." In reality, though, Mammy was more influenced by a handsome local Dominican priest. She respected and revered the clergy. The priesthood was clearly a prestigious profession and way of life. Though I had no inkling of this at the time, it made a lower class family middle class and proved to all that ours was a good and successful family.

Mammy admired those boys who went to the seminary. In particular she admired a neighbor of ours, Declan, a year or so ahead of me. I was never a friend of Declan—I considered him too "holy" and serious as he rode his bike to school everyday in a somewhat rigid posture. But Mammy was a good friend of his mother's. They were such a religious family that his sister, whom I thought attractive, also went away to the convent. I would realize many years later that when I was a child, mother had dreams of me being a priest, maybe even a bishop! Only after participating in pastoral counseling 25 years later, did I begin to fathom just how strong Mammy's influence on me was.

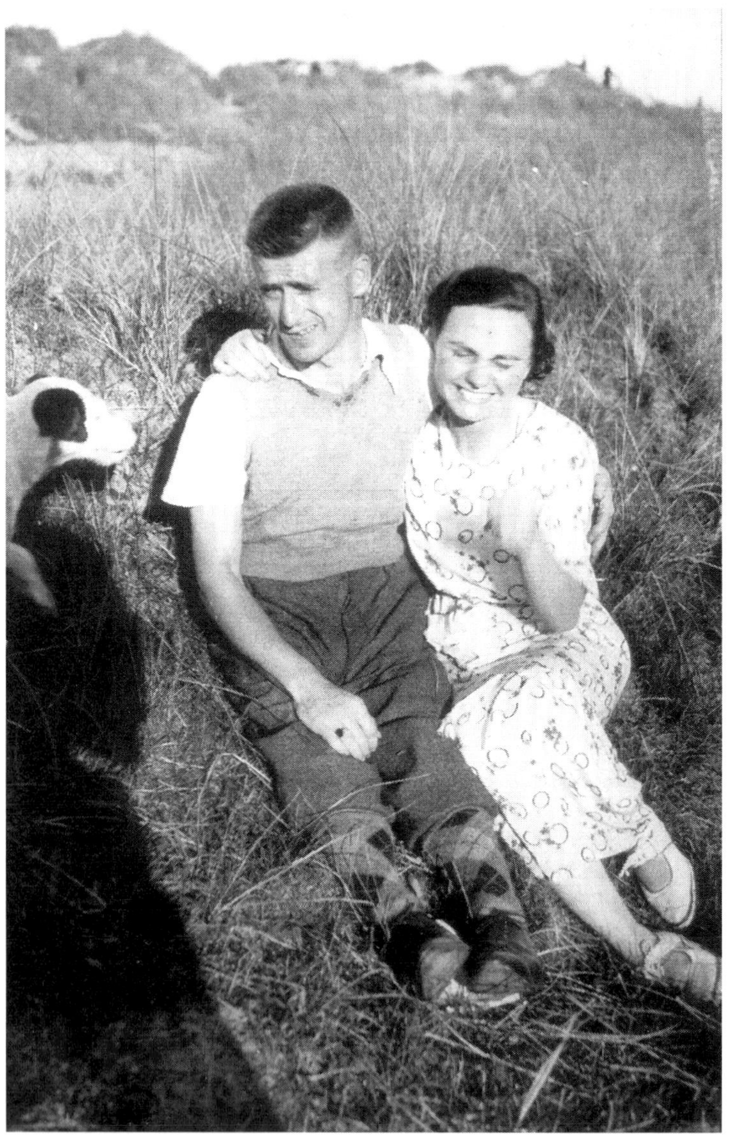

Jack Lennon & Christina O'Connor, courting, c. 1936

On that early summer afternoon I had to break the news to Mammy about "going away" to a seminary. "Mammy, a Mexican priest came into the school and when he asked was I interested in being a Missionary, I said yes."

"Oh, that's nice. You know, I always thought you had a vocation. You have always been such a good boy and never done anything to hurt Mammy's feelings."

As the day got closer, "Well, Father Coindreau, who came to visit the family, is inviting me to go on holidays to Bundoran during the summer". "Won't you miss your auld Mammy? But anyway, you might as well. Will the priest be coming 'round to the house?"

***

Sex

The most uncomfortable part of puberty for me, besides involuntary erections, was getting a bigger nose. I liked the deepening of the voice, though it made me a small guy with an incongruously big and sonorous voice. But the nose made me even more shy and self-conscious. Nevertheless, I always found a way of fitting in and being accepted by my peers. I was no lady-killer, but I had enough charm to get by. And a pretty good singing voice helped, along with my sports prowess.

Mammy was the enforcer of religion and morals—strict Dublin Catholic Victorian morals. In that environment "Sex" was a dirty word and could get you a slap in the face at home or at school. Sex and its pleasures were "dirty", and body parts were never mentioned except in those forbidden "dirty jokes" that abounded outside the home. The taboo was reinforced by priests, pope, politicians, and the ubiquitous Irish Christian Brothers. Premarital pregnancy was a family tragedy—girls being generally sent away. Extramarital sex was a crime, and sexual pleasure a shame. In fact, bodies were shameful, primary and secondary sexual organs were ugly, resulting in sexual acts being the main forbidden fruit. "Luscious in the bushes" and other phrases epitomized their furtive and clandestine nature. The flip side of this repressive regime, and ignorance or unavailability of birth-control methods—only dirty people used "frenchies" anyway—was that sexual intercourse was not entered into lightly by boys, and girls were in no hurry to lose their virginity. This was universally treasured, and not only by girls. For a large number of pious and proper young men of that generation, marriage was the only door into sex. Dublin teens also knew about love and affection, and hugging and kissing and touching. The more adventurous or experienced practiced what Americans called necking and petting.

For Dublin men who wanted to invest in heavy duty whoring outside the fold, there was always the B&I boat over to England on the week-end. One of the worse nights of my young life was a return trip on the B&I line across the Irish Sea from Holyhead after I had been to watch Everton play in Liverpool. It must have been in the late autumn of my 14th year and Dad and I had to find a place to rest on deck. We found separate places. Alone and cold, I couldn't sleep. I was shocked and disgusted by a conversation I could not avoid overhearing between two Dubliners—married, I assumed—comparing notes about the prostitutes they had visited "on the other side". They described the women in despicable terms and their trysts in lurid detail. Apparently, a small Russian sex-machine had given them a run for their money. That stands out as a particularly uncomfortable experience of my adolescence. For me that was sex—lust—and it was disgusting.

Perhaps Daddy made a faint-hearted effort to introduce me to sex or becoming a man once when we went around to the players' dressing room at St. James Gate to wait for my cousin Harry after the game. At home and at our soccer practice we changed modestly. Here the grown men were walking around in shorts or without shorts. I was neither attracted nor repulsed by the spectacle. I said nothing. Daddy said nothing. Anyway, as an introvert I probably wanted to find my own way without too much hullabaloo. I did not have an older brother to inform—or misinform—me about the secrets of sex. I was fortunate to have some positive sex education from Bro. Moore at thirteen back in the scholarship class.

I have a clear picture of my own psychosexual transition from childhood into puberty. The first eruption was sudden and surprising during a summer spent learning Irish in Connemara. But there were other challenges to fill my mind at that time, such as speaking the native language, going to school with the local preteens, and competing with the other boys in lifting and throwing heavy stones. It was that awkward stage of puberty when boys and girls start feeling strange, strong feelings towards each other and don't know what to do about it, and often don't do anything except furtively exchange glances; remarkable how I can remember my first crush in that small community. Nora was short with nut-brown hair. She was pretty and shy. We never exchanged a word. Besides, she belonged to a family that was maligned by my host family and our half of the community.

The reason was never mentioned openly. These men were fisher-farmers. They cultivated what they could of the rocky land and harvested what they could from the cold Atlantic sea. My tall weather-beaten host parent in the gray woolen jersey took me out in a rowboat or *currach*, and in a larger pitch-black sailboat, a Galway hooker, to go further out to sea for blue lobster, giant spiny red sea lobster and large crabs. I gradually discovered that the resentment sprung from an accident in which the ostracized family had not done enough to rescue the drowning during a shipping accident.

Quiet Páraic who spoke only Gaelic and talkative bilingual Mary Ned Joe—she had spent some of her youth as a nurse in England—shared all they had with me: the turf fire, fresh milk and hand churned butter, spuds and the local rockfish, the local rock bream. I can still remember them giggling apologetically when I told them the fish was called "bream" in English; it sounded like the word for "fart" in Gaelic. They were loving and kind to the little "jackeen" learning the language and culture.

Our farm bordered Carna's little harbor. I loved the smell of summer grass and salt sea air, and the feel of the water as it dripped off the fishing lines. Seaweed and sea moss, their slippery texture, subtle smell and tangy tastes were part of our daily lives. The regular stuff with the poppy pods was used as fertilizer and the Carragheen sea moss was highly treasured. Harvested in shallow waters and put out to dry on the sunny banks, it took on a pink mauve color. Local people chewed it for its jelly texture and bittersweet taste, and sold it in sacks for a good price.

The only uncomfortable part about that stage of my life, other than the wayward organ I was beginning to tame, was that everyone called me *Seán*. This is because my official name is John Paul, *Seán Pól*. I was too shy, or not assertive enough, to tell the organizers, the school teacher, and the host family, and everyone else to call me *Pól*.

However, the Connemara venture had other marvelous moments. I will never forget the local fair, a traditional Celtic festival with athletics, mostly feats of strength, and competitions of all kinds, including storytelling, singing and dancing. Young folk like me could sing, tell a joke, hum or whistle an Irish tune to win a prize. I won the whistling and was absolutely thrilled with myself. Thus the enjoyable novelty of living and learning with the people of the Irish-speaking traditional Connemara region was a marvelous environment for the onset of my puberty. A Galway hooker was involved. But other than that boat, no other hookers were involved in my sexual initiation.

There was at least one girl I avoided during late high school. Prostitutes were *hoors*, the kind of women you would see going off with sailors across O'Connell Bridge. I don't remember paying much attention to them. Girls that we figured were easy or from the lower classes were called "scrubbers" and were dismissed by my middle-class buddies. I remember my good friend Noel—though not much taller, he was so much more mature me that he was dating someone—warned me to stay away from a girl in his neighborhood. We would pass by her house on the way home from school in the 11 and 12 grade. She was blackballed in our circles. Though not a "scrubber" in the conventional sense—she went to one of our favorite girls' schools, Eccles Street—the curly dark-haired, full-bosomed, schoolgirl broke the norm for decent girls and had the reputation of being easy. We would politely stop and stay hello while she leered at us over her garden wall. I don't remember her asking us in, "Come into my parlor said the spider to the fly."

I have already mentioned the crushes at the tennis clubs. I remember a funny incident. At one of the hops, dancing rock 'n' roll with an attractive and good-natured heavy-set girl, I began whirling her around. As we gathered momentum she slipped my grip, lost her balance, and crashed to the floor. Courteously, I bent down to help her get up. But she was so heavy I couldn't budge her. I was too embarrassed to go near her again.

But now the Legion had appeared out of the blue whisking me away to permanent celibacy before I had to face that thorny and confusing subject of sensuality and sexuality. When I joined the Legion at seventeen, I was renouncing the affection I thought I knew, the raw sex I found repugnant, the being in love I did not yet know, and the monotony of marriage and family life I assumed.

4
RELOCATING
SUDDENLY TO SUNNY SPAIN

The first light of day entered the room. The Brahmin saw that Siddhartha's knees trembled slightly, but there was no trembling in Siddhartha's face; his eyes looked far away. Then the father realized that Siddhartha could no longer remain at home—that he had already left him.

The father touched Siddhartha's shoulder.

"You will go into the forest," he said, "and become a Samana. If you find bliss in the forest, come back and teach it to me. If you find disillusionment, come back, and we shall again offer sacrifices to the gods together. Now go, kiss your mother and tell her where you are going. For me, however, it is time to go to the river and perform the first ablution."

He dropped his hand from his son's shoulder and went out. Siddhartha swayed as he tried to walk. He controlled himself, bowed to his father and went to his mother to do what had been told him.

Siddhartha[4]

TRAVELING WITH FATHER MACIEL

Things happened quickly with the Legion of Christ. In the words of the brother of one of my earliest companions:

> "At home, Declan had decided to break the family mould. Having completed his Leaving Certificate at Synge Street (Irish Christian Brothers School)...he came home to my mother one Friday lunchtime in early July and told her he was heading off the next day, Saturday, for a week or so. An order of priests, the Legionaries of Christ, had visited the school and had invited some volunteers for a few weeks' holidays in their house at Bundoran in County Donegal...He was seventeen years of age at the time. He didn't see his family, nor they him, for the next nine years."[5]

We were allowed home for a few days in late August, 1961, to get measured for our black suits—the Legion paid for mine at Clery's on O'Connell Street—and prepare for departure to Salamanca. My mother was a bit shocked about the quick turn of events, leaving so quickly for Spain, but she did not want to go against something coming from a "clergyman"—and maybe she was inwardly thrilled by the prospect of having her "one and only son" become a priest. The blow was softened to some degree for us and our families by the news that we were going to Lourdes, a very special place of Irish religious devotion and pilgrimage. My father remained noncommittal, even though—as I learned many years later—he was going to miss his inseparable companion. I distinctly remember my mother asking Father Maciel at the airport when she would see her son again. "In a year or two, Mrs. Lennon," came the reply through the interpreter. That is what she wanted to hear.

Self-consciously wearing a new black suit and with the stiff clerical collar chafing my neck, I said good-bye to my parents and sister Patty at Dublin Airport as we headed for Tarbes, France. The "First Eight" were traveling with their leader: three of them from the July batch—Declan Murphy, Brian Farrell, and myself—together with five of the "old Brothers"—Pearse Allen, Declan French, Francis Coleman, Michael Caheny and Oliver Mc Gowan, renamed "Maurice" by Father Maciel. I later realized how Nuestro Padre had a penchant for certain names: *Mauricio*, in Spanish, and *Maurizio*, in Italian—there had been a handsome blond Italian boy who had joined about that time. He also liked to change unusual names, such as "Rigoberto" to more acceptable ones such as "Cristóforo." Thus there are quite a few "Cristóforos", re-baptized into the Legion, as it were, by the Founder and Superior General.

On the plane with Nuestro Padre we communicated through gestures and broken Spanish. I had never been that close to such a famous and holy person. One of the more outgoing postulants took an Aer Lingus brochure featuring a globe and pushed it at Nuestro Padre as if asking for an autograph. I blinked; he was not a soccer star or a cycling champ, and instinctively I felt uneasy with what seemed to me like false closeness. Nuestro Padre accepted it and drew "LC" with an arrow pointing at the globe to signify that we were going to conquer the world. Then I followed suit and got mine autographed. We felt like a bunch of kids with Santa Claus all to ourselves.

With Parents at Dublin Airport, August, 26, 1961

Our maiden voyage—my first airline flight!—took place on August 26, 1961, a landmark in the personal histories of the "First Eight", and in the history of the Legion of Christ in Ireland. The pioneer Irish Legionaries were landing on the Continent, beginning the first stage of their search for the Holy Grail, the Salamanca Novitiate. When the plane door opened at Tarbes airport, we were hit by a wave of sweltering heat rising from the tarmac. Deplaning in the company of our fearless leader was as momentous for us as the first man's landing on the moon. If we had not been this bewildered bunch of undemonstrative Irish teens we might have knelt and kissed the ground. I, personally, spent the next few days and weeks in a bewitched daze.

Despite its objective importance, a present-day history of the Legion would underplay this event or exclude it. The leadership cadre would re-write history in such a way as to exclude some troubling names, such as my own. Am I written out of official Legion history?

The morning following our arrival, after that strange continental breakfast, a bowl of coffee and a dry roll, we headed straight for the Lourdes Basilica, to dedicate our Legionary vocation to Our Lady at the Grotto. In hindsight we had only a vague idea of what this "vocation" meant and the demands it might entail. Father Maciel seemed happy surrounded by his first little group of Irish Missionaries; in his early letters the founder wrote about how he had dreamed of this since the late 40s as he passed through Shannon airport on his way to and from Europe. Perhaps it was irrelevant to him that we had not yet discerned whether we even had a vocation to the Religious Life, the Priesthood or the Legion. Feeling privileged and wanting to please this holy man, without second guessing, we just assumed we had.

***

Enchanting Spain

The little band's transition from Lourdes, France, to Spain in late August through early September 1961 marked another important step. We took a train out of France to Irun, in the Basque region, just inside the Spanish border. Full of expectation: in Spain we would soon be received by a large group of "real" Legionaries. Looking out the train window as it drew into the station everything was exciting and dramatic, dreams were coming true. I had been so bedazzled since Bundoran when I learned one of my fellow Dublin postulants had actually been to Spain, the land of great soccer players with sacred names like Jesús Santa María, teams like Real Madrid, bullfighters, swarthy gypsies and Flamenco guitar players. Enraptured by the exotic allure of this foreign clime, "What are the Spaniards like?" I posed. My fellow postulant explained how they carried knives, and you had to be careful. They were haughty and if you used the feminine form of nouns or adjectives when addressing a man, they might slit your throat. That was certainly good motivation to study Spanish grammar carefully! I excitedly pressed on: "And what do they eat?" "They carve a leg of ham with a flick-knife, tear off huge chunks of bread with their bare hands, and wash them down with a squirt of wine from a sheepskin they hold over their heads…" My Irish staples felt threatened: "And what about butter? Do they have butter?" "Of course, just like ours, yellow, except with a red stripe down the middle!" My jaw dropped, "Really?"

Such was the naïve and romantic Catholic boy who looked out the window as the train pulled into Irun on a sunny summer day in 1961. Examining the Spanish, or rather Basque, people in the station I was relieved to see they were shorter than the average Irish. But when I noticed that they all seemed to be shouting angrily at each other—even the women dressed in black shawls—apprehension crept over me. Then someone explained they were just gesticulating, that's the way they talk, and my stomach muscles relaxed. All was well again in Camelot.

***

San Sebastian

A large group of Legionaries had driven from Salamanca to meet and greet us. Now it was time to meet Mexico. I believe a certain Father José Bustamante, a sleeked-back-haired Mexican wearing tinted glasses and a broad smile, was at the wheel of the large and shiny Mercedes coach. Because of the historic occasion, three normally isolated Legionary "communities" were traveling together: the Theology student "Fathers" (*Padres Teólogos*), the Philosophy student Brothers (*Hermanos Filósofos*) and the Humanities student Brothers (*Hermanos Juniores*). We were showered with fraternal affection and hugs as we tried to communicate in Spanish and English. Some of the theology students knew a few words of English and they were thrilled to be able to practice, just as we to try our Spanish.

In hindsight, I remember Mexican Salvador Maciel among the welcoming committee—maybe because he had the same last name as Nuestro Padre; Roberto Gonzalez, who later as an employee at the Vatican's Congregation for Bishops would be temporarily "exiled" from Rome for poaching confidential information from a Vatican office; Mario Amezcua Maciel—his father was married to the founder's sister—who hung out with Roberto a lot—one of the few cases I can remember of close friendships going uncensored in the Legion; and handsome Raul De Anda, who would later become a confidant and important defender of the founder. They greeted us with this new thing we were learning, the Legionary *abrazo*. According to the rule, members could touch only in this way, hugging on the occasion of meeting or taking leave.

Along the way our newfound brothers sang wonderful songs for us in three-part and four-part harmony. Community singing, we discovered, was part of the Legion spirit. Pearse Allen, at six-foot-four, the leader of our group at that stage, had been there longer than the three Dubliners, encouraged us to sing. We had been rehearsing our group song since Bundoran. Pearse had taken that old British military standby "It's a long way to Tipperary" and changed the lyrics: "It's a long way to Salamanca; it's a long way to go—without your Spanish—it's a long way to Salamanca to the greatest town I know. Farewell Bun-drow-es, farewell Bun-do-ran. It's a long, long way to Salamanca and our hearts are there." It went off very well. The Legionaries gave us many cheers, or "porras," as they are called in Spanish. Learning and joining in on these hurrahs became part of our initiation into our new language and culture. We were gung-ho. And, anyway, the Irish are good mixers.

It must have been back in San Sebastián, at the *El Correo Francés*, that Declan played the piano for Father Maciel, a popular tune at the time which turned out to be the risqué Spanish song *Perfidia*.

To you
My heart cries out "Perfidia"
For I find you, the love of my life,
In somebody else's arms

Your eyes are echoing "Perfidia"
Forgetful of the promise of love
You're sharing another's charms

With a sad lament my dreams
Are faded like a broken melody
While the gods of love look down and laugh
At what romantic fools we mortals be

And now,
I find my love was not for you
And so I take it back with a sigh
Perfidia's won
Goodbye

Perhaps our leader's eyes twinkled mischievously at this was worldly music. Not knowing the Spanish or English lyrics I was not overly embarrassed listening to this music in front of a priest—though he was not just an ordinary priest but a veritable living saint.

5
RENOUNCING
THE SELF IN SALAMANCA

Siddhartha had one single goal-to become empty, to become empty of thirst, desire, dreams, pleasure, and sorrow-to let the Self die. No longer to be Self, to experience the peace of an emptied heart, to experience pure thought-that was his goal. When all the Self was conquered and dead, when all passions and desires were silent, then the last must awaken, the innermost Being that is no longer Self-the great secret!

Siddhartha[6]

SALAMANCA

As our Mercedes bus wound its way up and over the Spanish Pyrenees, Nuestro Padre bought cider for us and he was amused by our tipsy reaction to that peculiar alcoholic beverage. It was stronger than the Bulmer's Cider soft drink we were accustomed to at home. Some of the more scrupulous Irish may have thought twice before breaking their *pledge* of abstinence from all alcoholic drinks, made at Confirmation. But surely, why would we worry—echoing the Gospel verses—when we were like the Disciples in the Messiah's company? All in all this experience of camaraderie was pleasant. Santander, with its mountains, rivers, and green landscape, seemed like a sunny version of Ireland. Unfortunately, this bewitched phase began to draw to a close as we headed south through increasingly austere scenery toward our Castilian Novitiate in Salamanca. Mountains, rivers, and trees gave way to plains, stubble, and parched earth. Although Teresa of Avila was proud of the unending horizon, "more Heaven than Earth," this arid panorama, with no place to hide from the scorching sun, did not bode well for the "boys in green".

***

Crisis Counseling

A small spring gushed up in the midst of the geographical and emotional desert offering momentary respite. When we drove into the driveway at Ciudad Jardín, Salamanca, that first day in early September 1961, the gardens and the red-brick and glass building—built, we were told, to Nuestro Padre's specifications—were an attractive sight. Our companions pointed out to us the words in large bronze letters across the top of the entrance porch: *Christus Vita Vestra*, Christ Your Life. Jesus Christ would now be our model from this moment on. And I would have one whole year with nothing else to do except be transformed into another Christ. The ideal resonated deeply within me. Here was the Hero above all other idols and heroes: God and Man, perfect in his divinity and perfect in his humanity. Being ever a lover of books, I avidly read and studied *Jesus Christ* by theologian Karl Adam during my year's novitiate. But by then I was desperately trying to recover my faith.

Shortly after arriving in Salamanca in early September, 1961, lightning struck. Suddenly and without warning, storm clouds, gathering quietly since I stepped onto novitiate soil, exploded. I had come here to give it all up for Jesus, and suddenly Jesus was nowhere to be found. My mind blurred with fuzzy confusion; my leaden heart fell at my feet. I began doubting everything. My reason raged like a demon, demanding tangible proof. Had Jesus of Nazareth really existed? Had he risen from the dead? Was he really the Son of God? Where was he? I could not understand, believe or feel anything. Maybe Jesus was hiding, as St. Thérèse de Lisieux had once playfully remarked. But I was in no humor for games. My mind was a blank, black screen, my heart full of panic and despair.

During the week-long retreat before taking the habit on September 15, Feast of Our Lady of Sorrows, I had to unburden my soul to someone. I went to confession to the one Legionary priest who, thank God, spoke English, Father

José María Sánchez. His crinkly hair, large pudgy frame, soft voice, effeminate and creepy manner did not inspire a lot of confidence. But there was no one else to turn to.

"I feel terrible. I don't know what's come over me. My mind is blurred. My faith is confused. I can't feel or see God. I am doubting everything, including the existence of God!"

His advice was clear and reassuring: "Don't worry. That's a temptation from the devil. It will soon go away. Carry on, take the habit."

Here I was—thanks to Father James' meditations—feeling like Peter on the Sea of Galilee. The Lord was telling me, "Cast your nets for the catch," although I couldn't for the life of me see a fish around. I had to summon up some heroic faith from the depths of my doubt and blindly cry:

"In your name I will cast the nets". I received the Legionary uniform from the hands of our founder, Father Maciel.

Thus began what I believed were my *"Doubts of Faith"*, my own peculiar and personal *"Dark Night of the Soul."* That first big crisis of faith, probably a mixture of homesickness and a sense of dread, would not go away. Nevertheless my will—or my fear of God or of failure—spurred me on, and I never said I wanted to go home and out of there. I would struggle mightily, grappling myself to the mast by sheer willpower when imagination, emotions and intellect battered my ship.

***

A Feeling of Dread

I could not name or sort through the tangle of emotions sweeping over me as I numbly took the habit: homesickness, feeling trapped, a huge commitment bearing down on me like a Mack truck: overwhelmed by the rapid pace of events, I was making a choice that would bind me forever. No turning, no looking back, being cut off from family, friends, country. Today it's easy to suppose a muffled fear clamored to be heard: What am I getting myself into!

I remember Nuestro Padre joking later about how we first Irish were thinking of shanghaiing a boat in San Sebastian and escaping back to Ireland. A story he made up for his own reasons, perhaps to throw us off balance or lower our defenses. I, for one, at that moment lacked the awareness and bravery to carry out any such scheme. But the clever story seemed to distract attention from, or defuse, the real issues.

Borrowing from Eliezer ben Yehuda's 1882 arrival at Jaffa on finally reaching his beloved Holy Land:

> Yes! This was the coast of the land of my fathers! And the feeling of dread grew yet stronger within me. Nothing else did I feel, no other thought in my mind! I am afraid! After about a quarter of an hour my feet were standing upon holy ground, the land of our fathers—yet in my heart was no feeling of joy, and in my head no thought, no idea whatsoever! My mind seemed to have emptied itself or turned to ice; it would not budge. Only one thing filled my heart–that same feeling of dread. I neither rent my garments nor fell upon my face, nor embraced the stones, nor kissed the ground. I just stood there in astonishment. Dread![7]

***

Hanging in

José María Sanchez, the only English-speaking Legionary in Salamanca, approached me one day. It was during manual labor time. I was working in the garden at the back of the chapel, where the narrow stained-glass windows look ugly from the outside. He clumsily attempted to shame me into staying: "After all the trouble and expense the Legion and you have gone to, are you going to leave it all?" He mightn't have bothered. Despite the pain, I was still firm in my decision. Hadn't I given my word to Father Coindreau and to Father Maciel?

The other seven Irish novices who had traveled with me started getting sick. Maybe their immune systems were weakened. The food had been a problem from day one. This was a tangible obstacle confronting the first band of Irish Legionaries. Although butter was butter and did not have a red stripe running down the middle, we were unaccustomed to eating lentils or chickpeas—I had never eaten them before and considered them food only for very poor people, like putting margarine or Australian butter instead of Irish butter on your bread. Food was passed around on large dishes and each brother served himself. To the Spaniards, apparently, they tasted like Heaven. Our Spanish was poor at the beginning and we were still doing a lot of sign language. I remember personally having trouble with one of my old nemeses, *callos*, tripe, in light brown gravy, another delicacy, apparently; and the industrial quantities of white rice and peas. Even the *orejas de fraile*, fried batter in unusual triangular shapes, with eggs was hard to take because the friars' ears were sprinkled with sugar! "Where's the fish and chips?" we groaned. Survival being the mother of invention, the first Irish novices devised a method to beat the enemy. At the beginning we were allowed to sit at the same table in the refectory. One of us would test every new dish and give the go-ahead to the rest of the group or not. Each would take a minimal amount of the dangerous food, not to show disrespect or to disregard the rule that bade us, as brothers, all eat the same food. Signals would be sent under the table so as not to be seen by the rest of the community who, for their part, must have been amused by this new secret code.

For the most part those first days and weeks we lived on fruit. Spanish grapes and watermelons, as much as Faith, Hope and Charity helped the first batch of Irish Legionaries persevere in their vocation.

***

Novice Master, Father Arumí

After taking the habit, we were gently but firmly gradually encouraged to avoid English among ourselves so as not to create a division among the Novices. I was open to that suggestion and was always one of the most inclusive. I never had a problem with embracing Spanish and Mexican customs or people. Wasn't I going to be a missionary in Mexico? "When in Rome…"

My Novice Master, Father Rafael Arumí (maternal cognomen, Blancafort), LC, was at the same time my spiritual director, confessor, superior, and rector. He was one of several Spanish seminarians "poached" by Father Maciel from the Jesuit-run national seminary in Comillas in the '40s. Our craggy-browed instructor with the straight, dark sleeked-back hair saw himself as the formulator and explainer of divinely inspired Legion spirituality. Funneled into his ankle-length cassock, his head too big for his shoulders and the rest of his body, with shuffling gait, he scurried mole-like to the first floor conference room every day. With his nasal Catalan accent impoverished by slurred speech, he was almost impossible to understand when he expounded on "The Spirit and Mystique of the Legion of Christ" in interminably long sentences. Pious rumor had it that Father Arumí's tongue had been inadvertently sliced by a bungling dentist. But hadn't he heard about the new Spanish literary style that used short sentences? During weekly Spiritual Direction in his office, his semi-catatonic state would often slide into sleep, the drone replaced by silence. For the directee, it was most uncomfortable; one didn't know whether this was a pause in the conversation or if Father Arumí was gone. Padre Rafael seemed to suffer from catalepsy; maybe he had to take anti-seizure medication that caused drowsiness.

Who ever said that following Christ was going to be easy? Every evening, after mumbling the introductory prayer in Latin—only the first couple of words, "Veni, Sancte Spiritus" were distinguishable- Padre Arumí stumbled into the "Explanation of Rules": for a good Legionary, the lightest issues were serious, and all rules and norms, no matter how small, should be followed with the same exacting fidelity as expressions of God's Will. Key to the Legion Spirit & Mystique, explained Father Arumí, constantly clearing his throat from some dogging mucus and swallowing it, was that a member should bare his soul to his spiritual director with absolute trust but he should not disclose his personal feelings or problems to anyone else. It became second nature for us not to mention personal issues at all to anyone, neither to our companions nor to our relatives in our monthly letters home. As the song says: "Don't cry out loud. Just keep it inside..."

During my first and all subsequent "crises of faith" in the Legion it never crossed my mind, nor was it ever suggested to me, that I could consult with someone outside my assigned Legion spiritual director—usually my superior—or even with another Legionary priest. If on paper—to comply with Canon Law—recourse to another confessor or spiritual director was permitted, it was not part of my practical options. It was "not the custom"—Legion phrase for unwritten rules—to consult with an "outsider." "They would never understand our charism." Psychological or pastoral counseling were not offered, and I had never heard of them in the Legion. My resources were clearly defined: spiritual director—who in this case was also the rector—and Father Maciel via mail.

***

Roses and Thorns

Salamanca was our address, but we rarely ventured outside the cloister to visit the historic city. Isolated from whizzing Vespas and small uncomfortable Seat cars, on summer Sundays we could nevertheless hear the *Olé*s swelling from the bullring half a mile away. Oblivious were we to the groups of *estudiantina* troubadours roaming the streets at night and the crowded *tapa*s bars. Even so, from the top floor of the novitiate I sometimes espied strange sights in the surrounding fields: a tiny figure, poised on its toes, in the middle of a gray lentil stubble field, still as a bird; then in slow motion raising its left arm while the right held a stick parallel to the ground. The upper body swivels left, twisting at the hips and dragging the nimble feet around in the dust in a graceful backswing. A kid going to throw a stone or unleash a sling? Narrowing my eyes to focus, I make out a novice bullfighter. Maybe this *novillero* would have his *alternativa* this summer and become a full-fledged bullfighter in the *Plaza de Salamanca*. And the next *Olé* we heard as we prayed the Rosary strolling around the grounds on Sunday evening might be for him.

One break we got from our tight and monotonous schedule was the weekly outing. How conspicuous did I feel when we wore those white front-buttoned work-coats on our hikes through the Salamanca countryside looking like a bunch of escaped asylum inmates! And the hikes gave us little respite; they accentuated the freezing cold winter wind and the torrid summer sun. We missed the soft trees and emerald fields of Ireland, no matter how much our Spanish companions praised the austere beauty of Castile, home of Teresa of Avila and other luminaries of Spanish literature's Golden Age. Close by the River Tormes, where we often took ourselves in search of shade, they taught us that Fray Luis de León had composed his inspired poetry. In the nearby orchard, perhaps, he had written his devout literary treatise *The Names of Christ*. But for me Christ was nowhere to be found.

My Spanish fellow novices were good-natured, friendly and hardy, having grown up in the widespread poverty and austerity of Franco's Post-Civil War Spain. Hailing from neighboring towns with such Castilian names as Macotera, San Chidrián and Orcajo de las Altas Torres, their parents—teachers, civil guards and soldiers—had sent them to the Apostolic School in Ontaneda, Santander, at age eleven, seeking a good free education and maybe the service of God for their sons. My Mexican confreres were polite and ingenious, full of regional sayings and endowed with a vivid imagination to which they gave free rein during our weekly excursions.

On the ground floor notice board each of us was assigned to a *terna*, a small group of three or four under the guidance of a team captain. The captain was a companion sufficiently "integrated" into the Legion system and trusted by the superiors to make sure we behaved during the outing and to lead us in our acts of piety, such as morning meditation, midday examination of conscience, and afternoon Rosary. He would also report any bad behavior or conversations that were not full of edifying reflections and anecdotes. Lack of observance of the rules would be called out at the weekly Chapter of Faults.

***

Chapter of Faults

This was another traditional monastic practice that our founder had incorporated into his eclectic training system. One evening during the week we assembled in the conference room. The superior, seated on a dais at the head of the room, called randomly on a member of the community. The novice would go to the top of the room and kneel down facing the superior with his back to the community. The kneeling novice listened silently and humbly, without objecting or clarifying, as his companions pointed out concrete dalliances: "I have the impression that Brother Anthony broke the rules of etiquette yesterday morning when he gobbled down his porridge noisily." "Brother Anthony made a noise with his chair when he got up from the table". "I have the impression that Brother Anthony was looking around too much during our excursion yesterday, thus breaking rule number such-and-such regarding modesty of the eyes from the Rules of Modesty." "I have the impression that Brother Anthony was dozing in the chapel yesterday during Evening Prayer." "I believe that Brother Anthony was talking about his past life in a worldly way during recreation time on Monday evening." "I overheard Brother Anthony indirectly criticize the hairdo of one of the Assistant superiors in front of another novice last Wednesday." This petty activity I did not enjoy and for the most part abstained from calling out my confreres' faults. When I was called up I bore the nitpicking with Celtic stoicism.

***

The Agony of Prayer

Perhaps my problem was compounded by the meditation system indiscriminately imposed by the Legion on all members. We had to learn and practice the "discursive-affective" method. Legion spirituality was heavily indebted to Jesuit or Ignatian spirituality, and to an old and traditional version of it. Fr Thomas Keating summarizes

> The *Spiritual Exercises of Saint Ignatius*, composed between 1522 and 1526, is extremely important in order to understand the present state of spirituality in the Roman Catholic Church. Three methods of prayer are proposed in the *Spiritual Exercises*. The discursive meditations prescribed for the first week are made according to the method of the three powers: memory, intellect and will. The memory is to recall the point chosen beforehand as the subject of the discursive meditation. The intellect is to reflect on the lessons one wants to draw from that point. The will is to make resolutions based on that point in order to put the lessons into practice. Thus, one is led to reformation of life.

Apparently, this "one-size-fits-all" meditation method did not fit me and probably contributed to my inability to pray and to the ensuing distress and mental turmoil. I was never coached by the Novice Master in overcoming my difficulties, nor was it suggested I could try another method. This method tended to make me rummage around in my brain, "as dry as the remainder biscuit after a long voyage," like the fool Touchstone's in Shakespeare's *As You Like It*. Father Arumí unabashedly stated that the Legion was a totalitarian and absolutist organization: rules were meant to be obeyed without exception, methods followed and systems implemented without question; all members had to conform uniformly to the norm. "Like it or lump it" seemed to be the message from God.

Now, over forty years later, I find some consolation in Father Keating's wise words:

> If one attempts to persevere in discursive meditation after the Holy Spirit has called one beyond it, as the Spirit ordinarily does, one is bound to wind up in a state of utter

> frustration. It is normal for the mind to move through many reflections on the same theme to a single comprehensive view of the whole, then to rest with a simple gaze upon the truth. As devout people moved spontaneously into this development in their prayer, they were up against this negative attitude toward contemplation. They hesitated to go beyond discursive meditation to affective prayer because of the warnings they had been given about the dangers of contemplation. In the end they either gave up mental prayer altogether as something for which they were evidently unsuited, or, through the mercy of God, found some way of persevering in spite of what seemed like insurmountable obstacles.[8]

***

Automatic compassion pilot

The Novice Master appointed me assistant *enfermero*, male nurse, to the community of novices and *juniores* (Humanities' students who had finished Novitiate). He did not explain why. I would devote myself tirelessly and unselfishly to that mission all through my formative years in Salamanca and Rome. During Novitiate this job kept me busy, occasionally diverting the obsessive doubts that plagued me: "What if all this is not true, if there is no God, no Jesus, no Eucharist…What am I doing on my knees, going through the motions?" My spiritual director's advice—I would later comprehend—was along the lines of Spiritual Sublimation or Denial: "offer it up to the Sacred Heart"; "go pray in front of the Blessed Sacrament"; "forget yourself and your rationalism"; "be simple"; "deny yourself"; and "be more generous with Christ".

On a practical level, I was occupied taking care of the medical needs of my fellow novices. Besides the common colds, some took to bed in need of some compassion or someone to talk to or to take a break from the strain of the nonstop schedule. Our day was minutely regulated from 5:20 a.m. until 9 o'clock at night, interspersed with ten minute "free times" to attend to one's personal hygiene and needs. Between dinner in silence and Last Prayers we had twenty minutes of "Quiete," or relaxation, which was spent walking to and fro in groups of three of four—numbers mandated—talking of pious subjects and exchanging thoughts about the Legion or the holiness of Father Maciel.

I remember some of the brothers got hepatitis and as such were very irritable with me the nurse. But I offered up that suffering for my vocation and for the intentions of Nuestro Padre and Our Holy Father the Pope. One of my companions even came down with meningitis, which despite my ignorance and the lack of reaction from superiors, was still pretty scary. I could see that my companion was suffering intensely. Normally, we would handle all illnesses ourselves without outside help, just Father Penilla, a seminarian, and I. In case of need we had a doctor from Salamanca come visit. I was on automatic compassion pilot. It helped, because my prayer life was pure agony. There were no juices flowing in my soul during my hour-long morning meditation, my adoration of the Blessed Sacrament and my Evening Prayer. Spiritual reading consisted of Father Colina's arid Explanation of Rules, Father Rodriguez' ancient anecdotes, and Nuestro Padre's Letters. Midday and nighttime conscience examinations kept the spring coiled tightly.

***

Corporal Mortification

Denying the senses was never a problem for me. It's probably my Celtic monk. I got used to eating tasteless food, showering with cold water, drying with thread-bare towels, sleeping in patched sheets and mending my own socks. Using the discipline and the cilice was not a big deal either. Father Arumí it was who, a few months into my Novitiate, called me into his office at the end of the second floor to explain. Perhaps my Spanish was in its early stages and I did not ask questions. *La disciplina* was a small whip made from strands of hemp woven into the shape of a small cat o' nine tails. With this I whipped my thighs every Tuesday and Thursday night for many years. At this stage of my life my religious vanity blames my spider veins on this mistreatment. But in my better moments I know I am deceiving myself. Although it was intended to control the flesh, I found it neither calmed nor exacerbated my "carnal appetites". It was just a painful nuisance. The "*cilicio*", a kind of mini hair-shirt à la masochiste, was a three-inch wide garter of thin wire spikes, one end tied with a shoe-lace—a touch of class said it had to be black, matching our cassocks and socks!—to tie it snugly in place around the mid-thigh. It was the sign of a wimp to limp too much or to wear it so lose it fell off when you walked. Then you would have to bend down furtively and slip it in your pocket. It hurt when you knelt or bent down and when you were sitting at table. That was to be worn from the time you got up until after breakfast on Mondays, Wednesdays and Fridays. At least I think that was my regimen. When, that evening, in the twilight of his room, Father Arumí presented me with my arms as a *Caballero de Cristo,* the romantic part of me gallantly accepted this knighthood, and I continued to use them without comment or complaint for several years.

***

Soccer as a Means of Perseverance

The Constitutions and Rules of the Legion of Christ contain a long and detailed section on Means of Perseverance, consisting for the most part in various forms of prayer and participation in confession, spiritual direction and Mass. Playing soccer is not included.

But de facto the beautiful game contributed in no uncertain manner to my surviving the Novitiate and Juniorate. We Novices frequently played soccer among ourselves on the hard dirt pitch with a worn, light, and hard to control ball. The Irish left-winger strutted his stuff against Mexican companions such as Rosendo Silva, a nephew of Nuestro Padre, who after ordination went MIA in El Paso, Texas, and Jose Barragán, now a successful lawyer in Mexico. On feast days, together we competed against the Juniors, and beat them most of the time.

***

Recuerdos de Salamanca by Westinghouse Irving

(Hope that little play on words keeps the reader awake!)

The Novitiate, a rectangular, red brick and glass building—said to be designed by Nuestro Padre himself—was not well put together. The heavy "baldosas", cement floor tiles were never properly laid, so the silence of Holy Novitiate was constantly broken by the clip-clop of feet, including the clumsy tripping of absent-minded novices followed by the thud of a cassocked body hitting the deck; but there were no cries of pain, as that would have constituted breaking "relative silence" a double transgression. Repairs were constantly, if not consistently, taking place. The Rector, Father Arumí, assigned the job to the cook, Paco, in an apparent effort to help cut costs. Aside, one wonders how it was that the Legion central administration in Mexico City, usually swimming in dollars, kept poor Father Arumí on such a strict budget. Paco was large and loud, while his aide, Joaquin, was quiet and skinny; kind of like a reverse Don Quixote and Sancho Panza couple. When Paco was not in the kitchen throwing together the horrible food, he was up on the floors playing bricklayer. Our small cubicles were in the center, leaving a wide passage between our curtains and the outer walls. Each novice had a small table set close to the window where we studied; on the top left corner, lay a picture of Our Blessed Lady—the head of Michelangelo's La Pieta, and another of the Pope, held in place by a crucifix: you could tell a professed religious' table by the larger crucifix brought from Rome, compared to the skimpy novice model. Clippidy-clop floor was Paco's playroom. Our concentration was frequently shattered by piercing shouts of "Joaquin, more mix, for God's sake!" as Joaquin would come shuffling along hurriedly in his flip-flops, apologetically exclaiming, "I'm coming!" And Paco, "Hey, will you hurry up, the mix is getting hard!"

The heating system was another serious problem, even more painful than the floors. The radiators did not work. Or they had to be bled. Some of the novices earned their place in heaven wielding monkey-wrenches at all hours of the day and night trying to keep the radiators warm. Spaniard Rafael Barrientos and Mexican Jesus Navarro-Casillas, among others, cheerfully carried out this thankless task. Some of the Irish and Mexican brothers got serious chilblains during that first crude snowy freezing winter. Declan French from Waterford was affected, as was Octavio Acevedo, a hard-working, earnest and docile dark-skinned Mexican. Even with mittens, ulcers broke out on the tops of their fingers. It took all of my "supernatural spirit" to overcome my natural repulsion and treat those festering wounds with the limited resources at my disposal.

Hail, rain or shine, on Thursday mornings after breakfast we set off on our hikes. At the back kitchen door our supplies were handed to us in brown paper bags. The lunch consisted of a small Spanish loaf or *bocadillo* containing a slab each of straw-colored sweet quince and soft white Spanish cheese. During the hot months, for us Irish this was hard to force through our parched throats after a three-hour march on the blazing plateau. We had our sparkling water or *gaseosa* to wash it down. But there never seemed to be enough and it was a blessing to find a spring along the way.

A favorite destination during the dog days of summer was the "Salamander Spring," where I spied my first salamander, a rather unattractive amphibian barely visible in the shadowy crevices of a narrow nook. God's creatures, great and small, would always be a source of consolation to me. Another favorite haunt was a cool copse of fruit trees, nicknamed "The Wood of Imprudence" because of the day a team had been caught trespassing and the angry owner screamed indignantly at the timid novices: "This is the height of imprudence! How dare you!"

Another cultural gem was encountering the Spanish Civil Guard on our hikes. Mounted on their powerful dark horses, wearing blue uniforms, despite the incongruous black three-cornered hat, they inspired fear and respect. They seemed to look down on us lesser mortals on ground level, never sparing a word on us as they patrolled the roads. We walked in threes, they rode in twos. Did they have a code of silence like us?

I derived some pleasure learning Spanish during my Salamanca sojourn. As beginners we had a certain advantage when learning the modern Spanish style of short sentences, modeled by Azorín, in contrast to traditional convoluted Spanish syntax. "Platero y Yo," the deceptively simple narrative masterpiece by poet Juan Ramón Jiménez, about a man and his donkey, Platero, was an obvious choice as our first Spanish Reading book. My natural or learned modesty prevented me from realizing I had a certain gift, but I must have felt flattered when our teacher, *Profesor* Serrano, read a short story of mine in front of all the novices. It described a childhood episode when, with trepidation, I had approached the Dominican convent in Cabra West one early morning to serve Mass in that hallowed precinct and was disarmed by a nun's kindly face.

6
RETREATING
FROM THE WORLD

I have desired to go
Where springs not fail,
To fields where flies no sharp and sided hail
And a few lilies blow.
And I have asked to be
Where no storms come,
Where the green swell is in the havens dumb,
And out of the swing of the sea.

Gerald Manley Hopkins, *On taking the veil*

CUT OFF FROM FAMILY AND CONFRERES

Yes, I did read Gerald Manley Hopkins' verse; but it was wishful reading. My spiritual life continued to be plagued by doubt and drought, and by Legion "formation."

Soon after starting my novitiate, the Assistant Novice Master, Father Jorge Cortés, then recently ordained, told me not to sign my letters to my mother with just my first name, "Paul". Instead I should write "Brother Paul Lennon, n.L.C," meaning "novice of the Legion of Christ." All incoming and outgoing mail, even to relatives, had to be monitored and reviewed. The Legion was our new home, our new family, replacing carnal bonds with spiritual.

In our conversations, strolling in threes around the gardens, we novices never spoke of our families, our siblings, our previous life and experiences, our likes and dislikes, our opinions, our wishes, desires or difficulties with those who lived with us on a daily basis. Criticism or complaints of any kind related to our superiors or our Legion life were strictly taboo. Doubts and problems were a sign of weakness that we should never share among ourselves because it might "scandalize another brother and make him lose his vocation."

We novices spoke only to other novices in our community and to our superiors. We could not speak with the Juniors humanities' students, or they with us. Gregarious, curious, or talkative members would be given a penance for breaking the rules of communication, or *incommunicado*. Novices and Juniors could not speak with any Philosophy or Theology student "Padres" living under the same roof. We were permitted to send letters—reviewed by the superior—to individual members on other Legion "fronts". The phone was off limits. There was no internet at that time. Novices did not read the papers or watch television—always viewed in group, anyway, in the Media room—save on very special occasions such as papal elections, other Vatican events, or special treats like World Cup Soccer and carefully edited movies.

The only information we had about other "fronts" was what the superiors told us, what was contained in the carefully edited official magazines exchanged between the fronts, and what we could glean from the occasional circular "Letter from Nuestro Padre." We had no idea what was going on outside our own community of novices. We did not even know what was going on inside.

Under no circumstances could confidences be exchanged between members, as this could lead to "familiarity," which in turn could lead to "intimacy," which in turn could lead to a "particular friendship," which in turn would pose a threat to the vow of Chastity. This complex syllogism, citing a passage in Latin from one of the Early Church Fathers, perhaps St. Augustine, sounded like gibberish to my innocent mind but I wanted to be a good Legionary. Father Arumí explained how personal difficulties should be entrusted only to the "legitimate superior." So when you noticed a brother acting strange and then suddenly disappearing, you passed no remark. If you saw a brother having a nervous breakdown—in one case, I witnessed him burning the large drapes outside the chapel's glass windows—you did not ask questions and were given no explanations. If the brother you were playing soccer with the day before did not appear for breakfast the next morning, you kept mum. If the superiors noticed some anxiety swelling in the ranks—sticking out like a sore thumb—they might mention something vague in the weekly "Advice" sessions to contain any possible damage. With the greatest Charity they put our minds to rest about the brothers who disappeared during the night, "despicably selling out his Legion vocation for a bowl of lentils," or "sadly giving in to the pull of sensuality, softness, selfishness," or because of "lack of generosity with Jesus," or the excusable one of "having to leave because of illness," or the euphemistic "being granted special permission by Nuestro Padre to leave."

Every Legionary's access to the outside world is strictly controlled, albeit in varying degrees according to his level of initiation.

***

Legion's peculiarity

To understand the Legion's peculiarity, and how it differs from other Catholic orders, some knowledge of the structure and inner workings of the Catholic Church may be helpful.

> Properly speaking the Legion of Christ is a (Roman) Catholic Religious Congregation. By "congregation" here we do not mean a group of believers, the terminology in other Christian denominations. This community of believers in Catholic parlance is called the "faithful", or the "parishioners." In precise Catholic terminology, "congregation" is what people commonly call an "order"; except that orders, per se, are older and more venerable institutions than the more modern "congregations"; orders date back to Medieval and Renaissance times, suggesting names such as Benedictines, Franciscans, Jesuits, and

Augustinians for example. Nowadays female and male congregations abound by the hundreds in the Catholic Church.
Members of orders and congregations are under the direct authority of their superior, to whom they pledge obedience. The Vatican tries to hobble this unwieldy assortment of groups under the authority of a kind of government department, a dicastery of the Roman Curia called the *Congregation for Institutes of Consecrated Life and for Societies of Apostolic Life.*
One of the technical distinctions between the two types of institutions is that the members of orders profess "solemn" vows of Poverty, Chastity and Obedience, whereas the members of congregations take "simple" vows. The solemn are more difficult to quit by dispensation. And just to complicate things: Catholic diocesan priests, most of the ones you see in parishes, who are under a bishop's authority, who do not belong to an order or a congregation and do not profess the three vows, are nevertheless bound by a special solemn vow of celibacy which can only be dispensed by the Holy See.

The Legion's nature and structure is not monastic and does not have cloister like the orders of Poor Clares or the Franciscans. Legionaries live in "houses" from which they can go out, and into which lay people may enter. Neither is the Legion a contemplative order like the Cistercians in which members spend most of their time praying and performing manual labor. The Legion describes itself as a congregation "of active life": members spending a fair amount of time on active duty, going about their daily activities outside the mother house.

It is not easy for a Catholic to grasp all these distinctions; just as it is for the average American, indeed for any 21st century youth, to understand the Legion's high degree of information control. Here lies the paradox: the Legion, founded in 1941, and thus to all intents and purposes "modern," isolates its members from the outside world more than many ancient monastic and contemplative orders: no phone use, no access to the internet, no viewing TV or listening to the radio.

As a Legionary I never just turned on the television, surfed the web, or bought a newspaper or magazine at the corner stand. I could not step outside the house without my superior's explicit permission. The rules did not allow me to just pick up the phone and call another Legionary in another house—*front.* Much less could I call my family or friends—what friends? I had to have a motive and objective to contact *outsiders*; all activities not sanctioned by the very detailed rule had to be approved by my superior. There were literally hundreds of rules, some greatly detailed.[9]

My house superior monitored all my actions. I tried to act like a good novice, later a good religious, and I obeyed all these rules. Because of this isolation I never heard of Bob Dylan, The Rolling Stones, The Beach Boys, Peter, Paul and Mary...I was never interested in the Beatles and still cannot understand the celebrity cult of John Lennon and the reactions I get every time I use my credit card. I had no knowledge of the Cultural Revolution happening in Europe and the USA in the '60s and '70s, of Woodstock, or of the Civil Rights Movement. No knowledge or experience of pot or the sexual revolution. We were Babes in the Woods, or in the Desert.

***

My Personal Caesar

Father Maciel, despite his other multiple responsibilities, had a special interest in the first group of Irish Legionaries.

He came to visit us during our purgatory in Salamanca. I remember meeting him on the corridor in Salamanca and him asking me how the "*garbanzos y alubias*", chickpeas and kidney beans were agreeing with me. As a Novice, I experienced this brief individual exchange with the founder as a privilege. I cannot recall any other individual interaction with Nuestro Padre from that time, except one.

I must have sent home a photograph of me receiving my Holy Patron Saint from Father Maciel at the traditional "Distribution of Patrons" for it has survived to this day. The picture on the book cover captures a moment in this rather fun activity held in Legion and Regnum houses just after Christmas. "Holy cards" were carefully prepared with a picture of certain Catholic saints containing a motto or virtue typed on the back. When my name was called I walked up to the table where Father Maciel was sitting. I picked a folded number off the table and handed it to him. He matched the number with one of the holy pictures arranged on the table. The card he gave me was "St. John the Evangelist, Patron Saint of Fidelity to your vocation." The community reacted to this and was allowed some good-natured ribbing. Someone said out loud, "Oh, Brother Paul, careful with your fidelity!" It fostered that cheery, smiling bonhomie one often sees at Legion houses.

As co-founders we had the privilege of sending to and receiving correspondence from Father Maciel as often as we wished, without inspection by anyone else. He was not only our Superior General but also our Spiritual Director, presented to us as a holy man, with great wisdom and skill in directing souls. Fortunately, I was never gullible or superstitious enough to believe he could read my mind or my soul, as some other Legionaries did. It appears that the myth was present to some degree at the beginning and grew with the Legion's expansion. I was a believer than. It was recommended that all Legionaries write to Our Founder on a regular basis, totally opening our souls to him as we would to God. Thus we could have Spiritual Direction by mail with Our Superior General and Founder.

I began that practice soon afterwards, writing to him at least once a month, in Spanish, and receiving occasional replies—a total of about a dozen in 23 years—which I considered a personal and confidential treasure: the only objects—together with the crucifix of my religious profession—I could keep as my own, and take with me from one place to another. It was a sign of being a devoted Legionary to have received letters from the Founder. I'm not sure what happened to my collection of Nuestro Padre Letters when I left the Legion many years later. Were they taken from my room? Other ex-Legionaries report that theirs were.

Nuestro Padre, the Superior General, was also the Supreme Authority over every Legionary. In case of a misunderstanding with our immediate superiors, or when we needed privileges or exceptions to the Rule, we could appeal to his judgment and intercession. Just like a Roman Citizen of old, I could appeal to my personal Caesar.

***

Quick Passage to Profession

In the summer of 1962, as I struggled through my faith crisis, Father Arumí announced to the chosen eight that because our group was "special," Nuestro Padre was granting us the privilege of taking our vows after only one year of Novitiate instead of the customary two. Again I went through the consultation process with my spiritual director and hours and hours of forcing myself to "pray," reaching out to an invisible, intangible, and absent God. As part of preparation for profession I was able to make a General Confession to Father Maciel who had come to Salamanca for the historic event. There he heard the short list of peccadilloes of a very sheltered and innocent adolescence. As I kissed the end of his stole I could understand his advice in Spanish: "! *Adelante por Cristo*!" ("Go forward for Christ!") And I took it, blindly. My superior was Christ's representative on Earth. If I couldn't see, he would see for me. On September 15, 1962, trusting absolutely and blindly in him, I would take my vows, the Three Evangelical Counsels of Poverty, Chastity and Obedience. I also took a "Fourth" or "Private" Vow, regarding never to criticize a superior in any way, and to inform our superiors if we knew of another member breaking this rule. The special profession took place in the sacristy, secretively, in the presence of Founder and Superior General, *Nuestro Padre*. There we, the newly professed, received our crucifixes, brought from Rome, and kissed them as we took them into our hands. These would be our only possessions. True to that promise, I kept mine to this very day. I never really had a problem with Jesus or blamed Him for my odyssey. I did lose him for the first several years in the Legion's arid isolation. But I found him later in the lost world of Quintana Roo, paradoxically recovering my fascination for his personality and nature, his teaching and works.

More than 40 years later it is sobering to think my quick promotion to First Religious Profession, after only one year's Novitiate and just fourteen months—of emotional turmoil—in the Legion, may not have been due to my "success" as a Novice and my grasp of the Religious Life. Perhaps it was required by the expediency of moving the first Irish batch along the fast track in order to open the English-speaking and American market to the Legion. But any such realistic thinking was alien to me.

***

With Marie Brizard on the Beach at Nice

Exciting things were happening in the Catholic Church in 1962: Pope John XXIII, a pope that neither *Nuestro Padre* nor the Legion could ever truly understand or embrace, had just convened the Vatican II Ecumenical Council. Unwittingly, His Holiness was also doing some of us a great favor. Soon after taking our vows we would leave the extreme climate—and geographic isolation—of the Novitiate-Juniorate in Salamanca and travel to Rome to take care of a large group of Mexican bishops staying at our major seminary.

From 1962 to 1970 I would travel the Salamanca-Rome route on several occasions. Part of the Legion's PR program consisted of plying members of the Roman Curia, Cardinals, bishops, and monsignors with bottles of liquor and choice bolts of material. The material came from England; the liquor was transported by our Mercedes-Benz coach. Days before the trip cases of Spanish brandy, from the least expensive, such as Fundador, to the more expensive, such as Cardenal Mendoza, were stored in the belly of the bus. Anisettes, too, from the least refined, Anís del Mono, to the more expensive, Marie Brizard, plus many cases of Spanish wine, were carefully surrounded by other non- suspicious cargos. So the bus that ferried us seminarians from Salamanca to Rome had its luggage compartment full of contraband for the Kingdom of Christ. Apprehensive brothers, such as me, suffered when we came to the customs points in France and Italy where we had to stop and officers entered the bus asking for passports. Experienced brothers took it in stride.

Another embarrassing experience was sleeping accommodations. No matter how much our drivers pressed on through the night, we usually needed at least one night's rest. One of the strangest was the night at the Montpelier seminary, deserted during the summer. The single camp bed was bow-shaped head to foot, making it impossible to get rest. Had they arched them on purpose to air them while the regular seminarians were away? Was this some strange method of warding off wet dreams?

Rolling into another French city after midnight we implemented a money-saving strategy, for a higher cause. While expedition leader, Father José María Sanchez, checked in at the front desk—fifteen rooms for thirty—the horde of seminarians, pillows in hand, milled around the lobby. As the concierge counted out the keys, part of the confusing throng would peel off making a beeline for the rooms. In the resulting melee it was impossible for the desk manager to count the numbers. Eventually, sixty seminarians were able to rest in fifteen rooms. Mattresses were quickly tossed to the floor. Bed or mattress made no difference to hardened Legionaries. This deceit did bother me, but not much. You see, we belonged to this privileged group of seminarians with a mission for the world, and we had outwitted them, those ordinary, unimportant people.

On another occasion, traveling nonstop from Salamanca we arrived at Nice about 5 a.m. The bus pulled up at the famous beach and we fell out to stretch our legs on the promenade. Walking across the sand, we washed our hands and faces, and freshened up in those celebrity-hallowed Mediterranean waters. That part of the city was sad and deserted. Needless to say, at that time of the morning no steamy French beauty was afoot—not even an old lady strolling her dog. To catch a glimpse of Brigitte Bardot with her bevy of beasts would have been exciting. But my disheveled look and unusual attire might not have favorably impressed her. I would have to be content with my longing for sweet *Marie Brizard,* a seductive stowaway in the bowel of the beast.

***

First Defections

Four out of the five "older brother Postulants" who traveled with the three Dubliners and Father Maciel to Lourdes would not reach priestly ordination in the Legion; a couple were "casualties" of the Vatican II years in Rome, 1962-65, when Mexican bishops residing at our college poached them for their dioceses. Thus, three of the first Irish recruits—Coleman, French and Allen—left or were asked to leave, "walk-aways" or "throwaways", during the first few years after joining. To reinforce our perseverance in the Legion, or so I assume in hindsight, Nuestro Padre later told us the harrowing tale of Pearse Allen being abandoned in Mexico by a bishop who had lured him away from Rome to lead his Mexican seminary: Nuestro Padre described Pearse dragging himself to the Legion house in Mexico City in rags and tatters, begging for help, and the Legion mercifully paying for his passage home to Ireland. The fourth "veteran," Maurice Oliver, was "prematurely" ordained, circa 1968, and left within a few years. The fifth, Michael Caheny, after serving as a Legionary seminarian on a series of assignments for several years, left before ordination in the Legion and became a priest for the diocese of Elfin, Ireland.

***

The Wisdom of Father Alfredo

A year after Profession of Temporal Vows, and still in my "Dark Night of the Soul," following studies in Latin and Spanish Language and Literature, I returned to Rome to take care of the bishops and begin Scholastic Philosophy at the Gregorian University. Abandoning the enclosed atmosphere of Novitiate and Juniorate to act as "angel" to Mexican bishop Anselmo Zarza Bernal, and attend public college would disperse some of the fog in my head—but only to a certain extent. What better than Philosophical Theology to get you doubting about the existence of God as you read the likes of Sartre, Nietzsche, and Camus? Once more I approached my spiritual director, religious superior, and seminary rector—in this case Father Alfredo Torres—with my "doubts of faith." Father Alfredo was one of the few survivors from Nuestro Padre's earliest Mexican groups of hand-picked child Apostolics from 1941-42 and this was his main claim to glory. He was also a member of the Legion's first General Council, an ad hoc group Fr. Maciel created to lend legitimacy to his venture. An incredible tan hulk with a massive head of sleek hair, he attacked my problem with gusto: "Take a potato. See how it grows in the ground. Can you make a potato grow? Only God." Thus spake Zarathustra Torres of the slow gestures and cavernous voice.

The better Paul, usually a sensitive person who treats others tactfully, has at least one serious defect: he does not suffer fools lightly. The old smart-alecky Paul stirring inside felt like retorting: "And why the hell would I want to make a potato grow? It grows by itself, idiot!" The budding philosopher knew Father Alfredo's proof of the existence of God was a *petitio principii*, i.e. taking as a fact the proposition you are trying to prove in the first place! Such attempts at helping, never mind understanding or empathizing, were embarrassingly clumsy and dumb, and I decided not to bring my painful doubts up again. Maybe I would find something in C.S. Lewis or in Grahame Greene's novels. And anyway, Father Kocinek, our professor of Natural Theology, who had survived Communism, and was visibly moved to tears when explaining atheists' lack of faith, seemed to have some good counter-arguments

In retrospect, perhaps my crisis did not need more philosophy or reasoning. Maybe I was simply searching for a word of wisdom, a true and deeper spirituality, or some personal knowledge and experience of God. Or, perhaps, I simply needed to be listened to without receiving advice. What if I had learned to listen to myself?

A big "what if" surfaces now after forty years. What if someone in the Legion had listened to me, to what was happening to me, to what was going on inside of me? What if someone had been able to help me listen to myself, to go beyond the doubts of faith to the pain underneath, and below the pain to what this pain was telling me? But no, "spiritual direction" and "formation" contact with Superiors were the only instruments used to train me, to coach me on a daily basis not to listen to myself but to them, to the "Will of God"—meaning the will of Legion—which they knew and interpreted for me. From that very first consultation in September 1961, before taking the habit, I was being trained; I began learning to disregard my own thoughts, feelings, intuitions. Like the lobster tail readied for crab, the inner self had to be emptied out to make room for Legion doctrine. Whether the language was subtle or obscure, gentle or harsh, the lesson was clear: don't listen, disregard the self. To think, let alone talk, of one's needs would have been selfish. The self was identified with the "flesh" and had to be cleaned out. The constant drone of "be generous, forget your self" could always be heard in the background. Decades later I would find this kind of dysfunctional family described in the Adult Children of Alcoholics' literature: *Don't talk, don't feel, and don't trust*

Why didn't my superiors and spiritual directors adapt a more exploratory approach to discernment and spiritual guidance? Because they did not know any better. They themselves had been trained that way. They had never discovered the possibility, or learned the art, of listening. They had never listened to themselves, to their own thoughts, opinions, feelings and intuitions. The voice of God, the promptings of the Spirit had always come from the outside. As a result, I disregarded—repressed?—my own thoughts, opinions, questions, feelings, pain, searching, questing…I repressed my self. Where was my soul, my own soul, my personal, individual, and unique soul in all of this?

***

Coming up for air

Fortunately, during my Rome sojourn, because I needed to keep in touch with the English language, I was able to do some "personal" reading beyond the regular Legion fare. Partly because of my obsessive doubts, I became an avid reader of C.S. Lewis and his Christian apologetics, as well as other spiritual authors. These, beyond rote memorization of New Testament passages, unimaginative *Letters of Nuestro Padre*, and other mind-numbing assigned readings, would become a lifeline for me. I explicitly got permission to read each book, if not from the Rector, at least from the Prefect of Studies. However, I must be thankful for the kindness of the Prefect who supplied books of literature for me to review in both English and Spanish. Whereas Tolstoy and Dostoyevsky were considered safe reading, we were never allowed to read Sartre or other existentialists or dangerous liberal, non-conventional writers.

I creatively managed to carve out some intellectual freedom for myself by writing my philosophy paper on Gabriel Marcel, a Christian existentialist. In my "free time" I sank my teeth into Graham Greene, the Catholic author who describes the struggle of good and evil in every soul and God's mysterious action beneath appearances. What better than to read his *The Power and the Glory* to gain insight into Mexico's religious persecution? Did *The End of the Affair* help my faith, and what was the special fascination with Hemingway's *A Farewell to Arms?* I can only surmise in retrospect that human drama greatly attracted me, men and women of flesh and blood, with feelings and passions that made life untidy. The *End of the Affair* was a kind of solution to the celibacy problem: a man could renounce a woman for love of her; she could renounce him for love of God. I conjectured that troubled Hemingway revealed something about himself in the protagonist of *A Farewell to Arms*: losing the love of his life in a meaningless way could have turned him against the God he half-believed in. I knew what it was like to struggle with an absent God who seems to abandon us to our fate. Maybe there was a glimpse of hope in the unconventional God of Greene who is so unpredictable and writes straight on crooked lines.

Another breath of fresh air came via my occasional visits—I was still the community nurse—to the doctor's office in Lungotevere. Dr. Cesare Valenti, a World War II paramedic, was our pro bono physician and one of my only human contacts with the outside world. He liked me, *Fra Paolo*, and treated me as a fellow healer. He was a very down to earth man and often saw through the somatic nature of some of my sanctimonious brothers' illnesses, gruffly remarking in his *Romanaccio, Quello no ha niente!,* there's nothing wrong with that guy! Despite his apparent indifference to Catholicity he cared for me and for my vocation. When he saw me reading Curzio Malaparte's *Kaputt*, a lurid description of war atrocities, he remarked, "That's not clergy material. You should be reading (Manzoni's classic and devout) *I Promessi Sposi*!"

The Legion also depended on the kindness of generous strangers to take care of the seminarians' dental needs. We received no dental attention in Salamanca, except emergency extractions. I have no idea how the earlier generations fared in Rome. In the mid-sixties a new order of nuns came to our assistance, *Le Pie Discepole del Divin Maestro*. That versatile and prolific Italian priest, Don Alberione, founded them to attend to the health needs of priests and religious. Being a new foundation, *le suore*, sisters, were very young, and some were very pretty. I was fortunate to be personally attended by one of them, *Suor Angelica* of the heavenly touch, and I am sure the other seminarians enjoyed their visits to the well-equipped clinic. I was grateful to get any dental service I could because I had not seen a dentist in fifteen years.

And in the midst of all this, my parents decided to travel to Rome. It was September 1966, and I was beginning my first year of theological studies. It had been five years since I said goodbye to them at Dublin Airport. Together with John Devlin and Raymund Comiskey's parents they stayed at Hotel Fiume. We were allowed to visit the churches and other places of interest with them. It was a great treat.

They were so proud of me; although I felt silly wearing that ungainly clerical *cappello* on my head, and took it off whenever I could.

All in all this was a joyful occasion, though I felt estranged from my parents after such a long time of not seeing them. And they felt awkward toward me because now I was a Legionary religious and a future priest, and in a sense, no longer belonged to them.

St. Peter's Square, Rome

In December of that same year, tragedy struck for me. One evening Fr. Dueñas called me to his office and told me my dad was very ill, and that I would be leaving for Dublin as soon as possible. By the time I got on the plane I knew he had died. I was on my way to the funeral. I was devastated: three months prior he had been healthy and smiling, and I was enjoying his warmth and seeing myself reflected in his proud kindly eyes. Now he was gone. I was the future priest and I did not have any answers. I could neither console nor be consoled. I tweaked the rules and stayed on longer than my superiors would have liked in order to be with my grieving mother and sisters, two of whom were still young.

Roman Isolation

For seven years I was whisked through the streets of Rome in the beige Mercedes-Benz coach, screening my chaste eyes from provocative billboards of six-cylinder Alfa Romeos and twin-cylindered Gina Lollobrigidas. Our driver, Father Tarsicio Samaniego, would drop me and the other 50 Legionaries off on the steps of the Gregorian University, Piazza della Pilota.

Forever self-conscious, I was further embarrassed not to be allowed to chat with other seminarians at "The Greg." Despite this human isolation and control, at the university, with its theological effervescence, we were exposed to more ideas than at home. But because of the Legion's conservative bent, which I embraced at that time, we were never allowed to read "progressive" theologians of the day, such as Rahner or Schillebeeckx. Dominican Yves Conger, Walter Kasper, and the young Joseph Ratzinger were accepted, with reservations.

Dad all dressed up in Rome

***

But because of the Legion's conservative bent, which I embraced at that time, we were never allowed to read "progressive" theologians of the day, such as Rahner or Schillebeeckx. Dominican Yves Conger, Walter Kasper, and the young Joseph Ratzinger were accepted, with reservations. I was so gung-ho Catholic, I avidly read and agreed with "Cordula," von Balthazar's critique of Karl Rahner's overly optimistic thesis: all men of good will are "anonymous Christians" whether they know it or not.

And there was soccer to aid my perseverance. When we moved to Rome, as philosophy students we played against theology students on special occasions. Dirty play was kept to a minimum but there was always the odd player who got "stuck in", notably Tarsicio Samaniego. I have been accused of occasionally putting the boot in on some of the heavier opponents. But such allegations are, as Fr. Maciel so often says regarding allegations of sexual misconduct, nothing more than scurrilous rumors.

Intramurals I played as a philosophy student against theology students could get heated. Once I got rough with an impassive Raul De Anda. He was a tough defender. So I gave him some of his own medicine, ruffling his usually imperturbable feathers. Afterwards I was sorry about it and asked my community superior permission to apologize to theology student De Anda. When he opened his door I stated my apology briefly. He looked at me without blinking, and without any show of emotion, answered "I don't remember", as he closed the door in my face. Raul was always immaculately groomed and dressed in a clean black cassock. He was one of Fr. Maciel's personal secretaries, going in and out of the founder's quarters on the second floor at Via Aurelia 677. He left before ordination and got a Ph.D. in experimental psychology. With that impressive background, and ever faithful to Nuestro Padre, he was appointed clinical director of Alfa Omega family center in Lomas, Mexico City in the '70s. At that same time I would be opening the School of Faith not far away

***

A Slap and a Pat from the Founder

During the Second Vatican Council sessions, Father Maciel was busy coming and going between our college and the Vatican. One day as he came in through the main entrance, a large group of seminarians gathered around him to hear his news. There in the foyer, outside the chapel, he began to go on about certain theologians who were "destroying the Catholic Church." He reeled off a list of dangerous theologians, including Jesuit Teilhard de Chardin, then a real bone of contention among conservatives because of his mélange of spirituality, science, and theology. Suddenly I heard myself asking "and *Nuestro Padre*, what is wrong with Teilhard de Chardin?" I had never read this writer but was wondering why Father Maciel would condemn him without knowing much about him or while the jury was still out. The reaction was a swift and harsh public scolding: "Well, Brother Paul, if you want to read Teilhard de Chardin you can go somewhere else! The door is wide open! Out you go! We cannot allow our students to foster such ideas in the Legion!"

I wanted the ground to swallow me. What had possessed this quiet, timid religious to ask such a question? Needless to say, I was so scared, ashamed and helpless I did not follow his advice. Truth was, for several years, I had never been outside the seminary gate or had to fend for any of my basic needs. That is one advantage of being a religious: all your practical needs are taken care of by "the community." I would not know what to do or where to go even if the doors were wide open and a thousand dollars were placed in my palm!

Was this the beginning of my intellectual rebellion and of my clandestine reading of Teilhard de Chardin? Rebellion? Who knows? But I was really not all that interested in Teilhard when I asked the question, nor was I fired up to read his writings later on. Many years later would I peruse *Le Milieu Divin*. As it turns out, his thinking was too fuzzy for my liking: I could not grasp his "science", and his spirituality did not grab me. In reality, at that time I preferred other writers from the French school of spirituality and literature favored by Giovanni Battista Montini, then Pope Paul VI. I remember reading Bernanos, in vogue among us Legionaries; French lay intellectual, Jean Guitton; and convert André Frossard's *Dieu Éxiste, je l'encontré*, "God exists, I met him".

Though stung by the put-down, I blamed myself for my foolhardiness. I still believed in and revered the Founder, and Nuestro Padre continued to be my spiritual director through the mail, as he had been since the beginning and would be almost to the end.

Nor did the occasional clash totally exclude me from some downtime with Father Maciel. Nearing ordination, as a "Padre" or theology student, I was occasionally invited to Nuestro Padre's table chats. He always took his meals in the guest dining room, a rectangular space on the main floor, between the reception parlors and the refectory. In this more private setting, he could receive better treatment from his waiters, his special food could be more easily served, and he could let his hair—scarce as it was—down with a select audience. More refined, and discreet, Legionaries were chosen to wait on the founder and thus be privy to the repartee. Guests were allowed into this inner circle to entertain Nuestro Padre. The spirit of these chats around breakfast, lunch, or dinner was to "help Nuestro Padre relax and give his mind a rest" from his heavy workload. Levity was the leitmotif, and jocular the mood: the chosen guests were good at telling jokes, making fun of simple-minded members, or being a good victim.

I was never a good cocktail conversationalist, and there was also the danger that I might ask one of my awkward questions. Nevertheless, I did feel privileged to be part of the petit comité close to our leader. On several occasions, however, I witnessed Nuestro Padre gloating over how he had outsmarted some unfortunate Legion member, or even a priest, bishop, or monsignor at the Roman Curia whom he considered "an enemy of the Legion". His attitude was "Screw him; he got what he deserved!" amid loud guffaws. The founder would chuckle and wink an eye; the privileged few nodded approval.

Embracing Celibacy

You might suspect that vacation time in sunny Italy posed a challenge to our celibacy. Every summer we went to Monticchio Sui Due Golfi, a tiny town on an olive growing peninsula dividing the Gulf of Naples and the Gulf of Salerno. Pastor Don Miccio's eighty-year old mother and his very plain sister, the only women I could meet, in reality posed no threat. You see, though we were in the Napoli of Sofia Loren movies, we were staying at an old tumbledown monastery in a remote location. Ancient sisters with one foot in the grave inhabited a separate part of the building. The beaches we frequented were difficult to access and therefore very secluded. We scouted them out and made sure they were never frequented by "outsiders." We made them ours.

Ordained acolyte 1967 by Cardinal Confalonieri

***

Former apostolic schoolboys, now chronologically young adults, gave them innocent and adventurous names such as "The Ravine," "The Ghost" or "The Platform". Despite our stunning good looks I doubt we were a source of serious temptation to local or visiting *signorine* who occasionally sailed into these secluded coves in their launches.

The only local person I remember meeting on our hikes was an old Neapolitan owner of olive groves, Don Crescenzo. He would talk to us in the lazy dialect made famous by Dean Martin and make us listen to his rendition of "Torno a Sorrento," bribing us with some of his homemade wine. The greenish white liquid was tart and the layer of olive oil on top did not help. Belting out the chorus with Don Crescenzo was probably the closest I got to emotional release during that stage of my Legion training.

We went on hikes, always in designated groups of three or four according to Legion custom. Being competitive, I remember trying to beat others to faraway destinations. Brother Jose Luis Buenrostro, a horse of a man, was one of my greatest rivals. I believe I made it first to the top of Monte Faito, almost falling off a cliff in the process. But I must admit that he beat me to Amalfi on foot, a four hour trek. Once there, with his companions, he would not hoof it into the nearest hotel or trattoria for lunch but rather would find a quiet nook to eat his sandwich and drink his water.

At this stage, late '60s, the Legion was making a bold new fashion statement. Instead of the old white shop coat, now we wore long khaki pants and a white t-shirt under a light khaki jacket, called *chamarra* in Mexican Spanish. Nuestro Padre, always the good-natured leg-pulling and jovial leader, cracked the joke about the Irish brother who got the name wrong. So when he said "*Nuestro Padre,* I want to wear one of those new *chamacas*, he was really saying in Mexican slang, "I want to wear one of those new dames". Anyway, all wearing the same uniform wherever we went, we stood out as seminarians, or simply as a weird bunch of young men belonging to some kind of institution.

***

During the summer before my fourth year of theological studies, 1969-70, I found my superiors were promoting me to the deaconate. This was major: the deaconate, more precisely, the "transitional deaconate" in the Roman Catholic tradition, brought with it the solemn vow of celibacy. Nuestro Padre would spend some time with us in Monticchio, where we could talk with him individually regarding this big step.

Taking into account my long history of "doubts of faith", my lack of boundless enthusiasm for the Legion and its Apostolates—the strange Regnum Christi lay movement had just appeared on the horizon—plus the occasional "run in" with Father Maciel, I was uneasy. For years I was dogged with the guilty itch of not being "sufficiently integrated" into the Legion.

Never suffering fools lightly, and comparing theory and practice, could be risky in the Legion. Legion "poverty" is quite a paradoxical item. A Legionary can have everything he wants for his apostolate once he has permission from his superior. I was also aware that members on apostolic practices in Mexico often spent luxury vacations in the houses of rich benefactors—house maids, waiters, drinks, meal service and all. Hence Paul's sardonic comment: "Hey, brothers, this is great: our vow of poverty allows us to live like the rich without having to pay their taxes!"

Paul deacon celebrating Benediction, 1969, assisted by then Bro. McIlhargey (R.I.P.)

It probably comes as no surprise that I was never once a superior or placed in a supervisory position over other confreres. They must not have trusted me. But nobody ever said anything to me directly about my deficiencies. Maybe I did not notice the elephant in my living room either.

Nuestro Padre had set up an impromptu office at the edge of the cloister and I vaguely remember stepping across through the patio plants when I was told he was ready to receive me. With some trepidation—because I think an element of fear or religious awe had always been present in our relationship—but with some honesty and courage, I laid out my difficulties to the man of God. Maybe some part of me was awkwardly trying to find a last-minute "out". What I wanted to ask was: "Nuestro Padre, am I a good match for the Legion? Should I really be here and go forward?", but either my nervous words were too jumbled or he chose not to hear.

He appeared paternal, quickly brushing away my doubts and simultaneously closing the escape hatch: "You may have had your problems, but that is a separate issue. No, Brother Paul, you have never been a problem to the Legion or to me. Do not be afraid to embrace the deaconate. God will give you the Grace to fulfill your commitments. Trust in the Lord and step forward."

By this time I, Peter Paul of Galilee, had learned my script by heart. "In your name I will cast the nets!" I was convinced that my only problem was lack of generosity, lack of simple faith, my rationalism, stubbornness, my critical mind that analyzed the Legion and its doctrine in an excessively human fashion, my lack of "supernatural spirit," and my selfishness. The solution to all these limitations was the virtue that was harped on by my Novice Instructor, Father Arumí: Self-denial, *la abnegación*. Despite my Founder's reassurance, when ordained deacon during my 25th summer at the Church of Pastor Don Miccio, in Monticchio, Naples, I was still in some mental and emotional turmoil. But this step led the way to the jewel in the crown: priestly ordination and the wonderful supernatural powers that came with it. The Solemn Vow of Celibacy involved in ordination did not loom large on my horizon. When I was ordained a few months later, at the age of twenty-six, I was renouncing the affection I did know, the lust I found repugnant, and the romantic love I did not yet know.

Paul ordained priest by Cardinal Antoniutti flanked by Fr. Maciel

12 Legionaries ordained on Nuestro Padre's 25th ordination anniversary

8
REAWAKENING

He looked around him as if seeing the world for the first time. The world was beautiful, strange and mysterious. Here was blue, here was yellow, here was green, sky and river, woods and mountains, all beautiful, all mysterious and enchanting, and in the midst of it, he, Siddhartha, the awakened one, on the way to himself. All this, all this yellow and blue, river and wood, passed for the first time across Siddhartha's eyes. {. . .} Meaning and reality were not hidden somewhere behind things, they were in them, in all of them. {. . .}
But I, who wished to read the book of the world and the book of my own nature, did presume to despise the letters and the signs. I called the world of appearances, illusion. I called my eyes and my tongue, chance. Now it is over; I have awakened. I have indeed awakened and have only been born today.

Siddhartha [10]

Becoming a priest was an emotionally draining experience, and as I look back on a younger Paul Lennon ordained at an immature twenty-six I feel compassion for that struggling young man. Like Mario Vargas Llosa stepping into character to address Paul Gauguin's Pacific odyssey, I must step into third person to face my younger self.

Priestly ordination came in a blur of activities: rehearsals of the ceremony and practice of the minutiae of saying Mass in Latin according to the rubrics of the Roman Missal, culminating with the apotheosis of Nuestro Padre's 25th Anniversary celebrations. On November 26, 1969, at the Basilica of Our Lady of Guadalupe, Via Aurelia 675, Rome, Paul Lennon was one of Father Maciel's Twelve Legionary Apostles flanking him around the altar, ordained by Cardinal Antoniutti, surrounded by a host of Legionary priests, deacons, seminarians; sweating in white alb and chasuble under the blazing spotlights filming the historic event, his eyes dazzled and blinking at Father Tarcisio's camera flashes; his relatives' visit to Rome, his mother's joy and pride, the shock of seeing his younger sisters all grown up after eight years separation and now wearing miniskirts; visits to the Basilicas, the Catacombs...He could now celebrate the Mass and forgive sins: great privilege and grave responsibility. Indeed, it was a kind of out-of-body, an out-of-self experience. Finally, after more than eight years of striving he was there at the end of Harry Lauder's road, but it didn't feel so good. Another person takes over the narrative for a while.

Ordination private party:
Paul, Chrissie, Carmel & Christine

Surprises after Ordination

Paul remained in Rome to finish his fourth year of theological studies and receive his License in Sacred Theology. But there were no proud cap-and-gown graduation ceremonies for a humble and austere Legionary; he saw no grades and no diploma. These were handled directly by the superiors. Summer vacations in 1970 were spent with confreres, not in sunny happy-go-lucky Naples but in austere Salamanca, doing month-long spiritual exercises to prepare for his new life as a priest. As they drew to a close came a pleasant surprise: he was informed he had been chosen for a select group that would travel to New Haven, Connecticut, to take an MA in Psychology and Education at Yale. The group would include fellow newly ordained Padres Rodolfo Preciado, John Sherlock, Octavio Acevedo, Eduardo Lucatero, Rosendo Silva, and others. While accepting this honor and order, a wish, simultaneously worldly and spiritual, burst to the surface of his soul: travel to his home country to visit with family members who had not been able to be in Rome for that "first Mass." Paul's Community & House Superior & Spiritual Director, Father Juan-Manuel Dueñas-Rojas, expressed hesitation. It would require special permission from Nuestro Padre.

In reality Paul would have difficulty setting up any trip by himself because for the past nine years he had never had any money, had never bought anything, or made travel arrangements; he had always depended on the community administrator for all material and practical needs. In a word, he had little if any contact with the world outside Legion walls. When he eventually got back, Father Rector told Paul that he could spend twenty hours in Ireland on his way to the USA, making sure not to overnight at his home but at the local Legion house in Leopardstown, Dublin. The brevity of the visit was hard to digest but Legionaries are trained not to complain. Paul, however, could not avoid brooding—another one of his vices, *la cavilación.* Paul was being transferred from Spain to the USA; his parents did not live in either of these countries. Father Dueñas was "within his right" to deny this permission, despite the positive factors in his subject's favor: Irish born, newly ordained, not having shared this great event with all his siblings or extended family, and not having celebrated Mass in his home parish or country. In hindsight, Father Dueñas was right, strictly speaking; Paul did not qualify for a visit to his family according to Legion rules:

> Rule 300.4
> Priests and religious will be able to visit their parents for three days when they are transferred from one country to another, if the parents live in the same country or in the country to which they are transferred.

Soon after, Paul found himself between another rock and a hard place. Arriving at Villa Rosa, Woodmont, Connecticut that August he discovered a terminological inexactitude, a white lie: the university that the LC group was actually going to attend was not prestigious Yale but Southern Connecticut State College. The Legion had befriended the Dean of Students, Dr. Thomas Vitelli, and he made the necessary arrangements for the young priests' admission.

Paul also gradually learned that he would not be studying pure Psychology but rather educational psychology and administration, and his courses would to be selected by his community superior and rector. He wanted more psychology courses; his local superiors wanted him to take administration courses. Baring his soul in this new budding crisis, he wrote to absent Nuestro Padre, his Spiritual Director, and his personal

Caesar. He explained some of his heartaches, including the way Father Dueñas had handled the visit home, and how he was presently struggling with course selection, Fathers Acevedo and Ramirez giving him no leeway. Finally, he felt obliged in conscience to confess that his old "doubts of faith" were resurfacing with a vengeance.

This had all happened in September 1970. In November Paul received a letter from Nuestro Padre saying he was very concerned about the newly-ordained priest "losing his priesthood and his Catholic Faith" and that in order to salvage these at all costs he must abandon his MA studies, go to the Missions and learn the simple faith of peasants. Nuestro Padre would instruct Monsignor Bernal to prepare a place for Paul's arrival. For now, Paul should await further orders. Paul felt this was overkill. Efforts to engage his immediate superior's understanding and intercession were futile. Father Octavio Acevedo-Marín was as impassive, and uncooperative, as the proverbial Sphinx: there was nothing he could do until Nuestro Padre called or wrote again. Christmas came and went, by which time the "crisis of faith" had lost some of its edge, and Paul was actually enjoying the course of studies, interfacing with excellent teachers and friendly MA students of both sexes. Together with the other English-speaking Legionaries he was making a special effort to help his Mexican confreres finish their papers and gain credits.

Perhaps he was also making the great discovery of humanistic psychology, far removed from the philosophical psychology or the pedagogic psychology he had studied in Rome. His parched soul soaked up this psychology of living, and understanding of self and others. Maybe it was here he ran into Abraham Maslow's pyramidal hierarchy of human needs, something totally new and unheard-of until then; something that made sense; something missing in his Legionary worldview and which might have given him some insight into his predicament.

***

Prompt, Blind, Happy and Heroic Obedience

Having accumulated twenty-four of the thirty graduate credits towards his MA degree, in April 1970 the order came from Father Maciel for Paul to depart to the Quintana Roo Missions. He would not graduate with his companions from SCSC, even though he had been instrumental in their success. Prompt, Blind, Happy and Heroic Legionary Obedience was called for.

After nine years in the institution, Paul had learned that the Legion's real call was to educating and training leaders, concretely among the upper classes, and not founding or staffing foreign Missions. The drawn out order which was finally given had sapped his resistance. Mind and heart were already set on the MA with the prospect of working in one of the Legion's high schools, among the elite, engaged in the Legion's "specific apostolate." In a tight spot and not wanting to disobey, he attempted to bargain—in Legion terminology "clarify", and this was allowed by the rule—with community superiors Acevedo and Ramiro Fernandez to at least allow him to finish the MA in Education.

Despite lacking initiative and self-advocacy, Paul attempted to have his superiors delay transfer for three months. He was not savvy enough to know that his credits would remain active for several years or that he could have received his degree by substituting a project or making up the credits later on, even from Quintana Roo. In a kind of information and emotional cut-off, nothing was explained nor was he encouraged to contact his teachers or make alternative arrangements. No! Nuestro Padre had spoken and it had to be "prompt, blind, happy, and heroic obedience." Such was the description of Legion obedience in the Constitutions Paul was fed on.

The "blind" terminology was later changed to "motivated" to avoid conflict with Vatican II teachings and prevent perceptive clergy from raising red flags. In a typical Legionary revision of history, Father Maciel's evolving divine inspiration had a later version of the constitutions—circulated for American consumption—paradoxically state:

> Their obedience should never be blind. It should be fully conscious and loving; with the same characteristics of the obedience Our Lord Jesus Christ lived and practiced before his Heavenly Father: motivated, prompt, joyful and heroic.
> (Rule 301)[11]

***

"Get thee to the Missions!"

The Legion had just taken over the Quintana Roo Mission in 1970 from the Maryknoll Fathers by request of Pope Paul VI.

> Quintana Roo [kin, tana, ro] is a state of Mexico, on the eastern part of the Yucatán Peninsula. It borders the states of Yucatán and Campeche to the north and west, the Caribbean Sea to the east, and the nation of Belize to the south.
> The capital of Quintana Roo is the city of Chetumal. Quintana Roo also includes the resort city of Cancun, the islands of Cozumel and Isla Mujeres, the towns of Bacalar, Felipe Carrillo Puerto, Playa del Carmen, Puerto Juárez, Akumal, Xcalak and Puerto Morelos; the ancient

> Maya ruins of Chacchoben, Chakanbakán, Chemax, Coba, Dzibanché, El Meco, Ichpaatán, Kohunlich, Muyil, Oxtankah, Tancah, Tulum, Tupak, Xel-Há, and Xcaret; and the Sian Ka'an national park.
> This narrow state, running north to south, covers an area of 50,350 km^2, and the 2005 census reported a population of 1,135,309. The population is growing rapidly due to the construction of hotels and the demand for workers. Many come from Yucatán, Campeche, Tabasco, and Veracruz. The state, despite its status as a resort area, is also often hit by severe hurricanes due to its exposed location.

That part of Mexico was underdeveloped and sparsely inhabited in the 1960s and was considered a "territory," not achieving the status of Mexican statehood until the 1970s. At that time Quintana Roo was so remote it was still being discovered and explored by archaeologists, as reflected in the book, *The Lost World of Quintana Roo*, by Michel Peissel (1963). When the Legion took over the Mission in 1970, Cancun was a small sleepy village, not yet connected to the "island" strip between the sea and lagoon that would make it rich and famous.

***

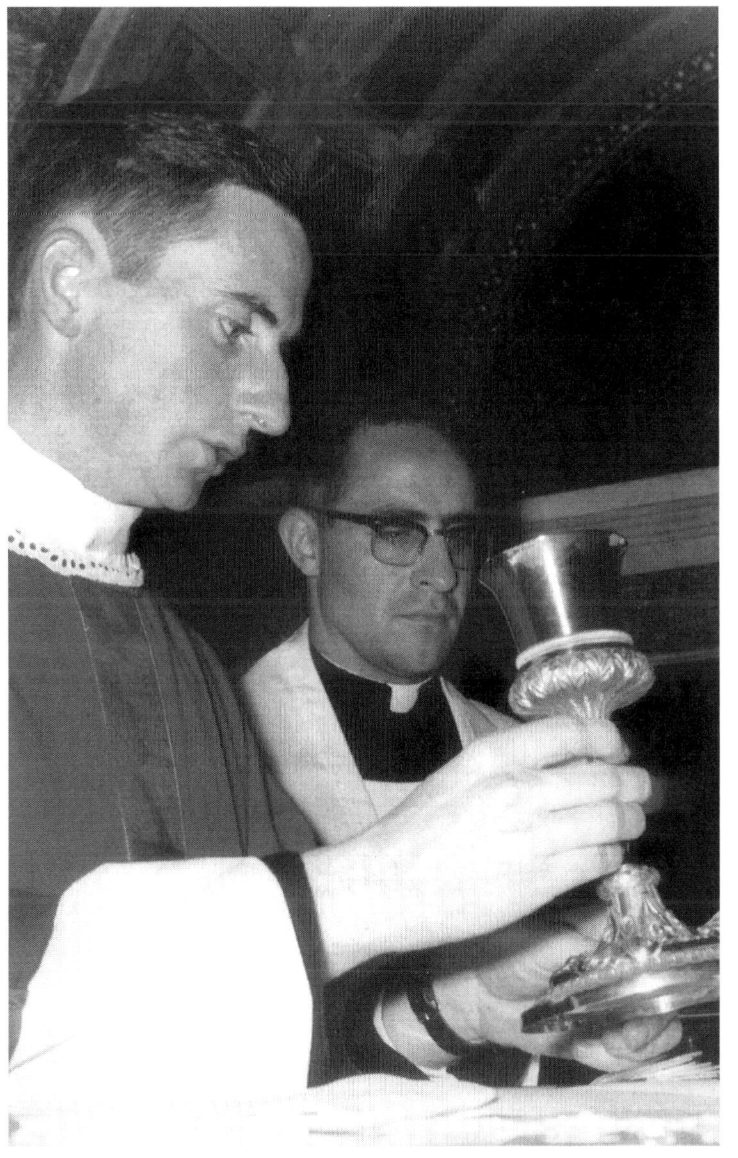

First Mass in the Catacombs

Sadly disappointed, but without conscious rebellion, Paul swallowed hard and obeyed to the best of his ability. He wanted to be a faithful Legionary religious and priest. The scent of rose petals still sweet in his nostrils and the feel of the holy oils still fresh on his hands may have contributed. And he was young and flexible enough to handle another twist of destiny: from naïve "Missionary" (vague adventurous concept in his adolescent heart) to "Legionary" (not "missionary" but rather teaching and forming leaders), back to "Missionary" (administering Baptisms, Mass, weddings, teaching people with a 3rd grade education).

Paul was put on a plane for Cancun, point of entry to the Quintana Roo Mission. Cancun was not much more than a one horse town at that time. Chetumal, 300 kilometers south, close to Belize, and capital city of the Territory of Quintana Roo, was Paul's destination. After meeting Monsignor Bernal, the bishop and superior, he hit the ground running. Assigned as assistant pastor in the small town of Bacalar, half an hour north, Paul lived in the Spartan parish house with fellow Legionary Angel de la Torre: no air-conditioning, no phone, no TV, no radio…He performed his priestly duties of saying Mass and hearing confessions in the mosquito-infested church. His lily-white elbows and ankles will remember forever with fear the dark, poorly ventilated confessional where the flying piranhas lurked and lunched. He drove the pick-up truck to the Maya villages accompanied by the Maya-speaking sisters, *Madres de la Luz*.

Paul was a newly ordained priest, less than twenty-eight years old and full of youthful enthusiasm and vigor. He was undeterred and his sense of humor was intact, his wit making light of the most difficult assignments and situations. And he came to dearly love the humble and noble Maya people he served. Grace of state had to be invoked when hearing Maya-speaking children's confessions. He could pick out the occasional Spanish word to get the gist of: "cussed out my sister," "hit my brother", "didn't feed the pig," or whatever. With true apostolic zeal, trying to explain and illustrate the rites, he conscientiously performed baptisms, celebrated the Eucharist, and presided at weddings.

After about a year, Paul was invited to live in the capital city of Chetumal, population then of 30,000. To a more cosmopolitan audience, he launched a Catholic radio program. Every Tuesday afternoon during Lent, at the peak hour, Roger Chan, in his most sonorous formal tone would announce: "'Christ Today and Always!' And here you have Padre Pablo Lennon of Divine Providence Parish!" Another highlight was workshops for religion teachers organized with confrere Father Bernard Quinn, L.C. Following the "mind of his superiors," and as a way of disregarding his doubts, he worked sixteen hours a day, six days a week, for four years.

Unfortunately, that is not always the case and Paul witnessed at least one other exiled Legionary literally falling apart during his Missionary assignment. Clearly needing serious psychological services, that confrere was attended by the local physician—beholden to the Legion—who prescribed some drug or other. Because of the strictures on outreach to a fellow Legionary, Paul's compassion could never approach his confrere to find out what was wrong, and Paul never learned what happened to this newly ordained priest later on. Paul was luckier. His genes, his resilience, his love of people, or some other unknown factor, saved him.

With catechists at Divine Providence Church, Chetumal, Quintana Roo, 1973

***

Life was "bustin' out all over," and perhaps the sap seeped into Paul's soul, just as the weeds burst through the tarmac and stubbornly encroached on the road from Cancun to Chetumal. Life in its vibrancy sprang from the humid heat opening the pores, caressing nostril hair, and arousing the senses. The sun blazed down from early morning out of a clear deep blue sky. In the dark green rainforest, filtered light revealed bromeliad rosettes, their leaf colors ranging from maroon, through various shades of green, to gold; many species sported dappled leaves with red, yellow, white and cream variegations; some spotted with purple, red, or cream, while others displayed different colors on the tips and bottoms of the leaves. The rich abundance was capped by bright scarlet and orange epiphytes leaping at the eyes from tree forks when Paul ventured into the forest. And this he loved to do in the company of Eulogia and Don Florentino, his Maya woodsmen.

Life-giving sounds abounded too: the chirping of unknown and unseen birds, the cacophony of frogs in concert after a rainstorm, and spider monkeys screeching as they played with the village children. Strolling the town street the stranger bristles at a wolf-whistle; quickly spinning around he catches sight of an impertinent green parrot mocking him from a porch emitting his whee-whee-o call; the taste of delicious fruit entices the most disaffected stoic to savor ripe bananas straight from the tree in the garden, papaya sprouting spontaneously like a many-breasted Indian goddess out of the fine cream limestone *sascab* outside everybody's house, and pineapple from the mother plant close to the sandy earth.

Paul would soon develop a weakness for the *chicozapote*, or sapodilla, fruit of the *chicle* tree whose sap was harvested aggressively by American companies in tropical Central America during the middle of the 20th century for chewing gum and other products. Its rough outer skin is similar to another tropical delight, *mamey*, but sapodilla is sweet but not too sweet. It has a burnt sugar taste, almost spiced, that seduces the taste buds. And then there is tamarind...

When venturing into the heart of the forest the greenhorn was stunned by the sight of the majestic mango tree: like a swaying giant, its red, green and yellow parrot-nosed fruit dangling from lofty branches, its gray hair rustling in the breeze; while at the talcum powdered beach, warm turquoise waters invited the landlubber to snorkel and explore a mysterious underworld teeming with life and striking color. Yes, in this earthly paradise Paul came to life.

Slowly he began to feel better. The "doubts of faith," while not disappearing, lost their bite. He had a kind superior, a friendly religious community of Irish and Mexican confreres, a more relaxed atmosphere, and dozens of people to nurture and by whom to be nurtured. He began to make friends with his parishioners, poor, good-natured people of the López Mateos neighborhood; men, women and children. For the most part these were *Mayeros*, people of Maya stock who were integrated to some degree into mainstream Mexican culture. The men wore regular clothing, while some women preserved the use of the embroidered hipil. Many of these families spoke Maya in their homes, Spanish being their second language. As Caribbean people they possessed a *joie de vivre* all their own: a sunny, uncomplicated disposition easily moved to laughter and to joking.

At Divine Providence parish Paul was fortunate to have a young, intelligent and resourceful "sacristan", jack of all trades, Eulogio Coyí, of pure Mayan ancestry. Paul spent many pleasant hours with him and his beautiful wife, Panchita, learning about Maya customs, popular Catholic religious traditions and picking up a few words of the native tongue. Eulogio and an older Mayero called Don Florentino Palomo introduced Paul to the forest and its tropical hardwood trees, the least of which was mahogany. Paul fell in love with the flora and fauna—and the people—of Quintana Roo. They did his soul good.

Padre Pablo experienced a deep sense of satisfaction in hearing confessions, healing, preaching, and teaching. He was known first as "The Bicycle Priest", *El Padrecito de la bicicleta*, because he rode his bicycle from the Sacred Heart Parish, where he slept and took his meals, through the oft-muddy streets of Chetumal to unpaved Divine Providence Parish.

Besides administering baptisms, weddings and funerals he set up catechetical enclaves throughout the parish. Because the sun was always so intense, he built wooden benches around "almond trees", or so the locals call them. These tropical trees, with large oval shaped leaves and the branches spread out in tiered circles from the trunk, produce an inedible almond-shaped fruit. This way the young students could sit in the shade. Noticing how some of the preteen boys and girls were bright and assertive, he created a group of *mini-catequistas* to teach younger children the rudiments of the faith close to their homes.

On top of regular ministerial duties, Paul fundraised to finance a cement Church roof to replace the corrugated iron one inherited from the former pastor, Father Vélez, who had returned to the diocese of Campeche when the Legion took over Quintana Roo. Paul organized parish fetes and built and raffled a house—personally selling the tickets to local shopkeepers, mostly Lebanese-Mexicans. He was happy to have a window into another fascinating culture.

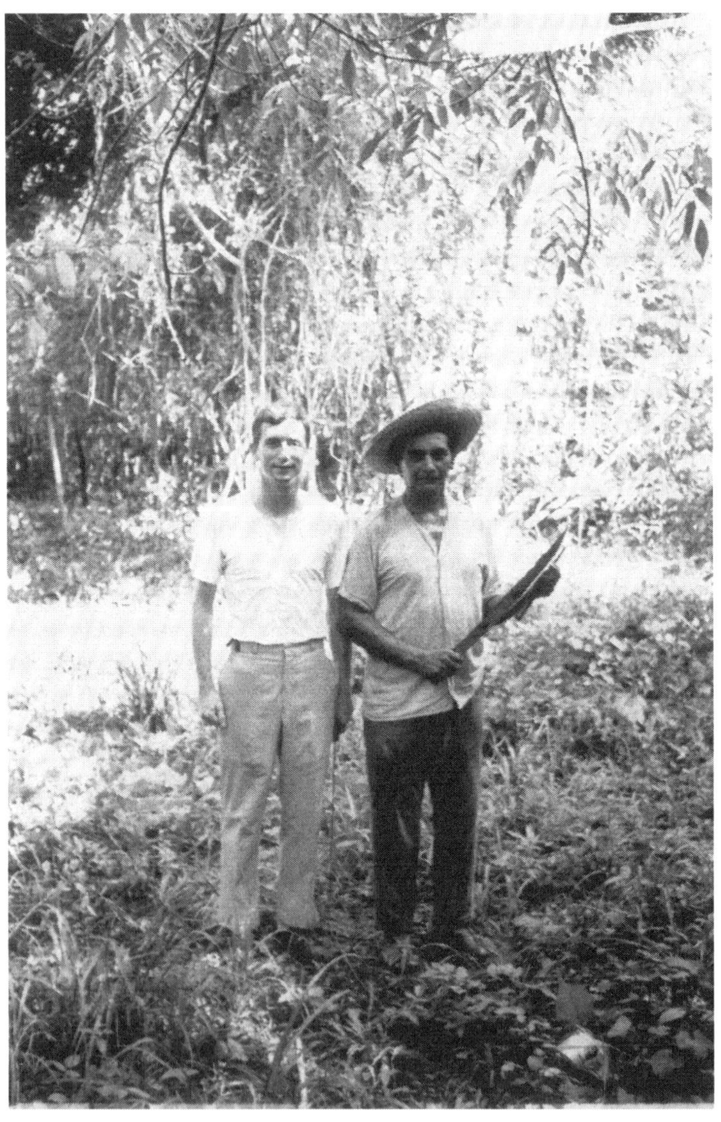

With Don Florentino Palomo, Quintana Roo rainforest, 1972

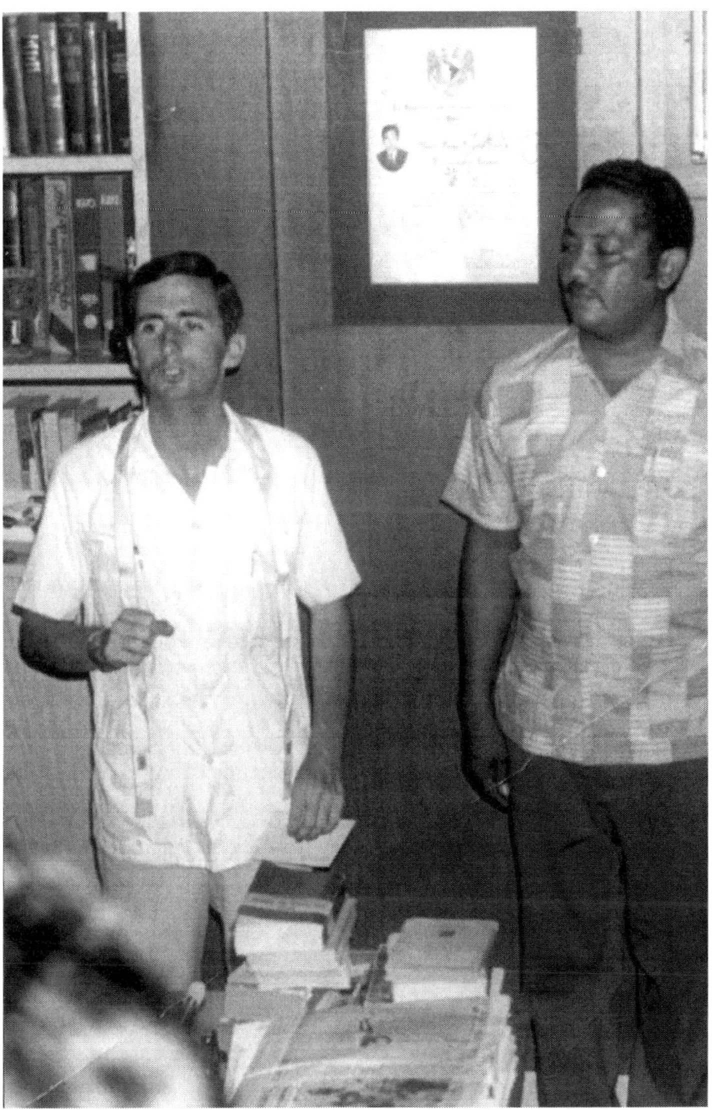

Blessing office in Chetumal, c. 1972, with Jesús Martínez-Ross, future governor of Quintana Roo

Noticing how non-Catholic missionaries hogged the local radio station, WXEROO, and despite the government's mistrust of Catholics in public life, he began a series of Lenten Radio Talks. The friendly radio announcer, not a Catholic himself, had to bow to the charm and zeal of the little Irish missionary. He enlisted his companion Padres to take advantage of the opening and deliver homilies on the radio: major success. By all and sundry, politicians and dispossessed, he was considered *Un Padre muy padre*, "a very hip priest." When, a few months later, Monsignor Bernal presented Paul with an old fashioned bone-rattling Willy's Jeep, he became *El Padrecito del jeep*, "The Jeep Padre."

***

Eros stirs

A virgin, with the scant sex education typical of his generation, Paul had always been leery of sexual pleasure. He was romantic, distinguishing clearly between lust, attraction and love. The C.S. Lewis he read in Rome laid it out so clearly in *The Four Loves*: Affection, Friendship, Eros and Charity. He would never enter love through the door of lust, which by religious upbringing he had already eschewed. On entering the seminary, taking vows and becoming a priest he would give up marriage, children, and romantic love—his notion of love: love as longing to get closer to the pretty nut-brown girl in Connemara. Though her hair was darker, it provoked the same feelings as Stephen Foster's

"I dream of Jeanie with the light brown hair,
Borne like a vapor on the summer air."

Soon after arriving in the one-horse town of Bacalar he struck up a platonic relationship that has lasted to this day. An intelligent and educated teacher-trainer who worked and lived in the town was to afford him many hours of friendship and learned conversation, something he could not get from his parishioners or local confrere. Lilí, who grew up with priests coming in and out of her house in Merida, and who cultivated healthy relationships with several Marist Brothers, kept her distance from the Legion's recruiting machine while treating the priests with respect and kindness. She noticed quickly that Paul lacked the wooden quality of most Legionaries, the impassiveness, the controlled facial expression, the stiffness and lack of spontaneity. "You're not like the others, Pablo; I pinch you and you cry 'Ouch!'"

Later in Chetumal another woman, warm and sensual, was attracted to him. He liked to visit and did not dislike the warmth of her home. One afternoon when her insensitive husband was not around, her feelings got out of hand and she began to caress him tenderly and kiss him on the face and neck. Though he enjoyed it and felt the pleasure, he somehow summoned up the self-possession to stop her and himself. He said something incredibly "mature" like: "Thank you very much for your affection, but we shouldn't do this as I'm a priest."

"Forgive me, Padrecito," she apologized, "I am very fond of you and got carried away."

The Padrecito: "It's my responsibility too, Rosa, I have to be more careful."

"There is no problem, Padre; I will never do it again, not even above the belt"

And she never did. Paul marveled at his aplomb and tact in handling this delicate situation; his pastoral commitment to Rosa and her family was a powerful deterrent. Besides Paul did not want to do anything that could affect the relationship of a married woman with her husband, no matter how tenuous or troubled that relationship might be.

The *Padrecito*'s ignorance, or gullibility, got him into other tight situations. He worked closely with an intriguing woman who helped him sell the 1,000-peso tickets for the house raffle. He visited her home, innocently, but often. Padre Paul was already on friendly terms with her other family members, so there was no reason for them to suspect any skullduggery. This was one of the characteristics of the people from southeast Mexico. They were less suspicious and cynical than their compatriots in some other regions when it came to man-woman relationships. Maybe they were less complicated and saw things naturally. Anyhow, Paul enjoyed spending time alone with this attractive single woman. In his foolhardiness he did not realize she might get attached or attracted to him. Then one day…he picked her up in the jeep on her way home from work. As they sat side by side, approaching her home where he was to drop her off, she said quietly, "Pablito, do you feel anything special between us?"

"Like what?" asked the space cadet.

"*Un calorcito*, warmth, welling up in your body."

Clueless, "No, I don't feel any particular warmth."

It was true. And she stepped down from the jeep and walked into her house. He continued to visit with her. Only much later did he learn how attached she was to him. Still oblivious, when he received orders to leave Chetumal and Quintana Roo, he went to her house, bid her goodbye, hugged her warmly, and went on his way. He did not realize that he, too, had felt some kind of attraction and affection, and that he had probably broken her heart.

Paul did not feel that these skirmishes violated his vow of celibacy. He did not mention them to his Personal Caesar, fearful by now of the draconian measures emanating from long-distance spiritual direction. Father Maciel, on the other hand, was mostly absent from Quintana Roo during the early 1970s. On one of his short visits to Cancun, Nuestro Padre did confide a tragic story to the scandalized troops: he had accepted into the Salamanca Novitiate an adult from the local town of Felipe Carrillo Puerto. This was an exception, because the Legion did not usually take people who had "lived in the world." But the Legion was eager to recruit members from the Yucatan Peninsula Missions and this man already had a career and a reputation. Nuestro Padre explained how this older novice had sexually abused some of his younger companions. "He destroyed the whole batch! I had to send them home", the founder lamented. We did not see how incongruent the remedy was: getting rid of the victims without acknowledging the abuse or offering them treatment; and the abuser was sent somewhere else, without dealing with the issue. That was the way the Legion treated such cases. If Apostolics or Novices were abused, they became soiled. There was nothing left but to send the damaged goods home as soon as possible, with some kind of excuse that would not arouse suspicions of parents or local pastors. There was no explanation given to the surviving community members. Silence can be a powerful instrument of control.

But now Paul was going off on a new quest. He was being "promoted", chosen by Nuestro Padre to start the School of Faith. This would entail some travel to check out what other orders were doing.

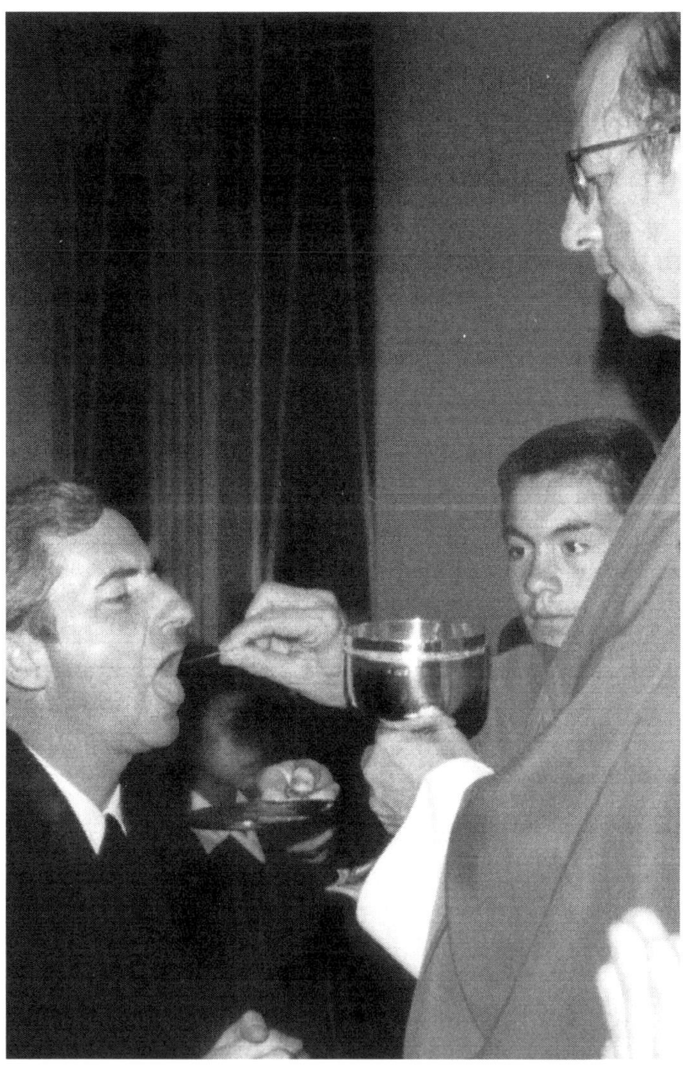

It was always a privilege, even as a priest in 1975, to receive Communion from the Founder's hands.

8
RESISTING

At times he heard within him a soft, gentle voice, which reminded him quietly, complained quietly, so that he could hardly hear it. Then he suddenly saw clearly that he was leading a strange life, that he was doing many things that were only a game, that he was quite cheerful and sometimes experienced pleasure, but that real life was flowing past him and did not touch him. Like a player who plays with his ball, he played with his business, with the people around him, watched them, derived amusement from them; but with his heart, with his real nature, he was not there. His real self wandered elsewhere, far away, wandered on and on invisibly and had nothing to do with his life.

Siddhartha[12]

DIRECTOR OF THE SCHOOL OF FAITH: THE GLORY WITHOUT THE POWER

Because of his success in Religious Education—and docility to superiors—in mid-1975 Paul was chosen by Father Maciel to set up a religious education center for adults in Mexico City. Assisted by Patrick, a big six-foot-four, bright ex-Legionary from Philadelphia, Paul opened the School of Faith officially in January 1976. It soon began to prosper, achieving relatively quickly the status of Pontifical Catechetical Institute.

Paul had been instructed by his superior general to consult with Father Alfonso Samaniego, LC, then Territorial Director, for help with launching Nuestro Padre's latest brainchild. Father Alfonso's fame, knowledge, and politeness had preceded him. As an elder brother he gave Paul some sage advice regarding the Mexican women from prominent rich families he had cultivated for years: older women would not be so helpful in the school because of their physical condition and the excessive attention they required; Paul should avoid menopausal women for the same reason. He would be looking for women in their thirties. These, on the other hand, had the drawback of being "problematic," and some of their marriages were in shambles. But they were energetic go-getters. Although Paul would have to invest time in them it could be worth the trouble...

Soon Paul and Patrick were invited to the home of Soumaya Domit de Slim, spouse of Carlos Slim Helú, in Lomas de Chapultepec where she had gathered a bunch of her friends. This presentation netted half a dozen intelligent, enthusiastic, and hard-working women who turned out to be very productive and ensured the school's eventual success. Paul spent hours preparing lessons, teaching students, and training his core group of future instructors.

***

Social Doctrine of the Church, a Taboo Subject

As Paul pulled together the curriculum, texts and questionnaires, he returned to Father Alfonso.

A faithful son of the Second Vatican Council (1962-65), during his forays down to the *Librería Parroquial* bookstore, Paul found sound and attractive texts to cover introductory courses on the Bible, the Creed, and Christology. For Moral Theology, Paul chose a synopsis of the groundbreaking summary of modern Catholic doctrine, the Pastoral Constitution on the Church in the Modern World—to insiders, *Gaudium et Spes.* Why complicate matters? The School of Faith course would shadow closely the document's three parts: Person, Family and Society. Father Alfonso had a quibble. Everything was fine except that third part, the section regarding the Church's social doctrine. He wondered whether Paul needed to include that. Weren't the articles of the Creed enough? Wasn't this the School of Faith? What need was there of the Church's social doctrine? That would be uncomfortable for the students from the upper social echelons. Paul could well imagine that and he was not looking forward to expounding on the great social encyclicals of the last popes, John XXIII and Paul VI, to such an audience. *Gaudium et Spes* reformulated such lapidary doctrines as "the universal destination of all wealth" and the Christian's fundamental moral obligation to share his wealth with those less fortunate. A truth as plain as a pikestaff to all Catholics, but not to the Legion and to the leaders it cultivates.

***

The Lovely Ladies of Lomas

In Mexico, *el Padre*, or rather *el Padrecito,* as he is called in the diminutive affectionate form, is an institution that crosses even the rugged barriers of social class. In most parts of Mexico, despite a history of government anti-clericalism, the priest is a beloved and revered key person in the community. Mexicans will open up to him when life's troubles overwhelm them. They will approach the *Padrecito,* anywhere and any time, to request *un consejo*, a piece of concrete advice, for their very personal problem, and take it to heart. A kind and available padre experiences this on numerous occasions during his pastoral life. On the occasion of the First Communion of a child, for example, the most lukewarm Catholic man can summon up the courage, swallow his machismo, kneel before the Padrecito and ask for God's forgiveness. Before getting married by the Church the most freewheeling groom gets down on his knees and tries to cleanse his soul because he really loves this woman, "the future mother of his children"—a little concession to machismo, perhaps, but also submission to the man of God!

Thus, a few months into his position at the School of Faith Paul had a large clientele of pretty, and pretty-messed-up, women. Whereas their spiritual directors with the Regnum Christi Movement simply responded with formulas, he would listen to their raw needs. He had no formal training beyond a course on pedagogic psychology, given in Latin by a French-speaking Jesuit in Rome and his truncated studies from Southern Connecticut State College. Here was the frustrated counselor finally coming into his own. He could empathize with their pain. Being sought after by these attractive and intelligent women must have increased his self-esteem and self-confidence, making him feel more competent and attractive.

Paul was never privy to the financial wrangling behind this apostolate. He knew the School of Faith had started off with a loan from Investigaciones y Estudios Superiores, AC, the Anahuac University Civil Association but he had never been directly involved in the financing. Don Francisco Lozano and his wife, Amparo, were the benefactors, as far as he knew. But Paul did not know the amount of their donations and had no right to ask for any explanations regarding financial management from his taskmaster.

A couple of years after helping Paul found the School of Faith, Patrick left for greener pastures. By 1978 Father Maciel was playing hardball. "Paul, the SF needs to be financially independent. You have to pay the loan back to the Anahuac University. You cannot be a burden for the Legion."

Who helped poor old impractical Paul solve that problem? Paul was joined by another ex-Legion seminarian, Iliano Piccolo. He was a great asset to the school, taking over teaching several subjects in the curriculum. He was a gifted teacher and well liked. For the most part he was helpful and supportive. Much later, when things started getting sticky for Paul in his relationship with Father Maciel, it seemed that the gifted leader would use Iliano's monthly reports instead of his, the director's, to get the lowdown on the school. Anyway, when it came to fundraising, the lovely ladies of Lomas were needed. They were the ones who organized a Nina Ricci fashion show, prêt-a-porter, at the Maria Isabel Sheraton Hotel on Paseo de la Reforma. Paul's religious superior reminded him the rules did not allow him to be present for that. It was a resounding success, bringing in several hundred dollars. All proceeds were duly deposited in the Legion account. Those ladies were efficient. And when it came to spreading the SF to the Mexican provinces? Along came Mr. and Mrs. Labarthe to take Father Paul and his team to lead weekend workshops in Irapuato, Querétaro, Aguascalientes and San Luis Potosí. Paul had contacts in Cancun and Quintana Roo to launch the Catholic Adult Education School there. But he was learning to rely heavily on the laity. Orders came from above, help came from below.

***

Disagreeing

The School of Faith as originally presented by Father Maciel and as implemented by Paul had a Church-wide dimension. It was meant to train religious instructors for Catholic parishes and dioceses, and this, from Paul's point of view, involved collaboration with the religious education centers of neighboring jurisdictions. It was also a school to catechize many parents whose children attended Legion schools. Because of the quality of the program and instructors, The School of Faith soon had *Regnum Christi* (the Legion's lay Movement) members from the young women's and men's sections thronging to the center. Some students favorably compared Sierra Vertientes classes to the duller "formation" fare being dished out in their respective Regnum Christ sections. The School of Faith was also co-ed, a place where both sexes could mingle naturally, safely and spontaneously.

Paul was hearing rumblings in the distance about the School of Faith being used as an Open Means of Recruitment, "*medio abierto de captación*", to get Catholics to join the Legion's Regnum Christi. To him this meant a narrowing of its initial focus and a twisting of its mission. He expressed his misgivings to the powers that be but the objections fell on deaf ears. Once more he felt restless and began, unconsciously, wanting to take some direction. Perhaps he had never adjusted properly to the introduction of the Regnum Christi Movement. Not on his horizon until a decade after he joined the Legion, now this lay section was supposedly more important than the priestly branch, the latter being absorbed into the greater whole. Paul's generation had seen "The Movement" evolve from vague ideas to a reality and he knew how important it had become for Father Maciel. But according to Paul's values, that should not justify its being placed above local dioceses and parishes or interfere with the original "universal" nature of the School of Faith.

Anyway, Paul's professional "moon" waxed during that period, 1976-82, together with his self-assurance and self-determination. His allegiance to Father Maciel and the Legion began to wane, perhaps in proportion, and prompted by a series of disagreements. By the end of 1979—he was now thirty-six—Paul was less hungry emotionally, and less insecure due to his success as the founder, creator, and director of the School of Faith. He takes this "Apostolate" with a bright future to other parts of central and northern Mexico. From his superiors' point of view, Paul is losing humility, docility, "spirit of faith," and "integration"; in a word, getting too big for his boots.

And he is becoming increasingly "worldly." On his long drives from Tlalpan to Lomas and back every day he turns on the radio of his little Renault and picks up an English-language FM station. He is able to reconnect with some of his old favorites of the '50's and early '60s and becomes a John Denver fan, singing along with him on those nasty and noisy Mexico City streets: "Country roads, take me home to the place I belong; West Virginia"—no idea where that was!—"Mountain mamma, country roads take me home." Maybe this was chicken soup for his soul. One of the more enlightened Ladies of Lomas bought him a Stevie Wonder record for his birthday in an effort to bring him up to date.

***

Take a walk!

In the spring of 1980, without notice, Nuestro Padre sent a fellow Legionary from Rome to replace Paul overnight at the School of Faith. Just like that. It was a rather sheepish Father Peter Cronin who mounted the flight of stairs and stepped awkwardly into the Sierra Vertientes' office: "I'm taking over the School of Faith. Could you tell me how to run it as quickly as you can?" Swiftly retreating to the top floor, Paul took a moment to get his bearings. He was being told to take a walk. The reason given was that he was urgently needed in Cozumel, Quintana Roo—a tourist destination but also mission land—to "accompany" a friend of the Legion, Cardinal Pironio, who was coming to relax. Pironio was Prefect of the Sacred Congregation for Religious and Secular Institutes and a friend of the Legion. He was instrumental in securing Vatican Approval for the LC Constitutions. Obediently, Paul took a plane the next day. When he arrived in Cozumel he found out that someone else was taking care of that particular assignment. Paul was relieved anyway as chaperoning church dignitaries, telling pious anecdotes, and fawning were not his forte. The local Legionary superior, Father Javier Orozco, LC, was kind but didn't need him.

Apparently, Paul was never "needed" in Cozumel—it was a ruse to get him away from the School of Faith. After a short rest in Cozumel, which included a bicycle ride around the island, the acting Territorial Director for America, Father Carlos Zancajo, had Paul back at the helm of the School of Faith. Father Cronin was sent packing to Monterrey, Mexico, and thence to Rome. One wonders why Nuestro Padre would not simply tell his subject Paul what he wanted him to do, instead of using this elaborate maneuver. The episode reveals Father Maciel choosing one particular tactic from his ample repertoire of manipulation to rock Paul and dislodge him from the School of Faith.

***

9
REACTING

"Govinda, I believe that amongst all the Samanas, probably not one will achieve Nirvana. We find consolations, we learn tricks with which to deceive ourselves, but the essential thing -the way- we do not find."

"Do not utter such dreadful words, Siddhartha," said Govinda. "How could it be that among so many learned men, amongst so many Brahmins, amongst so many austere and worthy Samanas, amongst so many seekers, so many devoted to the inner life, so many holy men, none will find the right way?"

Siddhartha, however, said in a voice which contained as much grief as mockery, in a soft, somewhat sad, somewhat jesting voice: "Soon, Govinda, your friend will leave the path of the Samanas along which he has traveled with you so long. I suffer thirst, Govinda, and on this long Samana path my thirst has not grown less. I have always thirsted for knowledge; I have always been full of questions"

Siddhartha was silent…Yes, he thought, standing with bowed head, what remains from all that seems holy to us? What remains? What is preserved? And he shook his head.

Siddhartha[13]

"GET RID OF THAT CONTEMPTIBLE WOMAN!"

El Puma" was the name coined by ex-Legionary Alejandro Espinosa, author of *El Legionario*, for his "Uncle Marcial". The puma (*Puma concolor azteca*) is the cleverest and strongest of Mexican fauna. Astute, it analyzes situations and sizes up its prey. *El Puma* Maciel instinctively intuits the quarry's vulnerability: pride, covetousness, lust, anger, gluttony, envy and sloth, or the myriad of human weaknesses which beset us all. El Puma will initially offer to fulfill your needs so as to eventually end up getting what he needs. El Puma prefers the stealthy approach, but can be violent when he has to be.

Paul's relationship with *El Puma*, as his religious subject and spiritual son, continued to deteriorate. In the spring of 1981 he was summarily called to meet alone with *El Puma* at LC headquarters in Tlalpan, in Mexico City's fashionable southern suburbs. This magnificent block of property, featuring a large artificial lake with canoes, a 100-seat luxury auditorium, royal palms and trellises had once been the scene of orgies when owned by the disreputable Mexican politico Morones in the 1930s. Encounters with Nuestro Padre were engineered in such an ambiguous way that the notified religious could only speculate about why he was there and what the interview would be about. This set up, naturally, placed the brother at a disadvantage. Paul got to the Legion property, baptized by Maciel *Quinta Pacelli* in honor of Pope Pius XII, Eugenio

Pacelli, housing the Apostolic School, the CEYCA K-12, and *El Puma's* offices. He waited—for a couple of hours—outside the building known simply as *La Tres,* Number Three. At that stage of his Puma-knowledge, Paul was not surprised by this, the delay tactic.

El Puma suddenly appeared and started walking briskly around the grounds with Paul in tow. He came right out with the blunt accusation: "I've been hearing things about you. There is a contemptible woman (in Spanish he used the pejorative "*tipa*") at the School of Faith. You need to get rid of her!" Paul took exception to that and countered, asking Maciel what he was talking about, as he did not know any "contemptible women." El Puma got impatient. "Well look, Paul"—he used the first name without title—you get rid of her, because I will not have adulterous priests in the Legion of Christ!" The thought flashed across Paul's mind: "Here I am surrounded by attractive women and breaking my balls trying to be celibate, and this *hijo de puta* is accusing me of adultery."

Paul was steely calm as he told *El Puma* he knew very well what adultery meant, that he was not committing adultery, and that *El Puma* was barking up the wrong tree. *El Puma* countered, "*Cuando río suena, agua lleva*", where there is smoke there is fire. Ironically, the phrase, and the suspicious philosophy behind it, would come to back to haunt Father Maciel. That day *El Puma* threatened to get rid of the impudent religious and banish him from the School of Faith. Paul responded in kind: if *El Puma* did that, Paul would go straight to Cardinal Corripio, Archbishop of Mexico, and report Maciel for falsely accusing one of his religious. Church hierarchy has some supervisory power over religious orders living within their jurisdiction.

Cardinal Corripio at first graduation of *Masters of the Faith*, Instituto Cumbres auditorium, Mexico City, c.1979.

> In his youth Paul had occasionally felt the rigors of education at the hands of the Irish Christian Brothers. One day in middle school Brother Kelly was complaining about the lack of cooperation for one of his fundraising or charitable projects. Sarcastically, he thanked the class in Gaelic. A voice from the desks responded "You're welcome", also in Gaelic.
> "Who said that?—asked Brother Kelly in Gaelic
> Me, Sir.
> Come up here, Mr. Lennon."
> Paul made his way to the front of the class to stand in front of Bro. Kelly.
> Without warning, Bro. Kelly's open hand exploded with full force along Paul's jaw, leaving his cheeks burning, his ears ringing and his head reeling.
> "*Sig síos*!" (Sit down!)
> Maintaining his composure, and balance, Paul turned impassively and walked slowly back to his desk, keeping the tears welled up in the corners of his eyes.

Though lacking physical violence, Father Maciel's attack was just as ferocious. The result was similar. The wary snail emotionally withdrew within its shell, with the conviction that this vicious attacker dressed in a black cassock could not be God, or Christ, or Church. But by now, in 1980, the snail, no longer a powerless schoolboy, had grown a hard shell and bigger horns. Even so, in the long run, what is a snail—or even a fox—against a puma?

Thus Paul experienced *El Puma*'s very human side up close and personal. Years back, before ordination, Paul had occasionally joined El Puma and his entourage for long gossip sessions in the private breakfast room at the college in

Rome. At these table chats *El Puma* began to reveal himself to the observing Paul as a man strangely bereft of gentleness, tenderness and compassion; his concept of women in general was low, referring to them without affection or respect. But this new episode was a personal affront to Paul and to the women with whom he worked. *El Puma* had also threatened and bullied, not a good thing to do with an Irishman. Paul took exception to this unholy behavior. Worse still, the confrontation definitively severed the already weakened trust in his spiritual father. Nuestro Padre lost Paul. Paul was beginning to look down on the man he had once placed on a pedestal.

Paul could not comprehend his own audacity. He was losing his fear of *El Puma,* along with his respect. He was also indignant: just because the complaint, gossip, or rumor involved a woman, *El Puma* immediately assumed something physical was going on, rather than other explanations such as loving feelings, emotional attachment, a working relationship, or even platonic friendship. *El Puma* seemed oblivious to the possibility that a heterosexual male could have strong erotic feelings toward a woman without having to act on them. Paul was incensed that this so-called holy man should have spoken in such an un-priestly and ungentlemanly way. They glared at each other for a long moment until *El Puma* stalked off with a scowl. The confrontation would distance Paul further from his former spiritual father. He would no longer trust or confide his troubles to *El Puma.*

Many years later, a close female friend of Paul's sheepishly confessed to him that around that time she had told her Spiritual Director, Father John Walsh, LC, of her concerns about Paul's relationships with his team of closest helpers—of which she was part!—at the School of Faith. In such a cloak-and-dagger atmosphere it is hard to reconstruct what really happened. Paul's friend's apprehension must have been reported quickly to *El Puma*; who then attempted to bluff Paul in an effort to find out whether the rumor was true or false. This helps to illustrate the porous boundaries between sacramental confession, spiritual direction and discipline possible in the Legion and Regnum. In order to achieve a "good" end, to "protect a priest's vocation", even dubious means—using information gathered from confession, direction, jealousy or rumor—are justified.

A week after the ugly confrontation, during Sunday morning retreat at the Instituto Cumbres Legionaries' residence, *El Puma* came up quickly, out of nowhere, and said in a low tone of voice: "Don't worry about that any longer. No need to do anything. I believe you." Without further explanation he slunk away, through the bushes and out the gate. Despite the unusual delivery, the message led Paul to believe he had won this round. But he was naïve to believe that he could win the entire bout.

***

Anonymous Accusatory Letters

Mexican women have traditionally confided their problems of all kinds to the Padre. He is the one safe man around. Usually, they do not perceive him as a potential threat to their marriage vows, irrespective of the state of said marriage. But despite the shield of respect, the padre can occasionally be the target of obscure or ambiguous thoughts, fantasies and desires. It would take Romantic Padre Paul a long time to realize this. Listening to the women confiding in him he was shocked to learn infidelity was rife among the elite where husbands' long hours at the office and close contact with attractive secretaries took its toll. There was a high degree of mutual tolerance between spouses. He was aghast to hear a woman say: “He can do whatever he wants outside my house, but don’t let him bring her into my home and introduce her to the children!” Despite Paul’s naïveté, he could usually pick up on words, feelings or touches that were overtly sensual or threatening his celibacy.

In the early ‘80s Paul continued his mission to afflict the comfortable and comfort the afflicted. Two passionate sisters, one divorced, the other still married, loomed on the threshold of his office, vying for his affection, and for a little more if they could get it. One of the sisters was imprudent, and began looking for excuses to consult with Paul in the evenings when no one else was around. She would come up very close to him, proclaiming her undying passion. By then Paul did know what the woman in Chetumal had meant by “el calorcito,” perceiving a sexual heat emanating from her body. And even though she went as far as to gratuitously share her gynecologist’s report on the prime condition of her sexual organs, the “assault” was too overt, clichéd, and soap opera-like to make a real impact.

Sometime after keeping the unwanted—if flattering and seductive advances—at bay, he received an anonymous letter. It was contrived in such a way as to appear to be from an incensed husband threatening to relieve Padre Paul of his genitalia. In ugly handwriting and in vulgar terms the alleged offended husband accused the padre of defiling his wife, offending his honor and that of his children. The logic was hard to grasp, and Paul wondered who the sender could be—hardly the spouse of the recently deterred lover. Knowing it was a lie, a false accusation, he kept the letter in his drawer without telling anyone. However, he became hyper-vigilant, not knowing who could have sent such a letter.

In July 1982, as his relationship with *El Puma* continued to unravel, and with it his career at the School of Faith, Paul was summoned once more to meet with *El Puma* at the Quinta Pacelli offices. Father Devlin, *El Puma*'s personal secretary: "You have an appointment with *Nuestro Padre*, "Nee-u-estro Pa-dray",—pronounced in his broadest Dublin accent—on Wednesday next at 4 p.m. in Tlalpan." That was it. It was always so difficult to get appointments when you needed them. But you always got one when *Nuestro Padre* wanted it, when he had something to say to you.

So Paul drove from Lomas de Chapultepec in the northwest to Tlalpan on the south side of Mexico City, near the foothills of the Ajusco Mountain. He rang the bell and was let in by the butler Ramón after he explained he was there for an appointment with Father Maciel. Going inside the property to *Las Tres* he knocked on Father Devlin's door. Nuestro Padre would be with him presently. About what? You never knew. The uncertainty affected the waiting religious. Paul stood, paced, waited, and ruminated: What is this going to be about?

After what seemed like ages *El Puma* appeared, polite and businesslike. They went into one of the studies alone. In contrast to the previous walking interview, this would be a sit-down meeting. Maciel sat at the head of the table, Paul to his right, in such a way that *El Puma* could see his face, expression and reactions, while Paul had to turn his head to see *El Puma*. After the usual courtesies he got directly to the point.

"Father Paul, I'm very worried about letters that Cardinal Corripio has forwarded to me. They concern you and it seems to be some man accusing you of getting involved with his wife. How can you explain this?"

Paul parried that heavy blow. He put two and two together and heard himself speak with composure:

"As a matter of fact, Nuestro Padre, I do happen to know something about that. I have received two letters like that over the past months and I knew they were false accusations. I did not tell anyone about them." Paul felt a bit guilty about this, as one is supposed to tell Legion superiors everything. He had not told anyone because he feared the way the superiors would deal with it, usually by taking control of the situation and the religious, and deciding peremptorily. "I have my own theory about this", Paul continued. "You see, they are anonymous. I can only suspect a certain person, because he is the one person I know who could even remotely doubt my integrity. He and his wife have been having a hard time and she has been seeking my advice. The wife has a sister who seems to be jealous of her, and so this whole issue gets really complicated. This is the only person I might suspect. I know I am innocent. I find the letters extremely offensive and vulgar." Father Maciel, perhaps realizing that he had not knocked Paul off his horse, continued in a paternal tone of voice:

"Well, Father Paul, I find your explanation very satisfactory and I will give it to Cardinal Corripio personally when I see him. Don't worry about this problem. It is all behind you." Paul was wise enough by now and felt the need to be respectfully assertive:

"Nuestro Padre, if you don't mind, I would like to see Cardinal Corripio myself. I did not know he received these letters. As I am a friend of his, I would like to meet with him, face to face, because I owe it to him and to myself." The wily leader and personnel expert would not be persuaded so easily: "Now, son, let me handle this. I will try to see him first and I will let you know as soon as possible about the outcome. I will make sure he gets your version. He did send the letter without any explanation and this may mean he wants me to take action." *El Puma* pressed on: "This unfortunate episode coincides with a decision already taken by your superiors long before this problem arose, to assign you to the Missions to work as you have done before for the good of the less fortunate souls." Then, to the intercom: "Father Devlin, will you please bring Father Lennon's file?" John Devlin brings out a manila folder containing one sheet of paper. Paul's eyes narrowed suspiciously, thinking "This one-page folder is my personnel file?"

There it was, in Paul's opinion, a letter predated two months, in May 1984. In formal words it announced that his term of office as Director of the School of Faith had expired and that in order to let younger religious gain experience in the Apostolates of the Legion...

With his heart tightening in his chest, his tongue dry in his mouth, Paul forced the words out. He could see the writing on the wall but he believed that despite all its challenges the School of Faith had been good for him. He did not want to let it go. He bargained desperately with El Puma to leave him in Religious Education where he had been for seven successful years, even if this meant going somewhere else—to Monterrey, Mexico, for example—where people were anxious to set up the program. Paul was willing to take the hit, to be separated from the Lovely Ladies of Lomas, so as to hang onto the School of Faith, the apostolate he loved and where he had felt most fulfilled in his ministry.

"No, Paul, we can't. You see, this is not my decision. It's out of my hands. This was taken by the superiors months ago before we knew about this new development. Your change had already been finalized before any of these recent events. As he felt *El Puma* closing the door, and as the non sequiturs increased, Paul became more and more skeptical, thinking "He just wants me to go. He is not listening. He already made his decision. I will just have to defend myself as best I can." After a little respite, *El Puma* carried on with the same implacable resolve:

"You may remain here in Mexico City until your replacement arrives so you can show him the ropes. Meanwhile, I'll talk with Cardinal Corripio and get this little mess cleaned up." Paul insisted, desperately playing his last "my good name" and "friend of Cardinal Corripio" cards: "It is my reputation as a priest that is at stake." Cardinal Corripio was archbishop of Mexico City and Primate of all Mexico. His blessing practically gave the School of Faith carte blanche all over Mexico. Perhaps El Puma would not want to stir up those waters.

It had transpired in the conversation that the bishop of Tlalnepantla, Mexico State, the jurisdiction where the School of Faith was officially registered, had also received one of the letters. Paul prevailed upon *El Puma* that while waiting for the replacement he could approach him also. He thanked *El Puma* and took his leave. Paul was beginning to scramble as he slipped into survival mode.

Paul had a policy of having open relationships with School of Faith staff and their husbands and was certain that no husband who knew him personally would accuse him of such a thing. But he has never been able to find out who sent those mystery letters: a suspicious or paranoid husband? Hell hath no fury like a woman scorned? At that time it did not cross his mind that a viable explanation lay closer to home. It could have been Father Maciel, or someone appointed by him. Strange as it seems, another Legionary, Father Manus McIlhargey, R.I.P., did discover how Father Maciel was capable of such "trickery". In a ploy to confuse and unbalance his charge—and make him more docile to moving orders—Maciel falsely accused that Legionary priest of having abused a young woman under his pastoral care[14].

***

10
REBELLING

On the same day, Siddhartha informed the eldest Samana of his decision to leave him. He told the old man with the politeness and modesty fitting to young men and students. But the old man was angry that both young men wished to leave him and he raised his voice and scolded strongly. Govinda was taken aback, but Siddhartha put his lips to Govinda's ear and whispered: "Now I will show the old man that I have learned something from him."

On the way, Govinda said: "Siddhartha, you have learned more from the Samanas than I was aware. It is difficult, very difficult to hypnotize an old Samana. In truth, if you had stayed there, you would have soon learned how to walk on water."
"I have no desire to walk on water," said Siddhartha. "Let the old Samanas satisfy themselves with such arts."

Siddhartha[15]

By this time Paul—that is, I—was no longer an obedient and docile religious. I stalled in Mexico City and on my own initiative set up appointments with the bishops involved. I was also struggling with a return to the Missions. "Been there, done that." This time I clearly perceived it as a step down, a form of banishment. *El Puma* had agreed to give me time to clear up the false accusations with the bishops. I requested appointments with Cardinal Corripio and with the Bishop of Tlalnepantla, Mexico State. I got some satisfaction when the latter personally told me in his office: "Accusatory letters about my men, I get many; anonymous, they go straight into the wastepaper basket. But this was about a religious; I sent it to your superior." (Was *he* telling the truth?)

The Easter Candle Trick

By August 1982 I was still hanging onto Mexico City by my fingernails. *El Puma'* valet and executive secretary, my former school pal, Father John Devlin, placed an envelope under my bedroom door at the Tlalpan residence one evening. It contained a note telling me to be at Mexico City airport early next morning. There Monsignor Bernal would be expecting me with a plane ticket for Cancun, Quintana Roo state.

I dutifully drove to the Benito Juarez International Airport in my dung-colored Renault (the cheap paint job hadn't turned out the way I wanted). I knew Monsignor Bernal pretty well from my first term on the Missions. He had always treated me well. But Bernal was also a wimp ("*collón*", his own term in a later confrontation). I spotted Monsignor waiting, walked across the waiting area and asked to see my ticket.

Priestly companions: Acevedo, Sherlock, Lennon, Lucatero, Moylan, Rome, 1969

***

I took it from his hand: "Monsignor, I will not be using this ticket today. Let me take it back to Father Devlin so he can get a refund." Grabbing the ticket, I bade him well, quickly departed the airport, drove back to the *Quinta Pacelli* headquarters, and put the ticket under Father Devlin's door.

Not long after Father Octavio Acevedo-Marin, then LC Provincial, phoned asking me to go to the Anahuac University chapel to pick up the Paschal (Easter) Candle and take it to the Instituto Cumbres' staff residence. I drove to the deserted chapel in Tecamachalco at midday that sunny Sunday. On entering the sacristy, I found Father Acevedo waiting alone in his usual ferret-like posture. He proffered a sealed letter. I took it, saw it was from El Puma, thanked my superior, and turned on my heel to go. Letters from he founder and superior general were private and confidential. "No, you have to read it here. That is an order!" Aha! So I had to do as I was told. The letter said in Spanish: "In virtue of Holy Obedience you are to go immediately to the Quintana Roo Mission." There was no wriggling out of that.

Back down on Maggie's Farm

Out of sheer obedience—and impotence—I finally took a plane to Cancun, Quintana Roo in late summer of 1982, trying as best I could to adjust again to that small-town lifestyle and pastoral work. I was being sent to Bacalar, the same isolated and sleepy little town to which I had been assigned eleven years before. The only phone was in the local *cantina*. The booth without a door, so everyone could overhear your conversation—and could understand it, if you spoke in Spanish. The key was to speak in English!

In missionary garb with First Communicant, Christmas, 1983

Once again I was at the bottom of the totem pole, Assistant Pastor. Only the pastor was different. Was he secretly assigned to watching Paul, to spying on him, beneath the facade of camaraderie? No longer "integrated" in the Legion, I arranged for some of my friends from Mexico City to come to visit with me and even engineered a trip for my mother. She flew into Cancun in 1983 and was able to see her dear son in action on his beloved missions.

It was just delaying the inevitable. I soldiered on bravely for another couple of years, once more losing myself in my work, conjuring up a new Radio Apostolate, and practicing my own "nature therapy": rising early in the morning to watch the sun come up over Bacalar's Lagoon of Seven Colors and strolling around the tiny plaza on my own every night contemplating the moon and the stars in the clear black sky, my reverie often interrupted by the throb of tropical *cumbia* music or the strains of a local ballad: *Mary es mi amor; sólo y con ella vivo la felicidad* (Mary is my love, only with her do I enjoy happiness). But there was little, if any, *felicidad* in Paul's heart.

Would this therapy, prayer, and the sacraments be enough to stave off my clamoring needs for honesty, friendship and support?

***

Lost Letter: Last Straw

One more episode further distanced me from the Legion, the mother I had then loved and served for twenty-one years. Several weeks after my arrival, Monsignor Bernal casually handed me a letter from Cardinal Corripio. You don't get a letter from a cardinal every day. I had requested an appointment before leaving Mexico City but had received no answer.

With Mom at the crèche, Divine Providence, Christmas, 1983

Now I saw that the envelope from Cardinal Corripio had an old postmark, the letter inside granting me an appointment at the Cardinal's office several weeks before. To my initial query Monsignor Bernal replied that the letter must have gotten lost in his briefcase:

"What a pity. What can be done at this late stage? Better just to let things go, pacify your soul, and accept the Holy Will of God."

I was quickly transitioning to a no-nonsense, problem-solving approach to the Will of God. I angrily confronted Monsignor Bernal at the Sacred Heart front office soon after, telling him that I believed he had purposely "lost" the letter: "I would not put it past either you or Father Maciel!"

Bernal backed off in fright. "You know I am a coward!"

I went on to tell Monsignor I would find a way of meeting with Corripio to clear my name.

Without asking for permission, I flew from Chetumal to Mexico City and questioned Cardinal Corripio about the letter. When I implied he had suggested to Father Maciel that I be moved—as El Puma had implied in our conversation—the normally unflappable Corripio testily countered: "I never tell religious superiors what to do!"

I found out years later from fellow ex-Legionary that El Puma had thought of sending me to Chile and not Quintana Roo but that he hesitated, fearing I would leave the Legion outright. El Puma had opted for the safer alternative: return Paul to the familiar Missions. But his decision to remove me from the School of Faith in Mexico City without discussion backfired, as it destroyed my trust and killed off any remaining filial affection. Disillusioned with the Legion and its Leader, I would henceforth dispense with human intermediaries in my search for self, truth, goodness and beauty.

***

A Storm Brewing

Over the years I had grown gradually more skeptical and critical of El Puma and the Legion. Like the Last Rose of Summer, my initial awe, admiration and respect had faded and died. That initial boundless and all-accepting enthusiasm, weakened by the never-ending struggle of self-denial, blind obedience, no dialog, and no answers for my questioning mind, became further debilitated by witnessing favoritism, mistreatment and injustice. The lonely, exhausting celibacy battle, waged alone because of my mistrust of Legion spiritual direction, decimated my resources. El Puma and other Legionary superiors increasingly became in my eyes the unhelpful imposers of the system, the Pharisees that laid heavy loads on our backs but were not willing to raise a finger to help. Their regimen was often arbitrary and unduly harsh, a cruel rack, and an implacable grindstone milling members into the dust. Some lay friends told me how some other "dissident" Legionaries were mistreated, further fanned the flames of my angry passion.

Two companions, a Spaniard and an Irishman, had been sent to French-speaking Gabon in West Africa by El Puma, for whatever reasons, to "learn their lesson."[16]

In that painful isolation they got on each other's nerves and quit the Legion. Soon afterwards, both abruptly left the priesthood and married. They were "personal friends" of mine—inasmuch as one could have friends in the Legion. The Spaniard had been ordained with me the same day in Rome, and the other Legionary was a fellow Dubliner whose father almost had a heart attack the day Big John suddenly showed up at his dad's Trinity College workplace. "Da, I'm back and

I'm out." I empathized with their suffering and identified with them and their families. Aware of how close I was to following in their footsteps, I was determined not to leave the priesthood impulsively, no matter what.

***

"Gunfight at the Cotija Corral"

Finally the thunderclap exploded, abrupt and fierce, although I had not been conscious of the storm brewing. In November 1984 the Quintana Roo "Missionary" community traveled to Cotija, Mexico, El Puma's hometown, to begin spiritual exercises. I was a changed person: unbeknownst to myself I was no longer afraid and would not be easily silenced. I did not realize there was an edge to me when I arrived at the retreat center on a pleasant November afternoon. It was customary to begin the week-long spiritual exercises on a Sunday evening. The main event of the Spiritual Exercises would be, as usual, El Puma's arrival and his delivery of the keynote address. As was also usual, he was late, and so the opening talk was rescheduled for the morning after the group's arrival. A score of Legionaries had come from the Quintana Roo Mission. These spiritual exercises were tailored to our needs. Finally, mid-morning, and amid certain fanfare, *El Puma* made his triumphal entrance.

The captive audience sat down to listen, admire, applaud and assimilate. He began by painting a rosy picture of newly recruited members basically breaking down the doors to enter the Legion and Regnum Christi training centers. How generous these young men and women were compared to the retreatants, lukewarm and tired religious and priests!

Fr. Maciel hugs Paul after ordination

The atmosphere around me was of acceptance and tolerance, if not docility. The fawning further frustrated me and my restlessness increased as I heard Father Maciel weave his web of wonder and felt the passivity in the room. They were all "yes-men," and he was going on an on in a way that devalued the efforts we were making on the Missions. How easy it was to compare and criticize! How easy it was to underrate humble parish work in the hot and humid tropics when compared to the flashy Regnum Christi recruitment activities among the elite! When was the last time he himself had experienced the physical discomfort of bugs and sticky heat? Many times had I witnessed his avoidance of a draft or a wayward sunbeam, his fussing over a glass of water not at exactly the right temperature, or his rejection of the wrong kind of mineral water.

El Puma extolled the virtues of the latest Legionary poster boy of the time, Florencio Sanchez-Soler, in Madrid, forgetting those who had gone before laying the groundwork or performing less flashy tasks. Everyone began with youthful enthusiasm, but what was left of it after ten or twenty years when the gloss wore off? What about those Legionaries who encountered obstacles on their path and began to struggle with obedience and with their human frailties? I was incensed by the despotic sending of the two men to Gabon; together with the fate of other admirable Legionaries who I felt had been unjustly sidelined.

I did the unexpected and spoke up, interrupting El Puma's discourse: He kept talking about all those coming in, but what about the hole in the bottom of the sack, all those Legionaries who were troubled, leaving or had left? Many who stayed were hurting, banished, or put out to pasture! An ugly argument ensued. El Puma told me to shut up; who did I think I was? I didn't know what I was talking about. It was none of my business what happened to other Legionaries. Leave that to the superiors. I fired back that it *was* my business because these who were being mistreated were my brothers. The names of Samaniego, Neftalí Sánchez and other formerly favored Legionaries came passionately tumbling out to illustrate my claim.

The fight response had kicked in and Hannibal was crossing the Rubicon. I would not back down, or sit down—by this time I was standing and shouting, firing with both pistols, at El Puma sitting erect at the table. Perhaps it was the exploding frustration of twenty-three years listening to the infallible, authoritarian and condescending Saint spouting out of him without ever being able to answer or reply. Few, if any, including me, had ever seen El Puma confronted in such a direct and head-on way. How long did the altercation go on? So intensely was I involved that I had lost all track of time. The "community" of about twenty priests and brothers looked on in stunned silence. Had they dived for cover under the saloon tables? Finally one spoke up—another former Dublin school buddy, now faithful servant of El Puma—Father Thomas Moylan:

"We have not come to hear a discussion but to listen to you, *Nuestro Padre*." To which the once Naïve and Sentimental Catholic Boy replied: "If that is the way you all feel, then this is not the place for me!" I walked out of that room, never to return to that house, or to the Legion.

***

"Jack and the Beanstalk"

The above happened in the heat of passion. I had not

planned my attack on Father Maciel. I was carried away by emotion, by an outpouring of suppressed complaints and accusations. It was not a controlled confrontation, although there was reason in my points. It happened to me as much as I laid it on *El Puma*. Ever since that day I have struggled to understand and make sense of it. It was if little Jack had wanted to chop down the beanstalk and kill the giant. I cannot help thinking of Bruno Bettelheim comments on this fairytale that seem to illustrate the subconscious drama that had just played out:

> "As the ogre pursues him down the beanstalk, Jack calls out to his mother to get the ax and cut the beanstalk.
> The mother brings the ax as told, but on seeing the giant's huge legs coming down the beanstalk, she freezes into immobility; she is unable to deal with phallic objects… Jack grabs the ax and cuts off the beanstalk, and with it brings down the ogre, who perishes from his fall. In doing so, Jack rids himself of the father who is experienced on the oral level; as a jealous ogre who wants to devour.
> But in cutting down the beanstalk Jack not only frees himself from a view of his father as a destructive and devouring ogre; he also thus relinquishes his belief in the magic power of the phallus as the means for gaining him all good things in life. In putting the ax to the beanstalk, Jack forswears magic solutions; he becomes "his own man". He will no longer take from others, but neither will he live in mortal fear of ogres, nor rely on Mother's hiding him in an oven."[17]

***

"So I'm leaving on a jet plane; don't know when I'll be back again…"[18]

No one followed me to try to prevent me from leaving, or

to dissuade me from carrying out such a hasty decision. Perhaps I could not have been stopped. Maybe it was too late. Walking to my room, I packed my belongings into the battered suitcase I had brought with me and went out into the street. Totally alone and left to my own devices for the first time in twenty-three years, now almost forty-one, I stood at the bus stop in Cotija. I did not know the bus schedule. Nor did I care. I would wait; though I was half-afraid someone might come after me. What would I do then? Although I had never read Siddhartha, I was resolute like him: "I can think, I can wait, I can fast."

Any bus was good enough to take me out of there, to Guadalajara, anywhere, far away from the sour taste in my mouth, the tightening in my gut, and the painful pounding in my temples. The second class bus with its cross-section of Mexican provincials and chickens in cages would do me fine. I was beginning a very long and lonely journey. Luckily, I did have some cash—on the Missions that was allowed—and a return plane ticket to Mexico City, which I hadn't planned on using on my own. Staying that night at a dingy hotel in Guadalajara, close to the bus station—the first time in my entire life I had ever spent the night on my own—I made sure to bolt the door against the many prostitutes, or *tipas*, as El Puma would say, who were surely going to burst in and take away my virginity. My romance with the Legion of Christ was over and I wanted to be alone.

LOVE ON THE ROCKS

Love on the rocks,
Ain't no surprise;
Pour me a drink
And I'll tell you some lies.
Got nothin' to lose,

So you just sing the blues all the time.
Gave you my heart,
Gave you my soul.
You left me alone here
With nothing to hold.
Yesterday's gone,
Now all I want is a smile.

First, they say they want you;
Gee, how they really need you;
Suddenly you find you're out there
Walking in a storm.
When they know they have you;
Then they really have you;
Nothing you can do or say;
You've got to leave, just get away.
We all know that song.

11.
REGROUPING

He breathed in deeply and for a moment he shuddered. Nobody was so alone as he. He was no nobleman, belonging to any aristocracy, no artisan belonging to any guild and finding refuge in it, sharing its life and language. He was no Brahmin, sharing the life of the Brahmins, no ascetic belonging to the Samanas. Even the most secluded hermit in the woods was not one and alone; he also belonged to a class of people. Govinda had become a monk and thousands of monks were his brothers, wore the same gown, shared his beliefs, and spoke his language. But he, Siddhartha, where did he belong? Whose life did he share? Whose language would he speak?

At that moment, when the world around him melted away, when he stood alone like a star in the heavens, he was overwhelmed by a feeling of icy despair, but he was more firmly himself than ever. That was the last shudder of his awakening, the last pains of birth. Immediately he moved on again and began to walk quickly and impatiently, no longer homewards, no longer to his father, no longer looking back-wards.

Siddhartha[19]

I am a survivor.

In a state of aloneness, agony, and abandon, only the will to survive was there, an instinctual drive to stay alive in a trapped and wounded animal. For some strange reason, despite all the devastation, the thought of suicide never crossed my mind. Maybe I was too depressed to even think of the effort. But what now? How to see through blood-drenched eyes? How to ward off the waves of pain? How to lift that tombstone off my chest? I was the walking wounded, with a gaping hole in my heart and my head. But being a total wreck and having nothing to lose had its advantages: I was wonderfully free, for the first time in your life.

The Underground Railroad

The morning after the Gunfight at the Cotija Corral, November 11th, 1984, I was on a plane from Guadalajara to Mexico City. There was no sense in checking in at the School of Faith in Mexico City whence I had been banished in 1982. I felt out of place and had chosen not to stay in any Legion house in Mexico City. Because of my conflict with untouchable Legion bosses, most of my Legion-based social contacts would shun me, or I would simply not feel comfortable.

At the Benito Juarez International Airport I went through a short list of numbers in a little brown booklet. At a payphone outside I called a faithful and "safe" female friend I knew through the School of Faith. Moved by that typically Mexican flexibility and generosity, she unquestioningly picked up the little guy in the *guayabera,* the Mexican wedding shirt, and took me to her home in Polanco. I confessed my showdown and was glad she was not too scandalized. I "holed up" there for a while like a knocked-out prizefighter recovering in the quiet of the dressing rooms. Actually, this was the person who had kept me updated on the saga of my confreres exiled in Gabon.

A few days later, from her home I called Father Acevedo and asked to talk with *El Puma*. Although my allegiance to *El Puma* and the Legion was shot, as a gentleman I felt obligated to apologize for my angry outburst and disrespectful conduct. The Territorial Director—the Easter Candle Padre, former fellow novice, who had tricked me and forced me to the Missions two years earlier—told me he didn't know where El Puma was. I refused to tell Easter Candle Padre where I was staying—perhaps my first clear-headed act of formal disobedience, or even assertiveness, in twenty-three years. I wonder what might have happened had I been able to meet with El Puma, or if Father Acevedo had appealed to my noble spirit or acted with more tact: "Father Paul, would you like to come in and discuss what happened, no strings attached?" It was not to be.

When full of angst I approached the Lozano family in Tlalpan to tell them I had a run-in with Father Maciel, they were bemused. "Mother", cried the daughter, Pablito had a fight with Maciel. Why don't we help him go home to Ireland to see his mother?" Out came the checkbooks, creating life raft number one.

As soon as I felt strong enough I said goodbye to those few generous and hospitable remaining friends in Mexico City and took off for the lost worlds of Quintana Roo. Part of my fledgling and confused recovery plan was to return to the familiarity and relative freedom of the Missions and pick up the pieces from the previous two years' work. Whatever belongings surviving my life in the Legion were there; with a strict Vow of Poverty that would not be much.

A feeling of relief came from losing all fear. And the loss of fear came from having nothing to lose. I just went back to Quintana Roo without asking permission from any of my superiors. I sensed that now that I was taking my destiny into my own hands they would not intervene. And they did not. It was a weird feeling. On arrival I took the car I had been using before my split and went back and forth about my business. I had never done that before, at least not to that degree. I was giving myself time to say goodbye to the Legion, my way, though I can't remember whether I actually did formally bid farewell to Legionary confreres; to a trusted few, perhaps. I said *Adios* only to my closest lay friends. Why trouble the ordinary faithful with my personal problems?

> Princess on the steeple and all the pretty people
> They're drinkin', thinkin' that they got it made
> Exchanging all kinds of precious gifts and things
> But you'd better take your diamond ring,
> You'd better pawn it babe
> You used to be so amused
> At Napoleon in rags
> And the language that he used.
> Go to him now, he calls you, you can't refuse.
> When you got nothing, you got nothing to lose.
> You're invisible now, you got no secrets to conceal.
>
> How does it feel,
> How does it feel
> To be on your own
> With no direction home
> Like a complete unknown
> Like a rolling stone?
>
> (Bob Dylan)

***

Having your passport, remote preparation for exiting!

"Remote" and "proximate" preparation are part of Legion spiel. These terms usually refer to morning meditation and the periods preceding it, but in my worldly travels they took on a different meaning. I could not have left the Legion without one essential element: my passport, remote preparation for leaving. In the Movement superiors hold the members' passports "for safe-keeping." This ensures that if the member is in a foreign country—and most Legionaries are—they cannot get going when the going gets tough.

Father Maciel handled my brand-new passport on that maiden voyage in 1961. From here it would have been passed to Rector, Superior, Instructor of Novices and Spiritual Director Father Arumí in Salamanca, Spain; thence, to Rome to be kept under lock and key by Rector, Superior and Spiritual Director Father Dueñas' or stashed away in the administrator's office. Did you, Vice-Rector, Father Javier Orozco, ever have it? I, Paul, must have used it to fly to the USA in 1970 and from there to Mexico in 1971. As a foreign priest I was an "illegal alien" in Mexico during my thirteen years with the Legion. My passport was kept at the central administration office on Melchor Ocampo Street in Mexico City, under the care of Mr. Armando Arias, an ex-Legionary who had always sucked up to Maciel and depended on him for his livelihood and other perks. Twice a year it was sent, together with dozens more, to immigration officials on the border in Reynosa, Tamaulipas, Mexico; the officers were bribed to stamp the Padres' passports without them being physically present and to issue new six-month tourist visas.

An exception could be made for those foreign Legionaries on the Quintana Roo Mission who could handle their own passports and secure visas more cheaply. They could travel from

Chetumal, Mexico, to nearby Corozal, Belize, just half an hour away, and have their passports stamped and visas renewed on the way through. For a few hundred pesos discreetly inserted between the pages, collaborative and understanding Mexican officials obligingly issued the padres' visas as they joked among themselves. During my second tour of duty in Quintana Roo, 1982-84, I did not purposely retain my passport with the intention of "escaping" from the Legion. Maybe, as a token of budding autonomy, I simply did not return it to Monsignor Bernal after processing. Having it would be an essential asset when I eventually wanted to get from Mexico to Ireland on the first stage of recovery.

***

Furtive Phone Call

My trek to freedom began with a preliminary trip from Mexico City to Quintana Roo to begin cleaning up shop. I continued to drive around the state from one Legion house to another in my vehicle. At the church offices of Christ the King Parish in Cancun, a furtive and tentative phone call in December, 2004, to ex-Legionary priest, my friend Declan Murphy, led to an acceptable planned exit out of the Legion.

In keeping with the Legion system of isolating communities and members into sealed cells in the Marxist mode, finding and communicating with Declan was no small miracle. There was no normal way an active Legionary could know what was happening to another confrere in another community, or even whether he was still in the Legion, on "special assignment," had left, or was MIA.

A year or so before the present episode a young American woman I never met personally, but to whom I will be eternally grateful, traveled to Chetumal, Quintana Roo, to work as an

English teacher at Our Lady of Guadalupe parish. She bore with her a business card from a certain ex-Legionary priest to be given to Paul. She found a way to get the card surreptitiously into my hands and wallet; I had no particular reason, or permission, to contact that confrere at that time, but I kept the card for the rainy day I never suspected would come.

I had not seen nor spoken with Declan for many years. That fateful day my survival instinct kicked in. I chose not to call from the Legion house because there was no privacy. I stole into the Cancun parish office during the secretary's lunch-break, locked the door behind me, and placed a long distance call to somewhere in the USA. It could have been Timbuktu for all I knew. This was the first long distance call I had ever placed by myself to a foreign country in my entire life. We did not have a phone in my home, and during my time in the Legion I never had occasion to place a call. The number led to Our Lady of Lourdes Parish in Bethesda, Maryland. Divine Providence had this particular priest pick up the phone personally, and precisely at that moment, to answer his devastated confrere.

"Paul, is that you? Where are you? Did you hear about my demise?" After all those years speaking Spanish I did not know what "demise" meant. "I'm out! I've transitioned to the diocese." I told him about my failure as a Legionary. "If you like, I can speak to the archbishop to see if you can try out your priesthood here. I am taking off for a few days after Christmas and will be flying home. See you in Dublin, at the restaurant on Abbey Street."

I now understand that in late November, 1984, I was starting a series of broad disjointed movements, perhaps a manifestation of anxious depression, in my effort to leave the Legion: Mexico City to Cancun, Quintana Roo; I moved around Mission territory to say some goodbyes and tie up loose ends. Thanks to the Lozano donation I could later take the transatlantic flight from Cancun to Dublin, meet up with two ex-Legionaries to open up a bridge to Washington, and decompress with family and friends. Later I would fly from Dublin back to Mexico City, to Merida, Yucatan, to Cancun and Quintana Roo, until finally taking my leave from the Legion and transitioning to Washington in February, 1985, in an effort to prolong my priesthood.

***

Dublin

During that harrowing Christmas 1984 in Ireland, my long-lost cousin, Collette and old friend Martin Devlin listened non-judgmentally to my tale of woe. They will never know how their understanding helped me to shake off the tremendous burden of guilt and to repair my damaged self-esteem. Meeting with my mother was another pivotal event: I could feel the Earth move under my feet when I told her I was leaving the Legion and she riposted that leaving the Legion should not interfere with my continuing in the priesthood! Mother was not particularly helpful but I was proud I had been frank with her about *my* needs and decisions. Notes I wrote in the margins of *The Second Journey* describe my human and spiritual quest.

> This book was given to me by someone (Declan) who has started his second journey a few years before me. It really helped me make it through the hell of leaving.
> O'Collins, Gerald (1978). *The Second Journey, Spiritual Awareness and the Mid-Life Crisis.* New York: Paulist Press.
> First reading: Ireland, December 19th, 1984 to January 27, 1985: very appropriate gift, reading slowly, no panic. I know my state; I have plumbed the depths. *De Profundis*

Clamavi ad Te, Domine, "From the Depths have I cried out to you; Lord, hear my prayer."

The Legion, 1961-84, was all part of my First Journey, up to my forty-first year.

I am forty-one. The Legion was twenty-three years; the priesthood fifteen. Where do I go? What do I do? I thank God that I am relatively free to make decisions, to decide on my life. Free to decide. Trying to see, to reappraise, and reevaluate these past twenty-three—indeed these past forty-one years.

What about me? Who's worried about me? Who's going to help me? Who cares about me? Who's going to save Paul? Only Paul. Paul must save Paul. Paul will save Paul.

Swords, Co. Dublin, 16-17 January, 1985

After speaking with Martin Devlin early yesterday morning, 1 am to 3 am, about my life in the Legion: "stifling, shit upon…"

Second reading, January 17, 1985, 12:44 am

Tonight, high school buddies at the Skylon on Drumcondra Ave: Rory Feeney, Noel Duffy, Mattie Martin, and Kenny Newman. Joy at seeing them again; they are successful businessmen. I'm proud of my generation. I'm also deathly sad. Do I want to close this 23 year cycle—July 1, 1961 until November 11, 1984? Closing the cycle of boyhood, youth, and early manhood? Finishing the first journey? Was the priesthood a way of making a decision without making a decision, of not facing life, personal responsibility, work, women, and a way of putting off options? Or was it as good as the decisions of my peers, according to our common degree of (im) maturity? What did I want to do back then? I was idealistic, enthusiastic: I wanted to serve, help, "do good," and "be close to God." "You had good family bonds," said Rory. "The most unlikely fellow to go away for the priesthood," said Mattie M.

Certain things become clear to me: money, making money, being rich is not an important value for me. People are important: friendships, intimacy, tenderness, compassion, service, contributing to others' well-being, sports, happiness, enjoyment. I wanted to do something for others: not use them, or dominate them, boss or intimidate them.

To be or not to be: a normal, ordinary man. I had repressed my needs, didn't think about them. They were latent, buried under enthusiasm and idealism. I had wanted a "helping profession." I had been "swept off my feet" by the Legion—what a good expression! I was wooed by the Legion.

Third reading: January 24th, 1985, on the train from Ennis to Dublin.

Two months after my rupture from the Legion, at the end of my Irish sabbatical month: no great relief emotionally; no enlightening intuitions. A few ideas: get out of the Legion; play for time; new approaches, understanding, without stubbornness.

Floundering fright;
No end in sight;
No harbor light
Beaming bright,
Lightening
My plight;
But thank you, Jesus,
For this book;
Bless you, friend.

***

Confession in Merida

On Sunday, January 27th, 1985, I left Ireland, flying from Dublin to London and from there via New York to Mexico City. On Monday I checked into Hotel Bristol, said more goodbyes to Mexico City friends, recovered some very personal writings, and left for Merida, where I was received by the Conde-Medina family on February 2.

Merida, Yucatan, "The White City," four hours from Cancun, had always been my friendly place. On previous visits I occasionally checked out the Church of the Third Order, sitting in at Mass to hear the padre preach. Despite its name, the parish was run by Jesuits. I had scouted out this padre before going to see him. "I'm a priest and I want to go to confession." Father Manuel López smiled in a brotherly way, patted me on the shoulder and said, dismissing the confessional: "Let's sit down in the private parlor." That was scary, but I was so beat-up it didn't matter. I opened my soul. He listened patiently, and at the end very unceremoniously exclaimed: *¡Estás jodido y encabronado!* ("So, you're fucked up and raging mad!"), a most un-Legionary summary. But the Prophet had spoken. The three Conde Medina sisters, Lilí, Diana and Mashi, gave their depressed and anxious friend hospitality and introduced him to a psychologist, thus facilitating my first ever therapy session. On February 3rd I unburdened my heavy heart to Alfredo Reyes Sandoval, an ex-Marist Brother, for four hours nonstop over a cup of coffee in a quiet corner of a city-center restaurant. Later, the Condes invited their troubled friend to the family beach house in Progreso. They remember how I sang compulsively, as if singing out the blues, in the van—the van of freedom!—and later walked alone the beach so agitatedly they could not keep up with me. They told me later that my engine could not stop running. One of them remembers that after dinner I kissed her goodnight on the tip of her nose. She will never let me forget how surprised she was that a priest would do such a thing. Maybe she was getting off lightly—this was the guy who had almost punched Father Maciel in the face. My boundaries were probably all over the place at this stage. Anyway, Paul, the priest, went to his room and she, the married lady, to hers…After a rest on the beach at Progreso I made my way to Cancun.

***

Cancun

Cancun was the place where I placed that clandestine phone call to my ex-Legionary confrere. And when I finally left Quintana Roo and Mexico for Europe it was from Cancun. I had been driving all around the Yucatan Peninsula in "my" car, but I was still officially a member of the Legion and so owned no personal property. When the day came for my flight to Ireland I asked Elda in Cancun to give me a hand. My personal belongings were in the car. I picked her up at her house and drove to the airport. Along the way I had visions of bridges burning in the haze over Cancun lagoon. I bade a subdued *Adios* to Elda and asked her to take the car back to my soon-to-be ex-confreres at Christ the King Parish down town. I did not want to owe the Legion anything. When that plane took off on February 11th, 1985, for Washington D.C. via Miami it definitively severed my ties with the Legion of Christ. I was out.

***

Felix Culpa, Happy Fault

Immediately after my showdown with Father Maciel I was overwhelmed by feelings of shame and failure. "Losing it" was precisely what I had consciously wanted to avoid. I had not planned to leave in anger, and I certainly did not relish making a fool of myself in front of the community. I felt I had done the unspeakable, that no one else could ever do something like that.

When I left, and for years after, I had no points of reference. My worldview had been limited to the Legion and only the Legion. I had no inkling I had been part of a high demand and high control group. Much less did I know what it meant to belong to a cult. Still learning after many years, and with the help of the International Cultic Studies Association and insights from Steve Hassan and Rick Ross, cult exit counselors, I found that helpful paradigm. Twenty-two year later I am struck by an uncannily parallel anecdote I find in the testimony of my friends, Dough and Wendy Duncan. For many years they struggled with their affiliation to Trinity Foundation in Dallas, Texas. Under the influence of charismatic leader, Ole Anthony, who convinced them that his was the true interpretation of Christianity, they were trapped.

> My own awakening came shortly after that, on that fateful spring day when I had my confrontation with Ole (...) I had been a member of Trinity Foundation for seven years. I knew that a true believer was always to be a peace and that everything was always perfect. According to the doctrine of the Trinity Foundation, if you thought anything should change, you were not at peace. Not being at peace was proof that you had crucified Christ afresh and had resurrected self....
>
> My confrontation with Ole that spring day produced an overwhelming fear that I was about to lose everything that was precious to me—my community, my new family, my sense of purpose, and my relationship with Doug. I believed that Doug was far more committed to

> Ole and the Trinity Foundation than he was to me or our relationship. I had committed the inexcusable sin of challenging the leader of Trinity Foundation. And yet, I could not let Ole continue to use his position of authority to distort God's Word.
>
> I snapped. Or rather, I snapped back. I snapped back to the person I was before I joined the Trinity Foundation. I snapped back and realized that I had somehow become part of a spiritually abuse and ultra-authoritarian religious group. "I can't hear God's voice anymore!" I had shouted at Ole. "Your voice has gotten too loud" I snapped, and in the single moment, I began to slowly find my way back to God[20].

It took me years after 1984 for me to gradually understand that passionate outburst was *my* only way out, while admiring those who are able to act with more forethought, self-control and dignity. I had to accept that after twenty-three years of immersion *I did not possess the tools to leave.* The Legion pruning knife had gradually stripped away the necessary mental clarity, self-determination, and decision-making skills. I was unable to rationally, calmly and purposefully walk out the door, away from Nuestro Padre and the Legion. Thank God for the subconscious, for that survival instinct. The Legion's coercive persuasion system, a.k.a. mind control, a.k.a. brainwashing, is so gradual, subtle and thorough it invades and takes over the conscious mind and the superficial conscience or superego. That is why it is useless to argue with a true believer Legionary or Consecrated member. That is why gung-ho members have no remorse when being unreasonable or cruel to their family and friends. With the conscious mind thus controlled, only at a subconscious level can the intuitive mind doubt, question, or rebel. Immediately after I flew into a rage at Father Maciel, my superego punished me. But perhaps at some subconscious level I knew it was ok, just as we subconsciously know love is right and hate is wrong. So perhaps, my subconscious—and true—conscience gave me permission to do the unspeakable: rashly contradict a saint in public, refuse to be browbeaten by a powerful authority, and stubbornly challenge an irreproachable figure.

I was immature when I entered the Legion at seventeen and immature when I left at forty-one. I had become *enmeshed and dependent on the Legion.* For years I held Father Maciel in holy awe. I had surrendered my mind and my will to the Legion. There were only shreds of me left for myself, and even these were supposed to be sinful.

After my "debacle", with further reflection and prayer, I began to accept the manner of my departure as my "fortunate original sin," the *Felix culpa* leading to growth and maturity, i.e. redemption. Besides, I have never sought to justify my actions—just to describe them as honestly as possible, spinning a cautionary tale of naïveté, deceit, disappointment, death and rebirth.

12.
RECOVERING
THANKS TO THE MILK OF HUMAN KINDNESS

"For when I was hungry, you gave me food;
When thirsty, you gave me drink;
When I was a stranger, you took me into your home;
When naked, you clothed me;
When I was ill, you came to my help;
When in prison, you visited me. [...]
Truly I tell you: anything you did for one of my brothers here, however insignificant, you did for me."

(Gospel of Matthew, chapter 25, vv. 35-36.40)

A TRIBUTE TO HIS EMINENCE JAMES CARDINAL HICKEY

Washington, D.C.
October 28, 2004

The walk from Farragut West Metro station to Rhode Island Ave. was pleasant under the warm gaze of a fall sun smiling from a clear blue sky. Inside the Catholic Cathedral of St. Matthew's, the light filtered shyly through the stained glass and alabaster windows dotting the marble floor. At 1:45 pm it was quiet, with a few people scattered around, sitting in the pews or performing their devotions at saints' altars. Two middle-aged men in black uniforms and plumed hats, Knights of Columbus, were standing guard at the top of the aisle, just outside the altar rails. A pair of kneelers was placed alongside the coffin where James Hickey lay robed in a chasuble, his fingers clutching his mother's Rosary beads. I plumped down on my knees to pray beside the man who had treated me well; a quiet man, who had dispensed to me the "milk of human kindness." My first encounter, in early 1985, at the Pastoral Center in Hyattsville, Maryland, was really quite serendipitous—or, in Christian parlance, providential.

When I precipitously left the Legion of Christ in November 1984, with twenty-two years of religious vows and fifteen years of priesthood under my belt, I was so devastated and disoriented I could have ended up anywhere. Unbeknownst to me, my situation had been aptly described in clinical terms by the American Psychiatric Association: "fatigue or loss of energy nearly every day; feelings of worthlessness or excessive or inappropriate guilt nearly every day; diminished ability to think or concentrate, or indecisiveness, nearly every day..." a Major Depressive Episode as described in the Diagnostic and Statistical Manual fourth edition.

But, with a little help from my friends, I was heading for Washington D.C. I was lucky, moreover, to reach the rendezvous. Due to my disorientation, and also because of lack of U.S. travel experience, I was confused by the fact there were three airports to fly into and I started to panic at the airport in Miami. Serendipitously, I got on the right plane to the right airport at the right time. What a relief when I found a priest friend, Father K-F, waiting for me when I came into the luggage area at Washington National. He remarked I looked like a prison camp survivor, and I made some comment about that old Hardy Kruger movie "The One that Got Away." This meant that my brain was at least partially alive. Another priest friend, D-M, also ex-Legionary, arrived later and we took off for dinner together. They brought me to a nice restaurant, I can't remember where. I think they wanted to get me drunk. But I was still wound so tightly they weren't successful. I looked so haggard, emaciated, so depressed, so shaken, that I suppose this was their male clerical method of helping me relax and lift a weight off my shoulders.

North from National Airport under Memorial Bridge, up along the George Washington Memorial Parkway we sped. The broad Potomac's black eyes winked knowingly up at us from the right through the barren maples. Safe in the custody of his freed brethren, John Paul O'Connor-Lennon, like thousands before him a hundred years back, fled under cover of night. He was not an African fleeing from a cruel Irish master, though, but a frightened Irishman fleeing from ruthless Mexican slave traders Maciel & Co.

That night, after hours of catch-up conversation spanning decades of lonely isolation, finally exhausted, I slept in the little guest bedroom at Our Lady of Lourdes with a great sense of relief; safe in that friendly strange rectory, knowing also that two friends cared about me and for me. I was on the road to recovery.

My good brothers had explained my plight to His Grace and I began living with another F.B.I., (foreign-born-Irish), priest in a quiet residential neighborhood. Winter was turning to spring and I relished the gradual budding of a variety of flowers and shrubs in my leisurely strolls. I became a self-taught expert on the stages of spring in the Washington area: first crocus, then daffodil, forsythia, azalea, dogwood, cherry blossom…After a couple of weeks, I was given an appointment with the Archbishop at the Pastoral Center. My mistrust of superiors must have been hard-wired at that stage, but Hickey was kind, plain and simply. I now wanted to be honest with myself and others; I was tired of the Legion's lies and my own. Catch-22: I needed to try out my priesthood in his diocese and for that I did not want to give a bad impression. On the other hand, I had to be honest about the fragility of my priestly vocation, after the hammering it had taken in the Legion.

"Well, Paul, I hope you are comfortable at St. Bartholomew's parish," was a good, disarming, ice-breaker. *So, here is a superior who appears genuinely concerned about my well-being,"* I thought to myself. Where had that been during the past twenty-three years? I was somehow able to convey to him my ambiguity and insecurity. He reframed it like a skilled therapist. "Yes, you have not been feeling well…Take a few months resting with Monsignor...and then let us know how you are doing. When your health improves and you are able to take on further responsibilities." I was being treated like a person, a human being, a fellow priest, with kindness and consideration, with respect for my situation and for my freedom of choice. I couldn't believe it. That is part of what His Eminence gave me: time to sort myself out in the most harrowing crisis of my life.

I was able to peacefully and enjoyably serve the people of God for another four years, thanks to James Hickey and the other good priests and faithful of that diocese. When the sad moment came to request a leave of absence from my priestly duties, His Eminence met me with the same pastoral and fatherly concern. "We would love you to continue serving the people of the diocese and working with your fellow priests, but I respect your decision." What a contrast to my previous experience where the superior was the one who made the decisions, and I had to accept no matter what I thought or felt!

When a year or two later I made the formal request to be relieved of my priestly duties, he personally received and oriented me. He told me he would be meeting soon with Father Maciel in Rome and would ask him for help with the process of my laicization—I purposely had not sought incardination into the diocese of Washington, and thus was still officially a member of the Legion of Christ. The Legion never responded to that request. His Eminence went beyond the call of duty and facilitated it through his diocese, assigning my case to my good friend, Monsignor Bernard Gerhardt—a kinder man you couldn't find.

Most people do not know that a dispensation from the solemn vow of priestly celibacy is not automatically granted with laicization. I remember I was embarrassed when His Eminence brought up this subject but extremely grateful when

I heard the words: "Paul, and would you like help with that too?"

Thank you, James Hickey, for showing me another, kinder, face of the Church and the hierarchy, when I felt like turning away in anger. People like you make the Church believable and worth serving; you are a credit to the priesthood and to the Savior you served. And blessed are you now, James Hickey, because whatever you did to the most insignificant of Jesus' brothers, you did to Him.

***

The Kindness of Family

Separation from family had been difficult for me; we had been, if not demonstrative, affectionate and close. When I joined the Legion I did not think the order would be so strict in this aspect, or so hard on me. The "weaning" from my father, mother, and four sisters began soon after entering the novitiate, cutting back on letter writing, the only communication I had with my family. A few years later I believed I was resilient enough for any sacrifice: not being allowed to go to my sisters' weddings; not being allowed to perform my younger sister's wedding after I was ordained…My dad died when I was five years in the Legion, just after a visit he and mom paid to Rome in September 1966.

I did continue to have a close relationship with my mother, with one letter a month…that was my total contact with her for years. She had visited me that one time after five years. The second time I saw her was at my father's funeral, three months later. The third time was at my ordination, when she traveled to Rome with two of my sisters and a few aunts. The fourth time was on my way from Spain to the USA in 1970 when I was allowed twenty hours in Ireland. I may have passed through

Ireland—staying at the Legion house in Clondalkin—during a trip to Europe in 1975 when commissioned to found the School of Faith. During my 1976-84 tour of duty in Mexico City, thanks to the hospitality and ingenuity of the Lovely Ladies of Lomas, I was able to wrangle a couple of visits for my mother. We enjoyed the time together and sightseeing immensely.

Relationships with sisters were almost totally lost during those twenty-three years in the legion. None of my Irish youth friendships survived, except one, and that to a limited degree.

When I transitioned to the diocesan priesthood, at age forty-one, I began "reclaiming" my family, and then when I left the priesthood, at age forty-five, I recovered my relationship with my sisters and my seventeen nieces and nephews. We are now almost normal, despite missing all the in-between years. Outside my family, I am a stranger in my native land.

***

The Fly in the Ointment

Recovery was not without suffering. My handlers in Yucatan had put me on Ativan, an anti-anxiety medication. They had committed a common mistake. When faced with an anxious depressive patient, you treat the anxiety instead of the depression. So for several months after my arrival in Washington I could not get better. I was taking a medication that was making me worse! Nobody read the small print: "Before taking Ativan, tell your doctor if you have a history of depression or suicidal thoughts…" Thank goodness I did not have a history of suicidal ideation.

But I was the guinea pig that got all the side effects during the trial run: light-headedness, drowsiness, dizziness, tiredness, blurred vision, sleep problems, sedation, amnesia and forgetfulness, trouble concentrating…That is what explains my walking into glass doors and hurting my nose and forehead and thus feeling more klutzy and depressed, lacking energy to do anything and dragging myself around, being clumsy and stumbling into things, my inability to think clearly and make self-enhancing decisions, and that sedation making me feel like I was not myself but a zombie.

My chemically induced agony ended when I ran out of the medication and let it lapse from inertia. I began to feel less bad. My therapy of stopping to smell the roses, i.e., my nature therapy strolling around the beautiful neighborhood, began to have a positive effect.

***

The Kindness of Strangers

At St Bart's in early 1985 I was still in a mental haze. A kind lady from the parish wanted to show me interesting pastoral activities in the area. She took me to a Pro-Life Center and introduced me to the coordinator, a serious young woman in her thirties. After the presentation of the foreign missionary by my chaperone, the young counselor took me to one side. God knows what she saw in me, or saw me in: "Father, it seems like you are going through a major transition from a religious order into a diocese…Have you thought of pastoral counseling?" I was stunned by her forthrightness and must have stared at her for a moment. She was not deterred. "Let me give you the names of a couple of counselors. You can choose the one you think best." This was a clear case of one very sharp sheep leading a disoriented shepherd.

After a few days—in my totally dazed and depressed state I had nothing to lose—I did decide to call one of them, the ex-Jesuit. He was also in transition, but on much firmer ground than I. He had recently made a good exit from his community and was still in touch with it. I knew that once I left I was anathema to the Legion. I was astounded when he told me that his Novice Master invited him, an ex-priest, to help the novices discern their vocations. What country, Church, or Religious Order was this?

When I had poured out my troubles in that first formal session he commented: "Well, it seems like you were bouncing off the walls in the Legion of Christ for a long time." It was such a clear and concise summary. Yes, I had been in a tightly closed pressure cooker…I gradually realized thereafter that perhaps those doubts of faith had simply been obsessive thoughts or ruminations, that those long periods of spiritual drought were manifestations of Dysthymia, and the harrowing bouts of my "Dark Night of the Soul" may have been untreated Major Depressive Episodes. Though depressing just to think of it, this insight made me grateful to God and boosted my personal esteem marveling at how I survived. Had there been too much unnecessary suffering? I never second-guess God now, but I do question the Legion's care of its members' mental health and human development. I would never put myself or anybody I loved in its hands again!

On my recovery journey, fellow Christians of all denominations embraced me on retreats, invited me to minister, and taught me how to pray. At Kirkwood ecumenical center, a wise Episcopal priest, Morton Kelsey, became my transitional spiritual father, being what Marcial Maciel had never been. Catholic parishioners at St Matthew's Cathedral in D.C. appreciated my ministry and still applauded when, during Mass, I announced my leave of absence. Monsignor Boland at priest personnel gave me a place to stay temporarily. The chancellor, Monsignor Bernard Gerhardt, fraternally secured my dispensation when the Legion did not cooperate.

Presiding at St. Matthews, D.C. 1988

Fairfax County Adult Education staff in the person of Nancy Scesney helped this disoriented forty-something-year-old with an MA and no real-life experience, secure his first job teaching English as a second language. Generous Portuguese friends, Eugene and Esmeralda Alcoforado, gave me their "lemon" as a means of transportation. A clinical supervisor trusted me with my first real—if part-time—professional position at a substance abuse detoxification center. A family services agency enabled me to work with my beloved Hispanic community. Further down the road my "boss" entrusted children and families to the care of this unknown, single, middle-aged Caucasian.

13
REVIEWING
PERSONAL CORRESPONDENCE WITH *NUESTRO PADRE*

"Your poetry is very good", said Kamala. "If I were rich I would give you money for it."...

"I also know the sacrificial songs," said Siddhartha, "but I will not sing them any more. I also know incantations but I will not pronounce them any more. I have read the scriptures..." At that moment a servant entered and whispered something into his mistress' ear.

"I have a visitor," said Kamala. "Hurry and disappear, Siddhartha, nobody must see you here..." However, she ordered the servant to give the holy Brahmin a white gown. Without quite knowing what was happening, Siddhartha was led away by the servant, conducted by a circuitous route to a garden house, presented with a gown, let into the thicket and expressly instructed to leave the grove unseen, as quickly as possible.

Contentedly, he did what he was told. Accustomed to the forest, he made his way silently out of the grove and over the hedge. Contentedly, he returned to the town, carrying his rolled-up gown under his arm. He stood at the door of an inn where travelers met, silently begged for food and silently accepted a piece of rice cake. Perhaps tomorrow, he thought, I will not need to beg for food.

He was suddenly overwhelmed with a feeling of pride. He was a Samana no longer; it was no longer fitting that he should beg. He gave the rice cake to a dog and remained without food.

Siddhartha[21]

POWER STRUGGLE

After I burst out of the Legion at the end of 1984, I was able—in spite of a veritable mental breakdown—to take advice from ex-Legion colleagues. I was to send a letter to Father Maciel notifying him that I wanted to leave the Legion. This way I would not be simply running away without permission but starting a process acceptable to Church authorities. They told me to sound strong and at the same time respectful, though at that moment I felt neither. I had to pluck up courage or, as they say graphically in Spanish, *hacer de tripas corazón*, "make a staunch heart out of quivering guts." I have been able to preserve some letters from Father Maciel because I was then safely outside. I do not know what happened to the ten or so I had received during my time in the Legion. Maybe they had fallen prey to the Legion superiors' system of purloining documents, i.e., stealing them, from our rooms as soon as they scented disaffection. Though it could also be they were simply lost in transition. Reviewing this painful period, even after ten years recovery, has been a grueling and galling experience.

***

Thy Kingdom Come!

Bacalar, Quintana Roo, Mexico
December 20th, 1984

To: Father Marcial Maciel, LC
General Director
Legionaries of Christ
CP 9031, Rome, Italy

Esteemed Father in Christ:

A series of problems, personal and relating to my superiors, plus my lack of trust and my inability to cope, have led me to a state of frustration, anger, aggressivity and depression, producing in me insomnia and neuralgias over the past few months.

This makes fulfilling my commitments as a religious in the Legion very difficult and forces me to be honest and ask you for a leave of absence. Thus, according to Canon Law 686,#1 I am asking you as Superior General permission to leave the religious life for three years so as to recover my peace of soul and be in better condition to freely and joyfully assume the obligation of my Christian, priestly and religious life.

I have the consent of the Ordinary {bishop} of the place where I plan to reside.

Grateful for all you have done for me up to now and hoping to count on your fatherly support,

Yours,

Paul Lennon, LC

My ex-Legion priest advisers suggested I send another letter by certified mail to Rome in case Father Maciel did not receive—or claimed he did not receive—the first. Although I was a nervous wreck, with some coaching I put another message together and sent it from my sister's home in Ireland:

December 26th, 1984
Cloughleigh Park,
Ennis, Co. Clare

Esteemed Father,

It is over a month since we met in Cotija during the Spiritual Exercises. I was sorry for the way things turned out and I tried to meet with you on several occasions but your other commitments made it impossible.

I have been reflecting a lot for some time on my relationship with the Legion and I have reached the conclusion that my personality (Sp. "manera de ser") does not seem appropriate for the life-style demanded by the Legion. At my age it would be difficult for me to change and I don't want to continue causing problems to the Congregation, nor can I bear the pressures and anxiety that endanger my Catholic priesthood.

Therefore I am requesting from you permission to leave the Legion of Christ in order to find psychological and spiritual peace. I do not have concrete plans at this moment but I will have to seek the hospitality of the diocesan clergy. I am grateful to you and to the Legion for all you have done for me during these years and I assure you I keep you present in my prayers.

Please reply to the above direction.

Yours in Christ,
Paul Lennon, LC.

On February 11th, 1985, I had arrived in the diocese of Washington DC, and was placed under the kind tutelage of Monsignor James J. Reddy, R.I.P. In late February or early March a letter from Father Maciel dated February, 2005, was forwarded to me. From the original in my possession I literally translate Father Maciel's—or his secretary's—type-written reply to my second letter.

Thy Kingdom Come!

MARCIAL MACIEL, L.C. PRIVATE

February 1985

Padre Paul Lennon, L.C.
Cloughleigh Park...

Dear Padre Paul,

Midway through the month of January I received your letter in Mexico, dated December, 26th, in which you communicate your decision to leave the Legion because you think that "your personality does not seem appropriate for the life-style demanded by the Legion". I believe that with a little effort and good will and with the always available grace of God, everything would have been possible.

Nevertheless, Padre Paul, I respect your decision, no matter how painful it may be for me to see leave one of our priests who for so many years has worked generously in the apostolic tasks entrusted to him. I thank you in my own name, in the name of the Legion and of the Church for these beautiful years that you have spent serving souls. All the good that you have done to confirm your brothers in the faith, first in the School of Faith and later on the Quintana Roo Mission, stands as your greatest work. Man may not adequately appreciate it, but Our Divine Lord values it and rewards you for all it is worth.

Let me know to which diocese you wish to go; ask the bishop to accept you benevolently and let me know so I can send my letter of request in your name, so that I can then negotiate your dispensation from vows with the S.C. [Sacred Congregation] of Religious at the Vatican.

Finally, Padre Paul, I entrust you to the Blessed Virgin Mary, protectress and inspirer of your priesthood. You pray for me and the Legion.

With an affectionate greeting for you and your family,
I remain,
Most affectionate and faithful servant in Jesus Christ,
Marcial Maciel, L.C.
(Signed in ink)

****

Without a doubt, Father Maciel is a wily letter crafter. He begins by taking control and goes on to make me feel guilty for not doing enough to "save my Legionary vocation": *I believe that with a little effort and good will and with the always available grace of God, everything would have been possible.*

"You say I let you down
You know it's not like that;
If you're so hurt
Why then don't you show it;
You say you lost your faith
But that's not where it's at

You had no faith to lose
And you know it."

Positively 4th Street, Bob Dylan

I saw the Father Maciel's previous phrase as patronizing and certainly minimizing my twenty-three year effort to squeeze myself into the Legionary mold. I did not find the above letter helpful; flowery, yes, but unhelpful. I had not trusted Father Maciel enough to initially tell him to which diocese I was heading. I decided to work with the diocese of Washington and get counsel there from Priest Personnel and other clergy and later present Fr Maciel with my plans—and to stop depending on Father Maciel and the Legion for my wellbeing and life decisions. I took psychological assessment tests offered by the diocese of Washington and was having weekly pastoral counseling which I paid for out of my monthly diocesan stipend.

***

Treacherous Transition

The ordinary reader, even Catholic, has no idea just how complicated the life of a Catholic priest can be, especially when he is leaving a religious order or is otherwise in transition. The Catholic Church does not allow any of her priests to "freelance", "float", or sell their pastoral talents to the highest bidder. In order to legitimately exercise his priesthood, a Catholic priest must always be under the authority, *jurisdiction*, of a bishop in union with the pope. Though the Sacrament of Holy Orders makes him "a priest forever, according to the order of Melchisadec" he cannot practice without the necessary authorization from a bishop or religious superior. There are to be no white, or black, knights in Holy Mother Church. In order to joust in this field of the Lord, Sir Priest must seek the favor of at least one feudal lord. And so, cantering out of his religious order enclosure, the priest finds the meadows strewn with thorny thickets, among which canonical rules and regulations rear their bloated carnival heads.

I was also negotiating with the archdiocese my migratory status and trying to get my "green card" of permanent residency in the USA. As a foreign priest I had been technically an "illegal alien" for thirteen years in Mexico. I remember approaching with apprehension the U.S. consulate in Merida after my break-up with the Legion. The middle-aged Caucasian woman who interviewed me was extremely kind and gave me a visa for the USA based on my valid Irish passport. She must have known I was a padre, for the visa reflected the status of a religious minister. I was so confused at the time I did not know I was holding something better than a tourist visa. My status as a minister would make it easier to apply for permanent residency as a priest of the archdiocese of Washington. It was still dicey. I had not incardinated because I did not want to deceive Archbishop Hickey into believing I had a rock-solid vocation. I was asking the diocese to do me a favor. Anyway, I am glad that diocesan administrators were kind and shrewd enough, or Uncle Sam turned a blind eye, and I did get my green card circa 1987. Not having it a year or two earlier prevented me from taking a de facto leave of absence when I felt the urge after scarcely one year into my diocesan ministry. How would I get a job without a green card? How about getting some financial assistance from the Legion through my own personal Caesar?

I had written to Father Maciel in December 1985 with some requests, my letter reflecting more peace and poise. In February, 1986, I received a reply. Father Maciel's reply reflects his greater prudence, now that he knew I was under the patronage of the diocese of Washington, D.C. Father Maciel, or his secretary, dots his canonical "i"s.

Thy Kingdom Come!

MARCIAL MACIEL, L.C. PRIVATE

Wednesday, January 29, 1986

To: Father Paul Lennon
St Matthew's Cathedral,
1725 Rhode Island Ave.,
Washington, D.C. 20036

Dear Paul in Christ,

I have received your letter of December 22, 1985 where you explain your present situation. I thank you for your Christmas greetings and I express my best wishes for the New Year that has just begun.

I appreciate your efforts and interest in being prudent and avoiding any kind of scandal or hurried decisions. I respect your intention, after consulting with the Archdiocese of Washington Chancellor, to take a leave of absence from priestly ministry so as to reflect on your priesthood and vocation in a quiet atmosphere. For my part I can only assure you of my prayer for the Holy Spirit to enlighten you and to sustain you in this very special time of your life.

I have given orders to Father Antonio Izquierdo, General Prefect of Studies to send you all the academic documentation in our possession or that we can get for you from ecclesiastical universities in Rome.

Not having any formal petition from you for dispensation from your vows, the Sacred Congregation for Religious and Secular Institutes has asked us to regularize your canonical situation. Therefore, I beg you to send me as soon as possible:

1. A letter to the General Director of the Legion of Christ, asking for your dispensation from vows and explaining the reasons;
2. A letter to the Congregation for Religious and Secular Institutes telling them of your decision, requesting your dispensation from vows and explaining the reason;
3. Enclose a letter from the local Ordinary (bishop) who has temporarily accepted you.

As soon as we receive these documents, we will present them, together with a letter from the General Director containing the Counsel's decision, to the Congregation for Religious.

I wish you, Father Paul, all the best for your life and I recommend myself to your prayers.

Yours affectionately, your servant always in Jesus Christ,

Marcial Maciel, L.C.

I did not react to Father Maciel's affirmation that "the Sacred Congregation for Religious and Secular Institutes has asked us to regularize your canonical situation." Experience had taught me how to interpret such apparent truths stated with aplomb. I had developed a sixth sense for discerning when

Nuestro Padre and the Superiors might be telling a fib, or at least stretching a point to their advantage. Had Father Maciel actually contacted the Vatican Department for Religious about the case of loose cannon religious Paul Lennon? Besides, my sixth sense also helped me choose my battles with the Legion. Well-meaning but naïve relatives of Legionaries often need to be coached by ex-members who possess this sixth sense when dealing with the Legion.

At that time I believed I had already complied twice with Father Maciel's first request. I did not see how his second request was justified. Point three I left for the diocese of Washington and Father Maciel to sort out. Newfound freedom outside the Legion and some empowerment stemming from being under the protection of Archbishop Hickey put me in a position for the first time in my life to wait, bargain with, and come up with some demands of my own for Father Maciel. It was also an opportunity to indulge in that other medieval game, casuistry, or persnickety debate. Thus the following:

St Matthew's Cathedral,
1725 Rhode Island Ave.,
Washington, D.C. 20036

February 25, 1986

TO: Father Marcial Maciel, L.C.
General Director, Legionaries of Christ,
Rome, Italy

Dear Father,

I received your kind letter dated January 29 in reply to my December letter. I appreciate your attention, your good wishes and I would like to continue our discussion.

1- I have not received any of the documentation you mentioned. I would like people to review my records in Salamanca so I could get some transcripts of my studies in Spain, and perhaps my certificates of Intermediate and Leaving Certificates from Ireland.

2- I would like you to answer me regarding financial help. I believe some religious congregations give their exiting members a monthly stipend or a lump sum to help them transition, a time that is often difficult and painful when re-entering a world they hardly knew. This way the gratitude you expressed to me a year ago could become tangible, gratitude not only of a person but also of an institution towards a man who has devoted twenty-three of the best years of his life to it.

3- In these circumstances, awaiting more efficacious help from the Legion, I am unable to step out of the ministry as I would be stepping into a vacuum. I will have to keep my options open and remain in contact with the persons who have offered me their hospitality up to now. For these two or three reasons I am unable to send you the documentation that you requested.

As I await your response,
Your affectionate son in Christ,
Paul Lennon, L.C.

***

Talking the talk…

Thy Kingdom Come!

MARCIAL MACIEL, L.C. PRIVATE

Rome, April 6, 1986

To: Father Paul Lennon
St Matthew's Cathedral,
1725 Rhode Island Ave.,
Washington, D.C. 20036

Esteemed Paul in Christ,

Yesterday on returning from Australia I found your letter from February 25, to which I now reply, hoping that you have received the academic documents by now.

Allow me, Father Paul, to again suggest you regularize your canonical situation. You can read the corresponding canons yourself (cc. 665, 691 and 693) and see how necessary my suggestion is.

At the same time, without wanting to influence you in the least, I would propose you do not abandon your priesthood but rather continue to serve God, by incardinating into the archdiocese of Washington, despite the difficulties you can feel about your vocation and the exercise of your priestly ministry: you can do so much good to so many souls, and God will always be there to support and help you in your difficulties.

Regarding financial help, you know very well how we do not lose interest in those who, on leaving the Congregation, are needy and require some help. And believe me that very willingly would I help you in a more significant way, if our financial situation were not going through serious difficulties provoked by Mexico's financial crisis. As the Legion continues to depend on the alms of Mexican benefactors, you understand the difficulties we have to face in sustaining our religious in training, who are more numerous every year.

But, if I can help you, independent of the decision you decide to make, I could send you about a hundred thousand

Mexican pesos a month, while you find a way to round off your budget.

I want you to know, Father Paul, that I remember you in my prayers, and heartily wish the best for you. I also ask you pray for me.

Yours affectionately, and your servant forever in Jesus Christ,

(Signed)

Marcial Maciel

In cases like this it behooves the exiting religious to read the corresponding canon laws carefully and take counsel. This prevents him from becoming overawed or cowed by vagaries or legalities. Once he has flown the coop the Legionary can consult with canon lawyers and monsignors within the diocese that is offering him hospitality.

In reality, the canons were not saying anything I did not already know and about which I was not being assessed. If Father Maciel was considering me a religious absenting myself from the house, according to Can. 665 §1, neither he nor the Legion ever applied part 2 of that canon to me:

> §2 Members who unlawfully absent themselves from a religious house with the intention of withdrawing from the authority of Superiors are to be carefully sought out and helped to return and to persevere in their vocation.

What the Catholic Church wants to prevent by these laws is priests wandering around the world without being under the jurisdiction of any religious superior. This happened a lot during the Middle Ages, and such priests were called "wandering clerics."

A more careful study of canon 693 shows how Father Maciel's interpretation is for his own convenience. Truth is I had crossed the Rubicon by confronting Father Maciel in public. The Legion never sought me after that, as was its obligation. Whether the phrase was ever pronounced or not, I was a *persona non grata*.

Basically, what I had done was request an indult from my superior, Father Maciel, to absent myself from the religious house while I sought a friendly bishop. This is a very gray area in canon law. On the one hand, the law appears to favor the superior and the institute over the individual. On the other, once a religious finds a friendly bishop he is "safe" from strong-arming by his religious superior because he in a certain sense under the protection of the bishop. Maciel kept insisting I tell him into what diocese I wanted to incardinate and that I should incardinate. He probably knew—the Legion had a house in Potomac, MD, half an hour away—that I was already living in good grace at a rectory in the diocese of Washington. Actual incardination was beyond the requirements of canon law, and was none of his business.

> Can. 693 If the member is a cleric, the indult is not granted until he has found a Bishop who will incardinate him in his diocese or at least receive him there on probation.

Father Maciel claims he did not consider my letters of request formal enough to constitute a petition of indult. But I had left my religious house and I was already on probation with a friendly bishop. According to canon law the Legion should have sent me the indult. This thrust and parry may have helped Father Maciel delay informing the competent authority and requesting the indult from the Vatican's Congregation for

Religious—in other words, he avoided telling the Vatican that one of his religious, an ordained priest, had left.

***

...But not walking the walk

In order to avoid revealing to the Vatican authorities the number of religious and priests leaving the order, the Legion has historically been purposely negligent in informing the Congregation for Religious about those who leave and in requesting the necessary indults.

There are presently many Legionary priests—dozens, scores?—working outside the Legion without the necessary indult, under a myriad of legal subterfuges. There are also many religious who have never been officially released from their temporary or perpetual vows. Case in point:

In May 2005, when Maciel survivor Jose-Antonio Olvera made his deposition to Vatican prosecutor Monsignor Charles Scicluna in Mexico City, after breaking down with the words "I am here, Monsignor, to denounce priest Marcial Maciel who destroyed my life," he told him that after more than forty years outside the Legion he had never been notified of his release from religious vows. Soon after Monsignor Scicluna returned to Rome, Jose Antonio proudly told us that he received the appropriate notification. I am assuming Monsignor Scicluna ratified Jose Antonio's canonical status directly with the Congregation for Religious without bothering, or bothering with, the Legion.

This same canonical irregularity is true also in the case of Neftalí Sánchez Tinoco—my Father Neftalí of Bundrowes House—who left the Legion about forty years ago and is presently a priest in the diocese of Morelia, Michoacán. Often these decades-long irregularities are covered up with "Father

X is on loan to the diocese of Y." But the bottom line is expediency. Why go to trouble for religious who are no longer of any use to the Legion! "Let the dead bury their dead!"

The Legion likes to point out the many potatoes falling into the sack. It does not want to look at the big hole in bottom of the sack; precisely my point of departure in the debate with Father Maciel in Cotija. "You shut up! That's none of your business!" were Maciel's words to impertinent Paul for daring to let that skeleton out of the closet.

Another very un-Christian chapter in the story of those priests who want to continue their ministry: Normally, before accepting a priest into his diocese, the bishop requests information from the priest's previous superiors. If the Legion superiors give a negative report, a non-committal report, or do not respond—as is their usual approach—the exiting priest is stuck in No-Man's Land. I know of one priest who was scared because his Legion superior had told him that because he read a girlie magazine he surely did not have a vocation to celibacy and he could not recommend him to the diocesan clergy! Thus the Legion will use holy blackmail to control the destiny of its exiting members. Its power to veto coupled with the blind faith many members still have in their superiors often determines whether an exiting member will go to a diocese or go into marriage.

The Legion frequently guides its departing priests away from some dioceses unfriendly to the Legion and towards other, friendlier, dioceses. In my generation four of us chose the diocese of Washington of our own volition or by happenstance. I chose it simply because I was unaware or scared of other options, and I knew at least one ex-Legionary there. The archbishop was scandalized by how we had been treated in the Legion and did not request information. Contemporaries of mine, Father

John McCormick—after a period of discernment—chose the diocese of Orlando, Fla. Father Rodolfo Preciado went to the diocese of Orange, Calif. Father Jack Sherlock is in the diocese of Wichita, Kan. Most of us went where we wanted. Because there were four dissidents in Washington D.C., the Legion tried to steer others exiting members away from us. They probably invented some horror story about us "with the best intentions"; "for charitable reasons", naturally, or "for your own good".

I had purposely delayed incardination because I was not sure I could continue to fulfill my priestly obligations. On the positive side Canon Law allows the religious member of an institute five years before having to commit to incardination. Without incardination, I remained a religious of the Legion of Christ and therefore under the Legion's care and responsibility. I, Paul, consider Father Maciel's suggestion to incardinate an attempt to dump a priest on shaky vocational ground on the archdiocese of Washington. He was quite happy with me living off the Archdiocese of Washington for over a year while still a Legion religious. Then he did a fine job of cleverly recommending I stay a priest. He finally suggested incardinating into the diocese of Washington so that the Legion could wash its hands of me and keep them clean.

***

Legion's support for exiting members

Note how Father Maciel played the poor-mouth when it came to offering financial help to this exiting religious. Gently, and cruelly, did he remind me that as an exiting LC I was less important than religious in training, eager to commit, while I, miserable me, was dying to get out.

I remember my disappointment and anger on calculating the amount of Father Maciel's offer. Maybe it was not a good time for a Legionary to leave the Legion. The Mexico City earthquake had precipitated a headlong fall of the Mexican peso's value from 450 to the dollar in 1985 to 922 in 1986.

So, if Father Maciel was offering me 100,000 pesos, which sounds like an awful lot of money, it really meant $109.20 a month. As an exiting member this is what I was worth to the Legion. Renting an apartment cost about $500. The Archdiocese of Washington was paying me, as a priest friend, a regular monthly stipend of $600 on top of bed, board and car. Father Maciel was offering me $100 to make it on my own. Besides the apparently generous offer of 100,000 Mexican pesos a month, I wonder how he expected me to "round off" my budget. He remained my "faithful servant in Jesus Christ." This reminds me of the King's words in Hamlet:

"Words, words, words…
My words fly up, my thoughts remain below.
Words without thoughts never to heaven go."

My options were limited. It was either stay in the priesthood in Washington, or starve. I let Father Maciel's offer drop and backpedaled on my original petition for a leave of absence. I would need the shelter of a second career before stepping out into the cold.

"You got a lotta nerve
To say you are my friend
When I was down
You just stood there grinning

You got a lotta nerve
To say you got a helping hand to lend
You just want to be on
The side that's winning

I know the reason
That you talk behind my back
I used to be among the crowd
You're in with"

Bob Dylan

***

Paul the Suave

Based on the shabby way he treated me, my natural inclination was to curse Father Maciel in my best Dublinese, "May ye die roarin'!" But my Christian spirit prevailed, as well as the fact that I was learning to combat fire with fire and ice with ice. After several drafts I wrote:

St Matthew's Cathedral,
1725 Rhode Island Ave.,
Washington, D.C. 20036

April 9th, 1986

TO: Father Marcial Maciel, L.C.
General Director, Legionaries of Christ,
Rome, Italy

My esteemed and remembered Father:

I hasten to reply to your kind letter dated April 6th, 1986 in which you refer to some of my concerns. I thank you from the bottom of my heart for all you have done for me up to now and I request you continue to have patience with me, lavishing on me your time and energy in the midst of the exhausting responsibilities as leader of the Legion. I have safely received the academic documentation sent me by the Prefecture of Studies.

Now I would like to request you send me documentation along the lines of verification of my priesthood as a first step towards my incardination. Facing your justified insistence on my sending you documentation I am obliged to read the Canons of Church Law you point out and to seek counsel with some assessors. My study of the canons prompts the following plan which I lay out hoping it will please you.

As you know, it was not Monsignor Hickey's criterion to grant incardination to ex-religious; but for the past few years he has done so. Thank goodness he is well disposed in my case. However, I do not possess any official document of the Legion accrediting me as a priest or referring to my priestly ministry; nor do I possess any official word of gratitude and acknowledgment from you as General Director of the Congregation of the Legion of Christ. I do possess personal letters such as that dated February 1986. I request you do this now in an official capacity, thus initiating the incardination process. Please follow the guidelines I am enclosing.

Hoping to count on your prompt collaboration,
Your servant in the Lord,
Paul Lennon, LC

Enclosed was a diocesan outline for Father Maciel to comply with the above canonical requirement. It took the form of a notarized letter containing the name of the superior, name of the priest in good standing, priest's date and place of ordination, etc. "Father…is hereby granted permission to serve in the Roman Catholic diocese of…in a permanent capacity.

We kindly recommend Father…to the Most Reverend Ordinary and Rectors of the Churches to the effect that he may be allowed to offer the Holy Sacrifice of the Mass and be endowed with the necessary faculties of which he may stand in need." The form ends with signature and title of signer.

Faced with a veritable official request from the archdiocese of Washington, DC, Father Maciel and the Legion quickly complied.

Thy Kingdom Come!

MARCIAL MACIEL, L.C. PRIVATE

Rome, May 11th, 1986

To: Father Paul Lennon
St Matthew's Cathedral,
1725 Rhode Island Ave.,
Washington, DC. 20036

Dear Father Paul in Christ:

I am replying to your letter dated April 19th which I received a few days ago. I am glad you received your academic documentation, and I hurry to send you a photocopy of the statement which, following the format you sent, I prepared and have sent to the Archdiocese of Washington's Vicar General.

I want you to know, Father Paul, that I will continue to pray much for you so you may continue to exercise your priestly ministry and doing good to souls. I say this from the bottom of my heart, knowing that this is the best for you and the way for you to make fruitful the gifts Our Lord has given you. Trusting that He will never abandon you, I renew my best wishes and the testimony of my esteem for you.

Please say a prayer for all legionaries and for the apostolic works we are carrying out.

Warm greetings,
Your affectionate and faithful servant in Jesus Christ,
Marcial Maciel, LC

This letter, on Father Maciel's personal stationary and signed by him in blue ink, postmarked New Haven, CT 065, May27th, was received on May 30th by the author in Washington, DC.

As I write I have before me on official LC stationary, Proto. LC. 236-86, the document granting Father Paul Lennon permission to exercise his priestly ministry, signed personally in black ink by Marcial Maciel, LC, General Director.

In a sense this letter marked the end of my correspondence with Father Maciel; a time to fight and a time to seek truce. He had my provisional promise to seek incardination into the archdiocese of Washington.

I had what I wanted: time. I had bought time to continue sorting through my befuddled mind and feelings.

***

Adios, Padre Maciel

A couple of years later I put an end to our correspondence with a gilt seal, sending Father Maciel a congratulatory letter for his priestly ordination anniversary. He replied with a typed business card bearing his personal signature which I translate exactly:

Thy Kingdom Come!
MARCIAL MACIEL, LC
Rome, 16-XI-1988
Father Paul Lennon
Washington, U.S.A.

Dear Father Paul in Christ:

I thank you warmly for your good wishes on the occasion of my priestly ordination anniversary, and I ask God to grant you the same graces and assistance you ask for me.

Affectionately in Jesus Christ,
(Personally signed in blue ink)

A corollary: When in 1989 I finally decided to take a leave of absence, I left by the front door, with the acquiescence of my protector, Cardinal James Hickey. A year or so later when I decided not to return to the ministry and told him, his kindness and respect never wavered. The Legion did nothing to help—although I was still officially a Legionary- but His Eminence followed through.

The requests for laicization and dispensation from celibacy were granted. Cardinal Hickey invited me to the Pastoral Center in Hyattsville, MD, to give the results personally and "instruct me on the restrictions" a laicized priest has to accept. Holy Mother the Church does give priests who back out a slap on the wrists, officially limiting their leadership in Catholic institutions and involvement in Catholic teaching. The bottom line was that I was now free from my priestly obligations and could marry in the Catholic Church if I so desired. In a nutshell, the archdiocese of Washington, to which I had devoted four years of ministry helped. Father Maciel and the Legion, to which I had dedicated my self from the age of seventeen through forty, stood back with folded arms, their hands unblemished. What to do with a person as scurrilous and cruel as Maciel? You express the anger, accept what happened, and get on with your life. Tardy truth takes time to shine through the clouds of deceit and justice to punish the wicked. Truth and Justice took their time before catching up on Maciel.

I had no further correspondence with Father Maciel, or with any other Legionary for that matter. We each went our separate ways: he to continued power and glory as Superior and General Director of the Legion of Christ, achieving great success in the amount of members, the Legion's financial stability and prosperity reflected in real estate, and in new Apostolates, including seminaries for the formation of clergy. Father Maciel would reach the apex of his Catholic glory being considered a personal friend of Pope John Paul II, being called by the pope "an efficacious guide for today's youth" and receiving honors and praise from the Vicar of Christ. Part of his glitter was tarnished by a Vatican investigation into his sexual abuse and drug abuse culminating in a censure from the Congregation for the Doctrine of Faith on May 19, 2006. Fraught with struggle, uncertainty and discernment, I went on to poverty without a vow, to the chaste love of exiting Legion and Regnum Christi members, and to the humble obedience of earning an honest living without clerical power, pull or privilege.

Out of nowhere the real and paradoxical God of "my ways are not your ways", regaled me with a second calling, almost by default lest I glory in myself: the Davidic task of pitting puny REGAIN against the Legion Goliath.

You see me on the street
You always act surprised
You say, "How are you?" "Good luck"
But you don't mean it

When you know as well as me
You'd rather see me paralyzed
Why don't you just come out once
And scream it

No, I do not feel that good
When I see the heartbreaks you embrace
If I was a master thief
Perhaps I'd rob them

And now I know you're dissatisfied
With your position and your place
Don't you understand
It's not my problem

I wish that for just one time
You could stand inside my shoes
And just for that one moment
I could be you

Yes, I wish that for just one time
You could stand inside my shoes
You'd know what a drag it is
To see you"

Bob Dylan

14
REVISITING FATHER MACIEL'S MODUS OPERANDI

In Mexico City, three months prior to the ordination of Jorge Bernal—now a Legionary bishop—in September 1957, Father Maciel told LC Seminarian Saul Barrales' parents to prepare to travel to Europe; their son, Saul, would be ordained together with then Bro. Bernal. The promise, alas, was not to be fulfilled. Saul had made one serious mistake. Following the spirit and letter of Legion rules, he had shown support for his then superior, Father Luis Ferreira (maternal cognomen, Correa), during that contentious period once known in Legion circles as "The War". In 1956 Father Maciel had been asked to step down from his leadership position and leave the Legion pending an investigation into his behavior. "Padre Ferreira," as he was known, was a co-founder and collaborator of Father Maciel, though always in a subordinate role. In 1956, however, when Father Maciel was separated from the Legion and silenced, Ferreira was officially appointed Vicar General of the Legion by Vatican authorities. Saul had accepted Ferreira's authority in Maciel's absence. Maciel, although officially separated from the Legion, would impede Saul's ordination.

BENEFACTRESSES & DOUBLE-FUNDING

Father Maciel has always been a master fundraiser. Since the beginning of the foundation he often was absent from his seminarians for long periods visiting benefactors. He possessed the knack of motivating generous Catholics, especially women, often widowed or estranged from their husbands, to contribute generously. He was also able to enroll Mexican entrepreneurs such as Don Santiago Galas and bankers like Don Manuel Espinosa Yglesias in the cause. It was not uncommon for the women to be considered the seminarians' godmothers, to exchange correspondence with them and to be entertained at the seminaries. These relationships were particularly strong during the foundational period from 1940 through 1980. Nowadays several multimillionaires, particularly in Mexico (The Garza-Sada-Zambrano dynasty in Monterrey), the USA (Thomas S., "Tom" Monaghan, president and CEO, Domino's Pizza), Spain (Alicia Koplowitz), and other countries financially support the Legion. The Legion also operates a sophisticated and aggressive mass mailing business from an office in Hamden, CT under the auspices of Father Anthony Bannon, LC. But in the beginning Father Maciel personally cultivated benefactors and they often visited the formation houses, giving us a break from the monotony of the austere "common life." For us this also meant that Nuestro Padre would be around and as enthusiastic members we looked forward to these special occasions.

My first benefactress was Doña Josefita. During the course of my training I was to have several other women supposedly contributing financially to the cost of my "formation," some individually and others collectively. Each one was considered, and considered herself, the godmother (*madrina*) of my priestly vocation. I addressed and wrote to these benefactresses with the honorable title of Doña, which means "lady": Edmé, wife of millionaire Santiago Galas; Flora Barragán de Garza, from the Garza-Sada dynasty in Monterrey, Mexico; and sensuous Señora Nora Mezerhane, of Lebanese descent, wife of a Caracas business magnate.

One person with whom I corresponded in a more individual way during my Roman sojourn was the widow Rosa Irigoyen, mother of prominent Mexican industrialist Manuel Senderos-Irigoyen. A truly influential Mexican of his generation, with a sense of civic duty, Don Manuel generously contributed to the construction of the Legionaries' Anahuac University and the Jesuits' Iberoamericana University. His labor of love became the IPADE, an Opus Dei higher institute for business leaders in Mexico City. Doña Rosa wrote personal handwritten letters full of real maternal affection for the future priest—I couldn't tell my mom!—and I will always treasure her memory. May God reward her. I assume that if her donations did not go directly to my training they must have helped defray the costs at least indirectly. Some of the more popular Legionary seminarians had real qualms of conscience juggling their various "godmothers," and got into very tight spots, especially if more than one arrived for their ordination!

***

Doña Josefita

I vaguely remember going to visit Doña Josefita at her villa in San Sebastian during those bewitching days in 1961. At that time the whole concept of "benefactress" was new to me. I never had previous contact with rich people or aristocrats. Like a fish out of water, more embarrassed than ever, I was introduced to this distinguished lady. What an extremely clever stroke of propaganda and promotion on the part of Father Maciel to have the first Irish recruits visit Doña Josefita! In order to get her name straight for this story, I had recourse to one of the best Legionary historians I know. His "note" will evolve into a story within a story, giving insight into some of the early Legionaries' and Father Maciel's way of treating them.

"Josefita Perez was the daughter of 1952 Venezuelan President (dictator?), Marcos Perez Jiménez. Father Marcial Maciel spent a lot of time with this lady in 1957. She accompanied him and the "Collegio Massimo" (Legion Senior Seminary on Via Aurelia, Rome) community to Lourdes, France, for the priestly ordination of Jorge Bernal Vargas on September 15, 1957. Doña Josefita presided over the special rehearsal dinner she offered to our large party of Legionary seminarians in the main restaurant at Monte Igueldo Hotel in San Sebastian the previous afternoon. On the 15th she attended Bernal's ordination at the Lourdes Grotto. The formal ordination banquet was held about four hours later at the Soubirous Fréres Hotel in Lourdes."

***

The Irish Connection

"It was at that hotel precisely where two Irish bishops visiting Lourdes heard us Legionary seminarians singing the popular Mexican song "Las Golondrinas" [author: a very romantic melody, almost Irish in its nostalgic goodbye]. One of the two bishops had studied as a young man in Salamanca, Spain, and had then heard some Mexicans singing that same song. The bishops approached our group and asked us to sing other Mexican songs for them. We obliged, and that is how Marcial Maciel's relationship with the Irish hierarchy began."

I would like to add two notes of my own—one serious, one picaresque—regarding Mexicans and Irishmen. Besides the obvious that both are Catholics, sentimental, and like the drink, Mexicans also profess an undying love for the Irish. During the Mexican War, 1846-48, a group of Irish mercenaries in the U.S. Army went over to the other side. The Saint Patrick's Battalion (*San Patricios*) was a group of several hundred immigrant soldiers, the majority Irish, who deserted the U.S. Army because of ill-treatment or sympathetic leanings to fellow Mexican Catholics, and joined the Mexican army. Most were killed in the Battle of Churubusco; about 100 were captured by the United States and roughly half were branded and hanged as deserters. For the United States they were traitors and received their just punishment. To the Mexicans they are heroes. A plaque honors their memory at Plaza San Angel in Mexico City.

The other strange coincidence is tooting the horn. In Mexico one way to get people's attention is to toot your car horn in a particular way: five in a row, a pause and then two more. Mexicans also consider this *mentando la madre*, "insulting the mother," about the worst thing one can do or say; blowing the horn this way can provoke an angry and violent response, even leading to bloodshed. In the streets of Cabra West we had the same thing, but without the lethal meaning. It was a kind of humorous ditty and did not give offense: "How is your auld one (mother)? Game ball (fine); out in the back yard, playin' ball!" Father Maciel did not know this latter cultural nugget but he certainly was aware of the "Land of Saints and

Scholars" and the San Patricios. Dreaming of having a battalion of these brave soldiers in his Legion, he took the first step at the Soubirous Fréres Hotel in Lourdes.

***

Attachment to finery and money

> "Superiors should vigorously put an end to anything that looks like worldly tastes as regards food, clothing, relaxation, trips or other similar things, and reinstate the proven customs of the Congregation."
> (Constitutions (Rules) of the Legion of Christ, the Vow of Poverty, #286, 2;[22]

Jose Barba continues: "At the time of Bernal's ordination, Father Maciel was driving around in a luxury special edition, two-tone, fully loaded Chrysler. According to him it had been donated by said Josefita Perez. Not so, according to other sources. On the first Sunday of August 1990, at the Hotel de la Soledad, in Morelia, Michoacán, Mexico, Father Neftalí Sanchez Tinoco (LC 1942-c.1969) told me it was not true that Josefita had given Maciel that car; au contraire, that he—Neftalí—had traveled in person with the Legion Founder to Tangiers, Morocco, and that there Maciel bought the car cash. Neftalí reconfirmed the story over lunch at the Hotel Alameda, Morelia City, Michoacán state, Mexico, in the summer of 1994. Presently a chaplain to a community of nuns, Neftalí also teaches Sociology of Religion at La Salle University campus in Morelia, capital of Michoacán."

Father Maciel always carries with him large amounts of cash. This is confirmed by testimonies of ex-Legionaries who have been administrators. Part of their job was to supply Father

Maciel with large sums of cash for his "personal needs," no questions asked. This privilege was, or is, one of Father Maciel's prerogatives as founder. It is universally accepted that from the beginning Father Maciel had access to money because he was the Legion's main fundraiser. Benefactors gave Father Maciel cash and checks in his name, and in the name of Legion institutions.

***

Saul, the Missing Ordinand

Father Maciel could be nasty. He would not let little Saul—one of the victims of his sexual abuse who would accuse him decades later—get away with a show of solidarity for rival Padre Luis Ferreira. With El Puma no favor is left unpaid. Ever ready for the pre-emptive strike, the Founder,—despite the Vatican's ban against him being personally involved in Legion activities—drove Saul from Lourdes to Madrid airport. On the way he told Saul he would not be ordained due to a decision reached by the Legion's Supreme Council, composed of co-founder LC Legion Padres Luis Ferreira, Jorge Bernal Vargas, Alfredo Torres, José-Maria Sánchez, and Carlos Mora. By that time, September 1957, the formerly favored personal secretary, Brother Dominguez, had been dropped by Maciel from the Council. Saul has steadfastly insisted that Father Ferreira denied such a decision was ever reached, and claims Maciel's explanation is a total fabrication.

I was privileged to experience up close the kind attentions of Saul and his wife, Tere, during a visit to Mexico City in September 2006 for Fernando Gonzalez' book[23] signing. Saul, 75 and recovering from a recent heart attack, ferried me solicitously to several meetings in his beat-up old American car. He actually had to stop, open up the hood, and make sure the fan was working. Weeks later I spoke on the phone with him to get his story right.

The fact of the matter is that Maciel, once in Madrid, exiled Saul, putting him on a plane to Tenerife in the Canary Islands. He suggested that Saul, now that he was not going to be ordained, should take some time off to study Gregorian chant, of which he was fond. He told Saul to go to a priest "friend" of his, called Padre Flores, in the coastal town of El Puerto, and there to await further instructions. Saul, the blindly obedient Marine, took himself to El Puerto, a lazy beach resort with lots of pretty señoritas. Saul did not see any connection with Gregorian chant. Could this really be to test his celibacy?

It turned out that Father Flores had little knowledge of Father Maciel, let alone friendship. He quickly dispatched Saul to La Laguna where the bishop resided. The bishop, not knowing what to do with this religious dropped by a superior general on his doorstep, did not want to be discourteous and put Saul up at a local guesthouse. Saul had no money. "What did you do while you were awaiting orders?" Saul lacked the strict regulations, routines that had guided every minute of his life for decades. Now he got up late, went to Mass, prayed, read, studied and tried to keep himself busy. Isolated from his Legionary community, completely forgotten—a *semper fi* Legionary without orders!—Saul was left to his own devices for about eight months. Finally, he swallowed his pride and asked for money. He cannot remember where he actually got the money for his return flight to Mexico City. Probably from his own brother in Mexico City who approached Father Maciel or the Legion. By the time he arrived on May 31, 1958, Saul had lost a lot of weight and looked gaunt. He was physically exhausted and in the throes of a nervous breakdown. This condition lasted for over a year after he left. Tere nursed him, fell in love with him and married him.

Saul Barrales is one of the eight living public formal accusers of Father Maciel. Known in the community of his time as "Brother Charity" because of his unflagging kindness to all, Saul was sexually abused by Father Maciel and also collaborated unwittingly in securing "medications" for the suffering Founder. As the community bursar, he administered some monies and often drove to pharmacies, dispensaries and hospitals at all hours of the night seeking medications for "sick" Father Maciel. When Brother Neftalí Sanchez told him that the ampoules they were procuring for Father Maciel were not real medications, Saul stomped on them in front of the founder and filially chided him.

Despite the reign of manipulation and fear surrounding the founder, Saul wanted to prevent others from falling victims by visiting El Puma's bedroom at night. Maciel demanded that members "take care of" him as he deserved. Saul described for me Maciel's entitled and impatient "*! Que me atiendan!*, "Tend to my needs!" Maciel systematically rejected and humiliated those who did not go out of their way to serve him or simply did not know how. From some handsome young members of his religious community Maciel demanded full "attentions" and service. Saul tried to interrupt the supply line. Saul was one of Maciel's trusted helpers. Under the pretense that he was keeping watch, Saul would lay on the floor just inside the door blocking the entrance to Maciel's bedroom—echoes of the faithful Uriah (2 Samuel 11, 9) betrayed by adulterous David.

***

Don't mess with Maciel!

I, Paul, had the questionable privilege of being one of the few Legion members who ever dared to publicly question Father Maciel's judgment or opinion. This happened at community gatherings or retreats when he, The Founder, would lecture us co-founders. Whenever I dared to ask uncomfortable questions, Father Maciel would humiliate me in front of the community: "I know where you are coming from," he would begin, implying that I was intentionally sabotaging the talk, and calling me a "rationalist" who lacked faith. I can reminisce, now with amusement, about certain escapades during El Puma's Conferences at the Interamerican Cultural Center, Tlalpan, Mexico City in the late '70s and early '80s during my tenure at the School of Faith. Some kind of "death wish" must have impelled me to speak up and ask awkward questions. More mature Spanish Padres, such as G. L. and Juan Manuel Amenábar, R.I.P., would whisper when I held up my hand: "For God's sake, don't ask a question. You know how he gets. We'll be here all night! Shhhhhh!" For them it was uncomfortable and entertaining at the same time. For me, because of my burgeoning doubts and questioning of Father Maciel and the superiors, it was an irrepressible need. During my stint in Mexico City I witnessed two examples of what I perceived as Father Maciel's despotic governing style. He banished two major superiors, Territorial Directors who dared question his decisions, or even opinions.

Father Carlos Zancajo, LC
Territorial Director

One casualty was Territorial Director Father Carlos Zancajo, sent packing to Caracas, Venezuela. What was the cause of his fall from grace? Perhaps for complaining about not being informed of one of Father Maciel's decisions that affected religious under Father Carlos' care. In the Legion, as in Stalinist Russia, one never knew the why, the where and the how one had fallen from The Leader's grace. The uncertainty spread uneasiness and apprehension, even a fear or paranoia, through the community. To this day, as far as is known, Father Carlos is in Caracas where he teaches at a modest university. He is a faithful Legionary, has no beef with the Legion, and would not want to be associated with any criticism of the Founder.

Father Alfonso Samaniego, LC.
The Legionary Prototype (*El Tipo Legionario*)

Since the beginning there has always been a "Legionary Model" theme. And in a certain sense, Marcial Maciel, as the founder, is the "prototype," the exemplar of what a Legionary should be. On our table, beside the crucifix of our profession, lay a card, attributed to our founder, describing the virtues of this ideal priest, A LEGIONARY SHOULD BE[24]. Nuestro Padre explained that because of his own frequent illnesses, whereby he participated in the Christ's Crucifixion, we should not look to him as the perfect Legionary. These sufferings, which often laid him low, forced him to stay in bed, and so be absent from community life, participation in which was en essential ingredient in the holiness of a consecrated religious. It was true; Nuestro Padre often had to take to his bed when assaulted by unbearable pain.

During most of my time in the Legion, early '60s through the early '80s, the person presented to us by Nuestro Padre as the best example of this Legionary "incarnation" was Father Alfonso Samaniego (Barriga). Our founder attributed this to the fact that Alfonso was a member of the earliest groups of 9-12 year-old Mexican recruits, hand-picked by him, and directly and personal formed by him in a way no other generation would be privileged. From this perspective, Nuestro Padre explained, those who entered later in life, or who had been subject to early worldly influence, found it much more difficult to capture the true Legion spirit.

Samaniego was the epitome of the suave and poised Legionary that Father Maciel admired: well-groomed, polite, intelligent, a gentleman in gestures and demeanor, and possessing good public speaking skills. Father Maciel referred glowingly to his psychological expertise (he read books on that always dangerous subject!) and his finesse with the opposite sex. Alfonso was first director of the women's Regnum Christi section in Mexico and a darling of all the rich ladies from the posh district of Lomas de Chapultepec, home of the *Instituto Cumbres* School. Samaniego scaled high on the Legion echelon: Director of the *Instituto Cumbres*, Territorial Director for Mexico and North America, Director of the Anahuac University, and first Legionary to speak on Mexican TV.

Samaniego met his Waterloo when he begged to differ with Maciel regarding Father Jesús Blásquez' recruitment system at the Anahuac University where Samaniego was rector. Those were the heady days of Regnum Christi men's foundation with such colorfully nicknamed college students as *'El Ratón'* (Mouse) Felix Sánchez Soler,*'La Coneja'*(Rabbit) Eduardo Robles Gil, *'El Gato'*(Cat)–whoever, 'El Santito'(Little Saint) the present Legion General Director, Father Alvaro Corcuera, and other important RC founders. (A less fortunate member of that fledgling group who became Legion General Administrator was Oscar Sanchez-Rosete. He appeared on Mexican Television some years ago ruefully describing sexual abuse in the consecrated men's residence in Mexico City.)

After this disagreement—the only time I ever saw Father Alfonso lose his cool—he, the Mexican-born founding Legionary priest and Father Maciel's own golden boy, never held another important position in the Legion. Since that fateful day during Holy Week Spiritual Exercises at the Interamerican Cultural Institute in Tlalpan, he has lived in reclusion. Alfonso, born and bred in the Legion, under the Caudillo's shadow, was never able to make a break.

It would appear that both exemplary priests are presently moored in Legion backwaters because they dared to question, or simply doubt, El Puma's judgment or decisions. The lesson was clear: don't mess with Maciel. These men were examples of great integrity and prestige among their Legion confreres and much beloved; could it be they were a threat to Father Maciel's continuing leadership, absolute authority and adulation? No rivals?

Father Maurice Oliver Mc Gowan, LC
First Irishman ordained as a Legion priest

Soon after his fast ordination, circa 1968, my fellow-traveler to Salamanca was appointed confessor and spiritual director to the consecrated women of the Regnum Christi Lay Movement at Dal Ríada in Dublin. Maurice, or Oliver, was smitten with one of them. The superiors acted quickly, shipping him off to New York where a distant relative of his lived. He was thus suddenly separated from the young woman in question, from his companions, and from the support of close family, friends and familiar environment. Shortly after, he left the Legion and the priesthood. As with the case of many other departed confreres, I have no idea of his present whereabouts. In fact I learned of his departure decades after the fact—after I too had left the Legion. It was engineered in a way which tends to illustrate Maciel's and the Legion's modus operandi. Once the superiors discover, no matter how, something they consider "dangerous" to the member or the organization, they will promptly act to "protect the member's vocation"—or the organization's interests—often without telling him or consulting with him. He will usually not have time or space to process or work through any difficulties, but will be ordered to leave immediately and secretively. The frequently applied "geographical cure" sends the member far away from the threat. The Legion will also go to great lengths to "avoid scandal" among "our own", i.e. members of the Legion and Regnum Christi lay movement, and "outsiders", preventing news of the defection from leaking out and negatively affecting the Legion's image of invulnerability and fidelity.

Father James Coindreau, LC
Recruiter of hundreds of Irish and American seminarians

An American ex-Legionary, KK, e-mailed me in January 2006:

During the summer of 1975 I was told to go to Cuernavaca to help Father Jimmie with his new recruits. As classes started again in late August or September, I was sent to replace Alejandro until the candidates left for Salamanca. Actually, I would have loved to continue working with Jimmie; but since the beginning of Holy Year, 1975, my calling was getting less and less clear. I was pretty fed up by Cuernavaca time and was just waiting for the word from Maciel that God indeed was NOT calling me!

James Coindreau was the one who recruited me and many other young Irishmen in the 1960s and Mexicans in the '70s for the Legion of Christ. James, Santiago, Jimmy was and is a charismatic bilingual Mexican whose enthusiasm and charm filled Legion novitiates. He was admired and loved by all his recruits. At the time he recruited me he was only a seminarian, but he hung in with great effort—most of his training years were spent on the road and little time spent hitting the books. But he reached his goal and was ordained to the priesthood in the Legion and continued to recruit in Mexico.

One day, in Mexico City, around 1975, I was waiting outside the famous Casa Tres, used as headquarters by Father Maciel, and where El Puma would show me the accusatory letters six years later. On that occasion he had summoned me to explain his new School of Faith project. Who should walk out from a previous interview but Padre James? It was so sudden I had no time to grasp the situation and react. When he saw me, Fr James quickly took off the clerical collar and breast-piece, only occasionally worn by priests in Mexico at that time, and handed it to me without a word as he passed me by. What did this mean? I was stunned by Father James' gesture. Was it Elijah passing on the cloak to Elisha (I Kings, 19, 19-21)? If that was the intention behind Elijah Coindreau's gesture, it was quite effective at that time for I continued striving to be a good Legionary and went on to be founding director of the School of Faith. I'm sorry it didn't quite work out in the long run!

After serving Father Maciel and the Legion very successfully for many years he left. He became a US AF chaplain and remains a devout priest to this day.

A year or so ago Father James sought me out and we have exchanged e-mails. I no longer hold him in the same awe as 46 years ago. For his part he seemed to fear I would be angry at him for getting me into the pickle. But that is not the case. However, I would have liked to learn more about him as a person, as a Legionary, and as a close collaborator of Nuestro Padre. Particularly I would like to know why he left the Legion. But nothing deeply personal is revealed. In this, Father James has remained a real tight-lipped Legionary. The following is his answer to my direct question about the Roman collar incident. Notice how he reframes his departure from the Legion as "moved to San Antonio", uses the Legionary "NP" code for Nuestro Padre, and speaks in glowing terms of the founder and his work. I can only speculate that El Puma must have convinced Father James that he could serve the Lord better outside Holy Mother the Legion:

The Roman collar incident had to be in 1975 since I moved to San Antonio that summer and I must have been given it to wear during my session with NP and probably was asked to pass it on to you. I saw NP next in Rome in 1978 as I was completing a flight around the world just before

joining the Army, and recently at the 50th birthday of the Legion in 91 in DF, at Juan Diego's canonization at Our Lady of Guadalupe's basilica, and at his 60th anniversary of ordination in Rome.

It's hard to believe that he was 32 when I met him at my Aunt Flora's home and he asked me, a 15 year old "gringo", to help him start the Legion in Ireland and the USA.

I am amazed how they are bursting at the seams with vocations to include a couple I have sent from the Army.

***

Disregarding Vatican restrictions during 1956-59 investigation of sex and drugs.

One of the special sources used in the recent Mexican book *Father Maciel, the Legionaries of Christ, unpublished testimonies and documents* is a series of authentic documents from the Holy See's official investigation conducted in 1956-1959. One document tells how an investigator is told to take Father Maciel's passports away from him, if necessary, to prevent him from traveling without permission of the acting Superior General, Father Luis Ferreira. In Saul Barrales' exile, Father Maciel also circumvented Father Ferreira's intention for Saul Barrales to be ordained.

The following is part of the author's e-mail correspondence with José Barba regarding Father Maciel's involvement with Legion members and the religious community during that special period when he was formally exiled by Vatican decree. Originally called in Legion parlance *La Guerra* (The War), because it was seen from inside the organization as a demonic effort by the forces of evil to destroy the Founder and the Legion, it was later renamed *La Gran Bendición*—The Great Blessing. *The Legion of Christ: a history*, an official LC publication, admits Father Maciel was "banished" from the Legion in October of 1956 and "settled in Madrid." It is a selective report, and certainly does not tell the truth about the Founder's movements and actions at that time.

November 6, 2005

"Dear Pepe,

I am still working on my Legion story with the intention of publishing it, albeit modestly. I need your help with the following: Father Maciel was present at the ordination of Monsignor Jorge Bernal in Lourdes and he exiled Saul Barrales to the Canary Islands during The War (1956-59), when Maciel was supposed to be separated from the Legion by Vatican order. How do I reconcile his presence in the life of members and intervention in the Legion's management with the Vatican prohibition?"

"November 7, 2006
Dear Paul

As of October 1956 Marcial Maciel was expelled from the Legion by orders of the Holy See. How could he stay involved in managing the Legion? He simply disobeyed. He was not supposed to have contact with us Legionaries but neither he nor our superiors complied with the Holy See's orders. Maciel was forbidden by the Holy See to "set foot in Rome" or to visit with us in the Legion community. But he slipped through this prohibition with trickery and casuistry. He would have the college bus pick him up outside Rome city limits and take him into the city. (Alejandro Espinosa can confirm this.) Getting into the bus Maciel would sarcastically comment: "Right, Brothers, I am not setting foot in Rome?" This was jubilantly received by the members who were privileged to accompany him.

Maciel even moved Legionaries from one country to another without the Holy See's knowledge or permission: Father Francisco Navarro was dispatched to the Instituto Cumbres in Mexico City, while Frs. Faustino Pardo, Rafael Cuena, and Gabriel Cortés were sent to Caracas, Venezuela, to twiddle their thumbs. Maciel wanted to punish them for lack of due loyalty to him during the investigation. Cortés told me much later that the fancy hotel where they were lodged was full of high class prostitutes.

Yours, Jose"

***

Holy Hypochondria

When I first met Father Maciel in Bundoran he presented as a vigorous and energetic leader. But he did not sleep in the same drafty house as us or take his meals there. Gradually I would learn that behind that healthy façade suffering gnawed at our founder. I discovered how his entourage and the superiors walked on eggshells, not only because Nuestro Padre was the venerable founder, but because of his varied "illnesses." During the twenty-three years I knew him he was always complaining of some ailment. Illness of one kind or another has been the leitmotif of his existence. Many seemed to be centered in his stomach: stomachaches, acidity, ulcers, and so forth, which in the short term meant bed rest and special diet. These ailments led him to visit specialists in Mexico, the USA and Europe. He had to travel in comfort, first class, because of his delicate disposition. He was the founder, and his life and wellbeing were precious and had to be preserved at any expense. He always appeared to be taking pills and liquids at his meals. I will always associate the Mayo Clinic in Rochester, Minnesota, with Father Maciel. He often flew there, from Mexico, Latin America, or Europe to be treated.

The relief of stomach or abdominal pain, as we now know from the testimonies of his accusers, was Father Maciel's royal road to genital pleasure Such accusations were finally made known to the English-speaking public through an article in the Hartford Courant on February 23, 1997[25].

Because of his illnesses, *Nuestro Padre* had to take medications and follow a special diet, excusing him from living "the common life" of consecrated religious, which includes eating the same food as everyone else in the community. Nuestro Padre's food was always prepared separately from ours and often entailed special and exquisite items. He demanded freshly squeezed juice and fresh fruit for breakfast, which could include mangoes, papaya or other tropical fruit. Sometimes he would take a liking to a particularly item he had eaten at a hotel or at a benefactor's home. It has been reported that during the 90s Nuestro Padre had a special kind of chicken from a Salamanca farm flown to Rome to be prepared for him there. It was his handlers' duty to procure these items for him. And he could be quite demanding. People were afraid of displeasing him. Anecdotes regarding Nuestro Padre's demanding nature at the table are legion.

> Our religious should observe common life faithfully as regards their food, clothes and furniture. [...]
> All our religious, whether Superiors or subordinates, are to strive for complete uniformity regarding the necessities of life.
> (Constitutions of the Legion of Christ, The Vow of Poverty, #281, 1 & #282)

Another area of illness for Nuestro Padre was the head—headaches, fatigue, and migraines—which also entailed special care, treatment and consideration. Often we would be told that "Nuestro Padre is tired and needs to lie down." Everyone in the house had to careful to avoid noise or any kind. His treatment could require a cruise through the countryside during the day or through the city streets of Mexico City, New York, or Rome at night, driven by his personally chosen Bro. Chauffer. It could necessitate a small group of religious "making conversation" for Nuestro Padre while he ate a meal in the visitors' dining room—which he used more than anyone else. It might mean that Nuestro Padre was confined to his quarters.

***

Father Maciel's quarters

The present Legion command headquarters at Via Aurelia 677 will forever be associated with Nuestro Padre's presence during the foundation period, and also with his illnesses and his habit of occupying and sleeping in special quarters. In the '50s he used the Infirmary when ill. In the'60s, during my time in Rome, he slept in a suite set aside exclusively for his use on the second floor. At times he would retire there for an undetermined length of time, "recovering" in bed. During this period he rarely left his room. All his meals were served to him there by Brothers Raul de Anda, Bonifacio Padilla, Juan Manuel Correa and a few others. Only certain people were allowed to enter the room and no one else was allowed to "bother Nuestro Padre" until he felt better. He would run the Legion from his sickbed. On some occasions, when "feeling exhausted" after "intense work" or a foreign trip, he could not enter the college at all because of "fatigue" and needed the comfort of a good hotel. He might stay at the nearby Agip Hotel where his Legionary team could cater to his needs.

As a young seminarian in Rome at Via Aurelia I once entered the chapel through the second floor entrance which opened onto a small choir balcony—we were encouraged to make frequent short visits to the Blessed Sacrament in the Tabernacle on the Altar containing the consecrated hosts of the Body of Christ. On this occasion I devoutly stepped inside the door and curtain and sank onto my knees at the center of the railing overlooking the chapel. I imagine it was to ask for faith.

I was not aware of anyone else's presence. As I began to collect my senses, suddenly I hear someone making a hissing snake sound in my direction, "sssssssssssst!" like they do in Mexico to get your attention. I turn to see Father Maciel with an imperious swing of his arm gesturing me to get to one side. Was I interrupting his prayer, or obstructing his view? I'll never know. I got up, went to one side, tried to be invisible, feeling I was being watched.

Outsiders, the American public, supporters and benefactors, and rank-and-file Legionaries and Regnum Christi members have no inkling of this petty and self-centered aspect of the founder's life and lifestyle. Father Maciel's illnesses would require a specific in-depth study. And there is so much we do not know about Nuestro Padre's secret and secretive life which he kept hidden like the contents of his crocodile skin briefcase. Only those who were close, the confidants and collaborators who went on special trips with him, who accompanied him to exclusive hotels and spas, getting to know his peculiar whims and tastes, can tell the true tale. But mostly their lips are sealed, either by choice or by need. Some of the ones I knew, such as Raul de Anda, Armando Arias and Jorge Luis Gonzalez, continue to work for the Legion in some capacity; their children enjoy full scholarships to the Legion's exclusive schools and universities, or they feel indebted to the institution in one way or another. There are many more stories to be told by those who were privy to Father Maciel's personal and secret life from the '80s through the present. I must mention the painful testimony of one of the new witnesses who gave testimony during the 2005 investigation into Father Maciel's proclivities. The story of Francisco Gonzalez Para's prolonged and harrowing sexual relationship with Marcial Maciel has yet to be translated into English.

Fernando Gonzalez meticulously documents other ex-Legionaries describing El Puma's lawless lifestyle and modus operandi[26]

15
REFLECTING ON SEXUAL ABUSE IN THE LEGION

"Whoever causes one of these little ones who believe in me to sin, it would be better for him if a great millstone were hung around his neck and he were thrown into the sea.

Gospel of St. Mark, 9, 42

MACIEL'S SEDUCERS IN SEVILLE

I

Approaching the Cristo de Burgos
For you I did penance and cried;
On the corner of Sales-Ferré,
Spied procession of Servite friars;
Amid Trappist', Jesuit' suspicions,
First Legionary adolescent needs,
-Bay of Cobreces, story Foundation-
Solace seeking with willowy priest.
In their budding homo-curiosity
-Close I to Granada's meet,
Home to Federico de Gay-
Their spiritual father in sheets?

Now one was robust and quite virile,
The other with sweet baby face,
A third was a fair-haired blue-eyes,
The next with a delicate grace.
They all had one thing in common
As for the seminary they signed:
To be fondled, aroused and pleasured,
Aye, ravished by their Father benign.

II

So facing the float of Dolores
Descending the narrowing street,

With long brown candles burning
Their hands peak-capped Nazarenes,
I prayed for the Christ of Cotija
Stretched across his mother's knee,
Grieving for her Jesus Maciel,
Broken, betrayed and bereaved.
They created the Myth of Abuser;
Accused him of tempting to prey;
Their saintly, innocent, Pastor,
True victim of calumnies vain.

Now one was quite strong and most virile;
The other, a round baby-face;
A third was handsome and blue-eyed
The fourth with a delicate grace.
Unbeknownst to their ignorant parents
-What little perverts they had raised! -
Had gone to the order with one plan:
His chaste body defile and debase.

III

The float forced its path through the lane-way,
Fairly crushing all bones to the wall,
My senses bewildered with brocade
Gold and silver, incense and pall.
Through the haze the halting procession,
Wending its way through the throng,
Cavorting, provocative altar boys,
All of eleven years tall.
When I tried to imagine their malice,
Fathom the evil they bore,

I coldly considered the "victim"
And burst into sobs for their souls.

So I wept for the blue-eyed conspirator,
And the boy with the soft baby-face;
For the virile, athletic and strong one,
And the one with a delicate grace.
They had come to the order with one mind:
To deceive the immaculate priest.
Were they wolves in babes' simple clothing?
Or prey to a Wolf and a Beast?

In the Glorious City of Seville,
Cradle of Christopher's Commission
And Torquemada's Holy Inquisition.

Poetic license provoked
By some Catholics' view
That sexual abuse by priests can be
Reduced to homosexuality, or gayness;
That the young ones are willing accomplices;
By testimonies of eight seminarians against Father
Marcial Maciel,
Founder and Superior General of the Legion of Christ;
By pro-Maciel defense and adulation of him and his mother;
By early Legion history in northern Spain where first rumors arose;
And inspired by walking the streets participating in Seville's Holy Week processions, 2003

Paul Lennon, author

***

Celibate or Hibernate?

In the light of sexual scandals in the Legion, which I learned about years after I left, I add the following considerations. During my nine-year training to be a Legionary, and indeed during the remaining fourteen years as a Legionary priest, I was never aware of sexual improprieties of any kind in the order. I was never aware of being approached by a confrere or superior in a sexually inappropriate way.

During seminary training leading to my deaconate vow of celibacy, I was never outside the "cloister" walls of a Legionary formation center on my own, and thus never met an attractive woman. Apparently, in order to be chosen as our cook, a woman had to be old and ugly. It seems reasonable to conclude that my commitment to celibacy was, like everything else in the Legion "formation system," an unprocessed foregone conclusion: "I assume, therefore I am a Legionary!"

I admit I felt fleeting attraction for that Venezuelan benefactress, Nora. Accompanied by her rather provocative daughter, she was allowed to flit around the college in Rome some time during my Theology studies. She must have been contributing in no uncertain terms to the "economy of the Legion" for Father Maciel to permit that. Although it was kind of strange to have a woman "in the community," with access to the semi-private areas in our house, all Legionaries knew that when The Founder was around exceptions could be made to regular observance of the rules. Anyway, my infatuation with La Señora must have lasted all of twenty seconds, that is, while we were together in the elevator between floors at Via Aurelia 677. And there were only four floors! I may have been slightly troubled about it at the time. Looking back, it just proves that I had not been totally neutered by the Legion.

Most Legionaries will attest that the atmosphere surrounding us regarding sexuality and chastity was eerily "antiseptic," like that sterile smell of ether you got when entering a hospital. Nuestro Padre sowed communal belief that the Legion had been protected from impurity by a special gift from the Blessed Virgin Mary. Thus, purity was a given, and impure thoughts, feelings, or actions were unusual, out of place, and unexpected in the Legion. It was an extreme case of "don't ask, don't tell." Some guys were kicked out because of voyeurism: looking into the showers or dressing rooms when other members were changing, or for other offenses that to mature eyes might not appear serious. But the superiors would never mention these transgressions. Sex was taboo, hidden, like the pasted over nudes in the *L'Enciclopedia dell'Arte* in our library.

According to the rules, or norms, we were allowed six 16mm or Super-8movies a year, never in a public theater, but in our own house. The projectionist and a superior previewed the movie beforehand. Whenever a remotely erotic or simple romantic scene appeared, a card was inserted between the lens and the film to block out the bad images.

There is a standing joke about the Irish Book on Sex: all the pages are blank. This reflects our Legion sexual education. We received no explanation of the physiology of the sexes, drives, attraction, falling in love, and love-making. Who would talk about something as "repulsive" and "impure" as that? Novice Instructor, Rector, Superior, and Spiritual Director Rafael Arumí, or obsessive compulsive Assistant Superior and Spiritual Director Octavio Acevedo, not-too-bright Rector, Superior, and Spiritual Director Alfredo Torres, or dog-lover and horticulturalist, Rector, Superior, and Spiritual Director Juan Manuel Dueñas-Rojas? Where would you find a manual, a booklet, or even some pictures? I'm sure some creative souls did their own research...but not me.

I had enough with my constant doubts of Faith. On the other hand, I must admit there was a helpful book about how to handle adolescent changes available in Salamanca. It was called "You are becoming a man." I felt I was a normal and healthy adolescent, with normal urges, practicing self-control and abstinence. There might be the occasional wet dream. That would be part of confession and spiritual direction. Father Dueñas, spiritual director, rector and superior in Rome made the recommendation: "Be more careful, and try not to let that happen again." I'm glad Irish Christian Brother Moore had explained things a little better back in the seventh grade.

So, regarding sex everything was silenced; it was not mentioned among us; no education, neutral, and frozen. As a heterosexual I never felt any intrusion from superior or peer. Father Maciel, in his later confrontations with me, appeared to express his sentiments: "Women, because of their sexuality, are the root of all evil."

Because we were forbidden from talking about anything personal among ourselves, I have no idea of how others fared—those struggling with their sexual identity or with homosexual feelings. Testimonies of ex-Legionaries now demonstrate that some members, no matter their orientation, were sexually approached by unscrupulous superiors, novice masters and spiritual directors. But many of us had no inkling of anything improper going on. This enigma is partially solved by the testimony of one of the original accusers, José Pérez Olvera, who exited as I was entering: "It seemed that nothing mattered more than the virtue of purity. We were wholesome boys, but they drummed the idea of purity into us to such a degree that we ended up being fixated on it. For us everything was a sin. The obsession with offending God was so great that I couldn't even touch my penis when I went to the bathroom. I ended up going to a Trappist monastery next door to confess. This from the time I was a boy, from the time I entered at age eleven. And I want to tell you that in Rome we were surrounded by paintings of nudes. A virgin breast-feeding a child was a sin. It was aberrant. The hypocrisy got to the point that they would put little pieces of paper on art book pictures so that things would not be seen [which produced the opposite effect]. I lived in anguish. One could never feel serene. It was as if God had not created sex. And to top it all off, Father Marcial was a total hypocrite; it did not matter to him that he had destroyed us."[27]

I know one of my Legionary colleagues was seriously troubled for years for having smuggled a girlie magazine into the seminary. Once discovered, he was haunted by his superior's warning that such an act of impurity demonstrated a serious moral shortcoming which seriously jeopardized his Legionary calling. That Legion-induced guilt hung like a sword of Damocles over his conscience for many years. He was led to believe that if he abandoned the Legion he would lose his priesthood: his depraved inclination would make it impossible for him to carry on as a priest, for no bishop would ever accept such a deviant priest into his diocese. Another ex-Legionary colleague, Hector Carlos—calling me out of the blue after 37 years—told me that when the Legion was trying to dump him, his spiritual director gratuitously announced, "You don't have a vocation to celibacy, because you masturbate." "Who told you I masturbate?" retorted my recently recovered companion.

***

El Puma's Accusers, flashbacks

I supported Father Peter Cronin when, in 1992, he initiated a newsletter to other ex-legionaries whose whereabouts he knew. We were unaware of the serious accusations of sexual abuse against Father Maciel at that time and for several years later. The bomb exploded in the American media in 1997 with the Hartford Courant articles of Renner and Berry. I had not read them and was still oblivious.

In 1998 I received a phone call at home from José Barba: "Paul, do you remember me? I am José Barba. Do you believe our testimonies?" It was too point-blank. "Testimonies, about what?" I was totally at sea. I lacked context and information. First, we had to catch up on the past interrupted twenty-five years of our lives. Such is frequently the disjointed existence of ex-Legionaries. I did remember José Barba, known as one of the most intelligent LC students ever, from a visit I paid him when he was an ex-Legionary teaching at La Universidad de las Americas in Puebla, Mexico. Then Legionary priest Juan Manuel Amenábar—who would later accuse Father Maciel on his deathbed—because of the relative freedom his fundraising activities then afforded him, found a way to visit his old confrere. I do not know why he took me in tow that day.

Barba now launched into an explanation of his efforts to bring the testimonies of ten ex-Legionaries accusing Father Maciel of sexually abusing them to the notice of the Catholic hierarchy. He mentioned other members I knew personally, Juan Vaca and Arturo Jurado. I was surprised but the stories seemed credible. He described the day he lost his virginity with Fr. Maciel. The story was faithful to the Legion atmosphere, and to the customs and character of the Marcial Maciel I had come to know beyond the aura of holiness and the legend of integrity. One thing I was convinced of regarding Maciel: he had no concern or respect for people. Nevertheless, I could not roundly condemn him without further information. I would be open to learning more about the accusations. After that I read the newspaper articles. They rang true. They were all different, but said the same thing. Maciel's method sounded uncannily authentic; the abuse sickeningly real.

"Dear Arturo (Jurado),

On Tuesday I received the videotapes (Mexican Canal 40, Círculo Rojo Program April 15, 2002) you sent and started watching them last night (April 4, 2003;), beginning with the first video: the "rough" version of the testimonies of three brave ex-Legionaries. On the screen appeared the face of Jose Barba whom I haven't seen for many years, and there he was, full of dignity, ruefully talking about his abuse. I was saddened and angry at Father Maciel listening to Jose's story. I, who love to sleep late in the morning, did not sleep well. I got up at six; a record for me. As I follow with the second tape, I understand better the nature of, and grasp the reality and seriousness of, this abuse. Hearing and watching Alejandro Espinoza talk about the recruitment of "pretty" boys I made an uncanny connection with my own "intuition." I seem to have stumbled onto the realization of Maciel being an "ephebophile", an adult who loves adolescents, a few days ago when I shared my reflections with our REGAIN group.

Memories and names from my own experience come to mind. When I arrived in Salamanca in September 1961, I do remember seeing a certain Arturo Jurado. He belonged to another community, and therefore we were not allowed to speak or communicate in any way, although we lived under the same roof. (You told me later, Arturo, that Maciel had you "quarantined" as a form of punishment.) At the time I assumed Bro. Jurado was already a Philosophy student in apostolic practices (i.e., a period when the Legionary takes a break from studies to get experience in one of the Legion's Apostolates or missions). From what I remember, although I could not talk to him, he did seem to be a particularly gentle and quiet individual. I certainly do not remember crashing into him during one of our "friendly" intramural soccer matches. But maybe that too was forbidden to you during your solitary confinement."

***

El Puma's Personal Assistants and Male Nurses

During Novitiate in Salamanca, 1961-62, I was trained as community nurse—which included giving shots of various kinds—by Jesus Martinez-Penilla. Called "Padre Penilla," he was probably just another philosophy or theology student appointed as "Prefect", i.e., assistant superior. I never had any problems with him, despite later reports linking him to sexual abuse scandals in Ontaneda, Spain. He may have been Father Maciel's nurse, administering intravenous, intramuscular, and subcutaneous shots to him. There was always a good stock of injections, from vitamins to sedatives, in the supply cabinet. Some medications were used exclusively by Father Maciel, "*Nuestro Padre's* medicines," or could only be administered with his authorization. I distinctly remember Largactil phials which, I believe, Father Penilla administered either to Father Maciel or other members of the community on an as needed basis. We all knew that Nuestro Padre was affected by a variety of illnesses that required rest, special care, and medication. Father Maciel's secretive nature more than likely kept his personal effects—including his exclusive medications—always close at hand, in his room, with his luggage, or in the infamous crocodile-skin briefcase.

I was never *Nuestro Padre's* nurse.

During my days in Salamanca, Brother Guillermo Adame was his personal assistant, secretary, valet, nurse and chauffer. This young man—a dark-skinned well built Mexican with chiseled features and jet black hair, who was never ordained—later had a nervous breakdown and left the order; a "throwaway"? His younger brother, Carlos, was also a member for a period and he too left without holy orders. Both were musically talented. I distinctly remember Guillermo playing Bach's Toccata on the chapel organ.

Other special "secretaries" to Maciel paraded by during my Legion training in Salamanca and Rome: Valente Velasquez, Raul De Anda, Bonifacio Padilla, Francisco Parga and others. In retrospect I thank God for not having the "privilege" of being particularly close to El Puma. He did want to be our "father"; he loved to be considered such by the brothers, and to be addressed in terms of affection. I remember feeling early on some anger toward a fellow Irish novice for using what I perceived as the even more endearing term of *"Mon Père"* when addressing the Founder. Although some of the older members used this name, the title smacked of too much adulation for me.

***

My General Confession to Nuestro Padre

I am at Sanborn's restaurant at the Plaza de las Estrellas mall in Mexico City's Anzures district on Saturday, September 10, 2005. Sitting across the table, Dr. Fernando González interviews me about my experiences with the Legion of Christ against the background of pedophilia. He is researching Maciel & Legion abuses, and will later publish *Marcial Maciel, the Legion of Christ: Unpublished Testimonies and Documents.* I tell him honestly I was never sexually abused in the Legion, nor was I ever approached in an inappropriate way by any member. Two years after Sanborn's I still must rack my brain to recall one unusual incident. It involved Father R.C., LC. I was already an ordained priest. During one of my few visits to Rome, we were strolling along the Via Aurelia Nova close to our Legionary residence. A woman passed by. I paid only fleeting attention to her. I can only infer that she was "a lady of the night" from R.C.'s question: "Ever thought of going off with a prostitute?" I said nothing but thought to myself: "What could have caused you to pass a remark like that? Don't you know I have sisters? I love and respect women. Of course, I find them attractive. But I don't use them! I forgive you because you are a Legionary. One never knows why Legionaries do things. Maybe you were on a special mission to spy on me, to look for chinks in my armor. What would you have said, thought, done if my answer had been 'Yes'? Was it just your own morbid curiosity? Yours was certainly not the kind of question sanctioned by the myriad of Legion rules, norms, guidelines and instructions."

Entering the LC at age 17 and 7 months, I admit I was immature mentally, emotionally, and spiritually; naïve and sexually unaware, too. However, as the son of a warm and structured home, I had strong relationships with my mother—her only son—and with my father; he and I were "boon companions." I did not need *Nuestro Padre* as a surrogate father.

I had the "privilege" of going to confession to Nuestro Padre for the first time before my Religious Profession in Salamanca, September 1962. I was 18 years and 10 months old. By then my Spanish was good enough. It was suggested to me by my spiritual director and superior that I make a general confession to Nuestro Padre' this way I would receive special graces through the Founder and as the best way of preparing for the religious life.

During the relatively uneventful and sheltered life I had lived before entering the Holy Novitiate at age 17, I had accumulated two "sins against purity" that troubled my somewhat scrupulous conscience and about which I felt extremely ashamed. Before entering the Legion I had unloaded one to a Carmelite friar at St. Teresa's Clarendon St., Dublin. In fear and trembling I unloaded the second to Nuestro Padre, Man of God. I do not recall any Earth-shattering advice or apocalyptic revelation. I felt he was kind. At the end, I kissed the end of his stole as a sign of reverence and gratitude. He may have brushed my cheek with the tassel in a fatherly way. I experienced a great sense of relief because I had been able to get rid of that sin. I don't remember any advice. Now, I had no sin on my soul, I was free through the Sacrament of Confession, and I was ready to take on my vows—although the doubts of faith continued to torture me.

My interviewer Fernando insists: was there nothing, not even the slightest sexual innuendo in this encounter with Fr Maciel? No, nothing. "And you were not aware of any abuse going on around you as appears from the testimonies of others?" Not at all.

Taking into account the two dozen testimonies of sexual abuse from the 40s and 50s, and those beginning to appear regarding the 60s and 70s, why were so many of us so totally unaware? Could it be that Father Maciel is a Master of the Game of secret societies, with their isolated concentric circles of information and power? Maciel in the middle, surrounded by a first cadre of "unconditionals" who silently acquiesce to his power? Only The Master knows everything. The unconditionals know more than the following circle, and so on. The victims do not necessarily belong to the inner circle, for it is now clear that those closest to Maciel were used to bring more sheep into the shepherd's fold. They appear within a separate circle, isolated from the community at large, which in turn is totally oblivious to what goes on behind the infirmary door or Father Maciel's sickbay? Reading the chilling descriptions in John Le Carré's *A Perfect Spy* and Solzhenitsyn's *Gulag Archipelago* regarding secrecy, isolation, and control lead one to such considerations.

I don't think I can fairly say that Father Maciel was an indiscriminate sexual predator, thought there is no doubt that he had a large harem to choose from for years as undisputed totalitarian leader of the Legion of Christ. There is no reason to believe that all who came within his "spiritual" radius or halo were potential victims. That said, could it be that the "sin" I confessed to Father Maciel in that first general confession, about being sexually accosted by an Irish Christian Brother, somehow "immunized" me against abuse? If so, oh blessed "sin"! Or could it be that my conscience was already gelling, thus making me impervious to molding according to this Spiritual Director's unusual criteria? Had I already gathered sufficient "ego strength" to avoid enmeshment with the guru? Or had he simply not found me attractive? Maybe I wasn't his type. Or my nose was too big.

***

El Puma's Lair

For Father Maciel's victims the logistics of the college on Via Aurelia Nova in Rome will never be forgotten. A pretty cream-colored E-shaped four-storey with large windows, it was surrounded by well-manicured gardens, and dotted with elegant Roman pines. José Barba even today refers to it by its Italian name, *Collegio Massimo*, a kind of special way to say major seminary. Because for us Legionaries, the Legion was special and its buildings had a charm of their own. Part of

Barba, the innocent intact youth, still radiates the idealism that inspired him when first he came to that holy and classical city, thrilled by the presence of ancient and modern cultures and languages.[28] But that charming place, housing ninety seminarians, ages 15 to 25, would be the scene of his holocaust. The torture chamber where he and others met their fate was Father Maciel's sleeping quarters; the bed his gas chamber. Not remembering any clear details about the infirmary, I sent an S.O.S. out to three of El Puma's victims. Here, fifty years later, Jose Barba tells us exactly where that infirmary was. Please note that, like other survivors from that generation, he uses the abbreviation, or code, "MM" for Marcial Maciel; always the unusual, the special, the mysterious, MM.

"Paul,

The infamous infirmary at the Collegio Massimo on Via Aurelia, 677, in Rome, was located on the first [ground] floor (Sp. planta baja), almost exactly in front of the billiards room and adjacent to the service door (puerta de servicio); it had a window looking out onto the basketball court, after (behind) which lay the tennis court.

Immediately behind the door to the infirmary there was a rather small space with three white doors: one directly facing the person coming in (leading to the bath-room), and two other doors; one on the left, and another on the right of the person entering. MM used to stay (lodge), sleep, and sexually prey mostly in the room on the left side, containing a window with a Venetian blind looking out onto the playgrounds. The room on right used to also have a window with a Venetian blind looking onto the Collegio's front gardens; an almond tree could be seen through the window. There was a small metal and glass cupboard with a regular set of ordinary medications. The room on the left did not have a closet, while the room on the right side had a tall one, similar to the ones we had in our individual rooms, which had three parts, each with its own individual door: the left door for the closet proper, the right door containing a washbasin with a mirror over it, and underneath a varnished wooden rack about twenty five centimeters above the floor. Finally, there was another section opening with a double door on top of the two parts already described that was (in our rooms) probably intended to store luggage.

Sometimes MM would change from one room to the other, and very rarely he would lodge at the suite reserved for the rector of the Collegio, which was on the second floor, directly opposite the choir and the chapel. Therefore, sexually abusing us there would happen directly across from the Blessed Sacrament.

During 1995, in less than six months, MM abused me in both rooms. Normally there was only one bed (in the room on the left). The right-side room usually contained a typical high narrow "infirmary operation bed".

At the same time I have a testimony from an ex-LC that once he found MM and another then-LC, both half-naked in bed composed of two twin beds pulled together. According to said testimony this happened in the '50s. For the moment, I am withholding the names of these Legionaries—now both ex-members, one a priest.

Jose"

To my same request for exact information regarding the location of the infirmary, Juan Jose Vaca wrote, chastening me:

"Dear Paul,

Your question about the enfermería in Rome: It was situated in the left corner [of the building], facing Via Aurelia, on the first floor, near the escaleras de servicio (service stairs), and next to the puerta de servicio (service door). The enfermería had three parts. As you enter, on the left, was the room used by MM to "sleep in" and sexually abuse his victims. Its window was facing [looking out onto] the basketball court and tennis court. Facing the entrance door a bathroom (with bathtub, sink and toilet) was located. To the right, was the "enfermería" room, with a cabinet for medications and diverse infirmary items, and a stretcher-bed, and a floor lamp in the corner.

Since you were the enfermero, after Penilla trained you as his successor in this egregious responsibility, I wonder why you don't remember such a notorious place. Maybe your memory is in 'denial'. Tell me."

Dear Arturo Jurado wrote me in Spanish. I translate:

"Paul,

My memory is slowly fading in the dark and ashen evening of my poor life. These are, more or less, my memories of that famous infirmary on Via Aurelia 677:

It was on the first floor. It was the last room, on the opposite end to the dining room. Through the shades of that infirmary, you could see the basketball pitch a few meters away. In my time it had, I believe, one bed. The entrance from the corridor led directly into the bathroom or toilet. To one side was a room with medications and a kind of patient couch. The door on the left led into MM's infirmary..."

Being stubborn, I insisted that I had associated Maciel with the suite on the second floor. To which Juan Jose Vaca kindly replied:

"Paul:

Yes, MM's "official" quarters (Nuestro Padre's room) was the suite you mention: his office, across from "the chapel choir" on the second floor; his bedroom, opening onto "the main staircase"; in between both rooms, a bathroom (bathtub, sink and toilet) was situated. But years before your time, MM also used la enfermería (downstairs) as his bedroom, where he used to sexually prey on his victims. He also used the second floor suite for the same purposes. At the time of our priestly ordination (1969), MM indistinctly used both rooms, la enfermería, and the suite on the second floor.

Hope you get your book ready for printing ASAP.

Un fuerte abrazo.

Juan José."

***

Hail to Maciel's Excalibur

E-mail sent August 18, 2005 by the author

Subject: Irish survivor accuses Maciel; confirms continuation of abuse; discretion requested

"Dear Friends

I believe I mentioned that in July this year (2005) at the Madrid International Cultic Studies Association International Conference I read a testimony I had just received in the REGAIN mailbox before leaving my home. A couple of circumstances made the two manila envelopes significant and poignant. One: they had been sent by mistake to Canada instead of US. (The writer said his secretary had made that mistake!) And two: I knew the sender personally, though I have not seen or heard from him in thirty-five years

(Nothing special about this, knowing the way you are isolated in the Legion and after the Legion). The sender did not know I was receiving them because he had simply sent them to REGAIN P.O. Box 3213, Alexandria, VA 22302.

Another interesting factor: this man is from my generation, the very first Irish-born Legionaries beginning their novitiate in Salamanca in 1961. He claims he was abused from 1962 up to 1969 at least. He clearly and brutally describes his own sexual abuse by Father Maciel. The perpetrator used the same technique which had served so well in the 40s and 50s: "Come massage my stomach" and gradually having the victim masturbate his erect penis.

> Maciel has a Rolex, eats the very best because he has "nephritis" and every time he gets sick new or old candidates are called to assist (attend him).How does Maciel proceed sexually? He complains of pains in his stomach and asks for massage and then gradually he brings the hand of the person down to his penis to masturbate him. At the same time he opens the zipper of his assistant's pants and squeezes his penis until he sheds sperm. When finished, you have to clean his belly and your hands of the sperm. He takes injections of Demerol regularly; if you doubt just examine his arm! He's an experienced Demerol taker. If you want to be popular always have a spare Demerol injection ready. But Maciel likes new flesh and change, so those naïve beautiful new men who are told to attend to "Our Holy Father's needs" go without knowing what's in store!—Problems of conscience forever!

This witness speaks clearly of Maciel's drug of choice, Demerol®—a narcotic analgesic prescribed for the relief of moderate to severe pain. Use of narcotic analgesics over time can result in addiction and physical dependence. According to the Irish witness, the drug loosened Maciel's tongue, causing him to lower his defenses, reveal lurid details of his sexual life, and specific details of his victims' genitalia.

Personal contacts and phone conversations with Saul Barrales confirm Father Maciel's modus operandi. There was always the cloak of illness, exhaustion, not being able to sleep, stomach pains. He would arrive at the Legion house and demand to be taken care of by the superiors. "I need attention" he would always say. The brothers were supposed to "attend to his needs." How could they refuse when he was the founder, the provider, the superior general and a saint? He surrounded himself with a group of concerned members who wanted to take care of him and cater to his needs. Not all knew that Nuestro Padre needed full service, including oil change and tuning. Anyone who did not know how to do it, would be despotically dismissed by him: "go away, you are useless. You are no good to me! Can I have someone who knows how to assist me?"

This recent Irish testimony confirms the embattled original testimonies, denied by Maciel and the Legion and by such luminaries as the Rev. Robert J. Neuhaus. I accept this new testimony as confirmation that the abuse done to Barba & Co. did not stop there but continued at least through another generation. Sad but true. I was filled with indignant rage at this person who abused one of my own companions; Michael and I traveled together with Maciel by Aer Lingus from Dublin to Lourdes on August 26, 1961, and took the Legion uniform together in Salamanca on the same day. On the other hand it is heartening to see another brave survivor come forth and demand the truth be told about Maciel's sick and destructive behavior. Initially I had been remiss in sending part of this new material to Monsignor Scicluna, Vatican "promoter of justice," or chief investigator, before finally getting it done. I gave a copy to Jose Barba when I met him in Madrid on July 20th, 2005, at the International Cultic Studies Association Conference. He took it to Rome, and so I am hopeful it got into the right hands. This survivor had sent his testimony to the Pope and to twenty cardinals, without success or response. Naturally, I can imagine sending a letter to the Pope or the Vatican is like sending a needle to a haystack. I feel happy that REGAIN has some clout and a voice to draw the Church's attention to this scandal, and I am also glad the investigation was formally reopened in April, 2005, bearing some fruit.

Kudos go to Pepe, Juan Jose, Arturo, Alejandro, Pepe Antonio, Félix and others for all their pioneering work, and to the new men who are now bearing the flag. In December 2005 my testimony vouching for Father Maciel's original accusers before the Vatican investigator was posted on the REGAIN web page[29] and is available as an appendix here.

Pray for this fearless new witness who is still hurting after all these years: Michael Francis Caheny, residing in Natal province Brazil. Many more still silent victims will carry their secret to the grave. He demanded his story be told before Maciel dies.

***

The number and consistency of testimonies must have overcome Vatican resistance to touch the untouchable Father Maciel, who did not refrain from touching his members' members, coaching them how to excite his glistening Excalibur.

Irishman Caheny supports Mexican Espinosa's testimony that in his drugged stupors Nuestro Padre extolled the merits of his extremely large tool and its mighty feats. The New St. Paul did not distinguish between Jew and Gentile, freedman or bondsman, Greek or Roman, as he brought salvation to all. He even relaxed his own self-imposed high standard: "Gentlemen prefer blonds," as his boundless and irrepressible zeal for the salvation of souls occasionally even overcame deep-seated prejudices and taboos of color and race. According to the Saint in his delirium demens, his sword was two-edged, wreaking havoc among both male and female. In his transfiguration the New Christ revealed to his confidants his sexual prowess with hungry widows and estranged spouses, and how he covered all with his sacred robe. Faced with such supernatural power, the writer, another unworthy Pilate, can only exclaim "Ecce homo," "Look at the man." Behold this epitome of human dignity and integrity!

16
REGAINING
TRUST IN GOD and MYSELF, and in my BROTHERS and SISTERS

"It is a good thing to experience everything oneself, he thought. As a child I learned that pleasures of the world and riches were not good. I have known it for a long time, but I have only just experienced it. Now I know it not only with my intellect, but with my eyes, with my heart, with my stomach. It is a good thing that I know this.
He thought long of the change in him, listened to the bird singing happily. If this bird within him had died, would he have perished? No, something else in him had died, something he had long desired should perish. Was it not what he had once wished to destroy during his ardent years of asceticism? Was it not his Self, his small, fearful and proud Self, with which he had wrestled for so many years, but which had always conquered him again, which appeared each time again and again, which robbed him of happiness and filled him with fear? Was it not this which had finally died today in the wood by this delightful river? Was it not because of its death that he was now like a child, so full of trust and happiness, without fear?
Siddhartha[30]

FATHER PETER CRONIN AND THE LADS

After leaving the Legion and Mexico, and moving to Washington, I met up with three other Irish-born ex-Legionaries in the nation's capital. They brought hope to my broken heart.

Peter Cronin joined the Legion a few years after me and always struck me as a bit of a country boy, even though he went to school in Dublin. Give him his due, though, he was an upright, direct and likeable country boy. Peter was a wiry six feet, with sand-colored wavy hair, quiet and gentle demeanor, with a nice deep voice, and a twinkle in the blue eyes behind his glasses. "A true Israelite in whom there is no guile" (John 1, 47), as Jesus would have called him. And I think that set him up to have his leg pulled quite a bit in the sharp-tongued Legion. He was an earnest and hard-working kind of religious who believed in Father Maciel and the Legion and just went about his business without attracting attention. He was a good student and, perhaps, more intelligent than on first impression. Underneath the somewhat goofy surface, behind the thick horn-rimmed glasses, he was pure gold. He was also at home in the Legion's intellectual training system and became a talented teacher of Latin, New Testament Greek, Philosophy and Theology.

Peter was that tall galoot who walked into my office sometime in 1980 and told me Nuestro Padre had sent him to take over the School of Faith. If he wasn't so low-key and unassuming I might have ripped into him. Of course, he didn't know he was just a pawn in Father Maciel's Kingdom of Christ chess-game. Poor Peter, the local superior, Zancajo, gave him the boot to Monterrey, and thence back to Rome.

When I arrived in Washington DC in February 1985, I found Kevin and Declan already here, by then members of the diocesan clergy. Six months later Peter arrived. So we became the Four Musketeers: four Dublin-born former Legionaries, Spanish-speaking internationals, in the same diocese. We were as thick as thieves, and the other priests did not object. The first thing we had to learn after leaving the Legion was how to buy clothes. So on our day off, for several weeks, we spent hours scouring our local Syms store at the Georgetown Pike Plaza in northwest Washington buying colors. We went to the movies together and ate out. What a ball! And to think we were not committing any sins, even though our Legion mythology assured us that we would never make it outside the Legion: we would become reprobates without our Legion Mother's structure and strictures. In reality we were just four forty-year-old adolescents enjoying life for the first time; four forty-year-olds, previously hampered by mental and emotional straitjackets, who could finally be friends.

Why would a nice guy like Peter leave the Legion? We did not ask each other that very personal question, but there were some common themes in our conversations over lunch at Kenwood Golf Club, where Dec had secured the cheap clergy membership. Each one had his personal experience with Maciel and with the Legion, and his own idea of how to cope with it. We accepted each other fully and without reservations. Our friendship was honest and unconditional. I was not aware at that time how much thought Peter had given to his departure from the Legion.

When I left the active ministry in 1989, I had my companions' acceptance and support, and we continued to meet and have good times together. It wasn't as easy as before, because our lifestyles and situations were diverging: I was making my way in the world for the first time, free on weekends, while they were off on Fridays and busy on weekends. As priests, my friends were better off financially than this struggling newly-laicized nobody. I had no inheritance and no severance pay from the Legion.

Peter was good at keeping in touch, and he showed real brotherly concern for me. Every year he would give me these wonderful presents of Irish crystal ware and other household items, as if encouraging me to settle down and get married. At times he invited me down to Myrtle Beach at a parishioner's condo when he had a few days so we could relax together. I didn't realize how close we were until after he died and found he had bequeathed a number of personal valuables to me.

On one of our "beach retreats" in 1992 he revealed his plans for Network and I encouraged him to launch it. This effort would later gel into REGAIN.

***

In the beginning was Network

Peter, tenacious and organized, had put together a short list of about twenty ex-Legionaries he knew where to find. At that time, the Legion isolation system worked so well that members left in isolation, lived in isolation, and died isolated from those who had once been their close companions. There was no webpage, discussion board or directory. But Peter had his short list of Irish, American, Mexican and Spanish xLCs, and in late 1992 he sent out the first message. In it he formulated, for the first time in English, a critique of the Legion as an organization.

> Introductory number of NETWORK, October, 1992, from REGAIN archives
>
> Dear Friend:
> Greetings and Welcome to NETWORK. This newsletter is an effort to create a network of former members of the Legion of Christ, a way to keep in touch, communicate ideas, share our personal experiences (and maybe a few laughs), analyze and evaluate our past and, hopefully, offer support to each other. The past is prologue [Shakespeare].
> As you can see from the list of names, we have the beginnings of a network that extends to many states in the US and other countries. Please contact others you know who would be interested, mail the list and articles to them, and invite them to send me a letter or an article, a personal history or bio, thoughts or reflections which I will be happy to copy and send on to all Network members. Send all communications to:
>
> Peter Cronin
> St. Bartholomew's
> River Road,
> Bethesda, MD
> ...
> You can FAX letters to me at...or reach me by phone at (301)...
>
> I think all of us agree that in the realm of social phenomena leaving the Legion of Christ is a unique experience. Is there anything quite like it? It is unique for several reasons:

Firstly, the lifestyle we shared prior to leaving. We progressed through a series of stages—Postulancy, novitiate, Juniorate, philosophy, apostolic practices, theology and maybe even ordination and the priesthood. We were the Curso Intensivo (shortened course of studies for Irish and American students) in Salamanca, Prefectos de Disciplina (Prefects of Discipline) in Mexico, Vocational Directors in the US and Spain. We moved in a clearly defined world in which we absorbed ideas on the spiritual life, the priesthood, the Church, the apostolate, the Legion. [Spanish key] Words such as quiete (conversation time) Primerísima (feast day), Cesare (our cook in Rome), Cotija (Father Maciel's birthplace, Cumbres (Legion's first school, in Mexico City), Kranz (one of Father Dueñas' favorite German shepherds in Rome), modestia de la vista (modesty of the eyes), Nuestro Padre, Tercer Grado [Regnum Christi 3rd level of commitment], Monticchio (little village in the Province of Naples where we spent summer vacation), la Sección Femenina (female section of the Regnum Christi with whom male members had no contact) and so many others became part of our everyday vocabulary and even ingrained in our subconscious...

Secondly, leaving the Legion is unique onto itself.

It is not easy to leave the Legion. One is encouraged, advised and directed to stay by the Superiors. We went through a lengthy period of personal discernment before taking the step.

Prior to leaving we could not share the crisis with anybody except the Superior. This resulted in gradual isolation that we had to cope with and overcome.

Before leaving, we went through a difficult period of disagreement with the Legion on basic issues: aspects of priestly formation, Apostolic Schools, lack of diversity or individual freedom, lack of dialogue, the practice of confession and spiritual direction with the superior, relations with one's family. With whom could we share these concerns? Where did we seek counseling? What forum was there for a free, healthy, honest discussion of these issues?

When one leaves the Legion it is kept a secret within the order for as long as possible. Why?

Thirdly, our experience after leaving the Legion is quite special in that we emerged from such a close-knit organization into a world in which we are faced with the excitement and challenge of personal decision-making everyday.

Un Legionario se es o se despide (You either are a Legionary or you take your leave!). That is precisely what we did. However, it was our decision. The time came when we realized that it was not what we had originally looked for; the Legion did not meet our expectations or answer our needs for spiritual growth, or respond to our vision of priestly life or religious experience. We left because we had to leave. Personally, I consider my decision to leave and my departure from the Legion as a grace-filled, liberating and ultimately salvific event. It was the will of God!

After I left, I found the company and support of Declan Murphy, Kevin Farrell and Paul Lennon in the Washington DC area to be most helpful. Thanks, guys, if I never said it before! I am very happy now as a priest in the Archdiocese of Washington. I find my ministry to be diverse, challenging and rewarding. If any of you are ever in the DC area you have a place to stay right here. Is that Espíritu de Cuerpo—esprit de corps- or what!

We have all gone our separate ways, adjusting to our new reality; some in the priesthood, others in the lay state, married or single. But, we have a common past and experience—which was wonderful, fulfilling, graced, happy, funny, silly, disappointing, sad, horrendous, unjust, inhuman...(Add your own adjective). We have a lot to share. I will try to send out Network every other month. Mail or fax your articles to me or call me on the phone 24 hours a day (although, preferably, in the normal waking hours).

It has been fun putting these thoughts together. I look forward to hearing from you.

Yours truly,

Peter Cronin[31]

***

REGAIN's Genesis

1. In Mexico in the 1970s, nine of Father Maciel's one-time seminarians—unbeknownst to the fragmented Diaspora of other ex-Legionaries—had begun, individually and later together, to demand accountability for the sexual abuse he perpetrated against them. Their first revelations were addressed to confessors and spiritual directors, many of whom told them to leave it all in God's hands. They insisted, approaching monsignors and bishops, and finally taking their case to Rome. Receiving no response, they took their cause to the Mexican media, meeting with limited success. Their story finally got USA and worldwide attention with the Hartford Courant articles in February, 1997. The book, *Vows of Silence*, by the same investigative reporters, broke the conspiracy of silence and gave them a voice.

2. Network: Father Peter Cronin ex-LC had been the pioneer. He was very balanced and had a sincere interest and open-minded love for people. Peter launched a communication newsletter to a group of 20 ex-Legionaries in 1992 that slowed

down in 1998 as his pastoral responsibilities got heavier. Peter was made Pastor of St. Michael the Archangel Parish in Silver Spring, MD, and only managed to send sporadic letters to the his ex-confreres. When Peter died suddenly and prematurely at the age of fifty on September 19, 1999, Paul took up the torch.

3. Ex-Legionaries: Paul Lennon and others—who, for a variety of reasons, wish to remain anonymous, and that is why so few names appear—continued to network as best they could reaching out to ex members and administering to their spiritual, emotional, and career guidance needs.

4. The Pat Kenny Talk Show, in which Peter Cronin was prominent, broke the untouchable taboo and unmasked the Legion in Ireland, seriously damaging its future as a religious order of priests.

5. The Connection: an Irish ex-Legionary living in the USA contacted with and met Jose Barba after the Hartford Courant articles. Later, Jose contacted Paul, telling him about the sexual abuse and what the Mexican and Spanish survivors had been doing. Thus Mexico joined with the American and Irish ex-Legionaries to continue to break down the Legion's barrier of silence.

6. New Blood: around 2000, American ex-Legionaries Glenn Favreau, Keith Keller, JB. TJC, et al. (who wish to remain anonymous for fear of Legion reprisals; the Legion has now become as legally aggressive as Scientologists), began to pump new blood into the fight for truth and justice on the American front.

7. Campaign for Truth: the union of Mexican, Irish, American and some Spanish ex-Legionaries strengthened the group's resolve. Jose Barba & Co in Mexico gained greater visibility there and in the US, culminating with the Brian Ross

20/20 expose of April 2002 where Paul joined with Mexican brothers Barba, Vaca and Jurado. Emboldened, small number of former Legionaries appeared on NBC.30 in New Haven, CT.

8. REGAIN: was born of the collective efforts of all members spearheaded by a webpage guru who finally set up the website to coordinate efforts.

9. Dallas Conference 2002: As we worked on our New Haven project the idea of a REGAIN conference jelled with local members. That conference could not have taken place without the organizational skills of the newly-exited Americans, the logistical generosity of Tony F., the earnestness of Jose Barba and the enthusiasm of the "Mexican boys", and the women and men from near and far.[32]

***

Personal notes on REGAIN's 2002 Dallas Conference

Before

En route to Dallas, June 28, 2002

I have been preparing for this conference for forty years. At the age of seventeen, with seven other naïve and enthusiastic boys, placing myself in the hands of Marcial Maciel, I stepped on a plane bound for Lourdes, France, and thence to Salamanca; and thereafter lost my self. Today, forty years later, alone, with no external validation, but fully aware and free, I take a plane and fly to Dallas, to reclaim and Re-GAIN my self.

After

Upon leaving, July 1, 2002, Dallas to Houston

The spirituality that guided me during this trip was: IN GOD I TRUST.

I did not have everything planned to the very last detail, as a Legionary would—and, I must admit, I did not consult with any superiors. There were times when I did not know what was going to happen next, what to do. I was almost, but not quite, flying by the seat of my pants. The team and I were constantly pulled in various directions trying to attend to the diverse needs, insights, desires, and plans of the other participants and the journalists. But we were united in our desire to stem the tide of deceit, bad faith, manipulation, abuse and power of the Legion of Christ. We all were, like the vast majority of RC men and women and LC priest and student survivors, people of good will who had broken out of a vicious system over which we had no power and which hides its viciousness behind a benevolent façade: conservative orthodox Catholicism.

My own spiritual journey, particularly over the past two years, has been of learning to trust God. It had not been my forte previously to joining the Legion at seventeen (I had to be good and "do the right thing" so God would like me). And I never grew in trust during my twenty-three years in the Legion.

I sadly ask myself why I never learned to trust God during all those years in the Legion. Is it because the Legion is more about trusting Father Maciel, the superiors, the institution, the self-righteous cause of the Legion, its infallible methods, strategies, plans, and playing the numbers and money game? Thus, one was taught to mistrust oneself, one's brothers, and all "outsiders." In the Legion one also learned a radical mistrust of Human Nature, "the condemned mass"—more Augustine than Aquinas, more Lutheran than Catholic—and to mistrust one's personal judgment, personal freedom of choice and self-determination. In practice, a Legionary could never be trusted to be on his own, or to make choices and decisions without consulting with his superior. Someone else always monitors him, and his brothers inform on him, even as he, too, is under obedience to monitor and inform on them. Thus the much vaunted LC auto-formación ("self-formation") is, in practice, a formation from the outside in, an operant conditioning. So-called "dependence" on the superiors is actually co-dependence of the worst kind. As I reflect in my plane seat I can see the ugly flaws behind this seemingly beautiful, impressive, and wonderful spirituality which deceives thousands of gullible Catholics. I envision the apparently impregnable Legion as a pack of cards held together by the pins of manipulation, mind control, deceit, trickery, empty promises, appearances, fear, and threats—a pack of cards about to fall.

The searing pain of trust betrayed or unlearned in the Legion also undercut my faith in "spiritual direction" and "confession." I became wary of mediators between my soul and God, especially those who had co-opted my mind and will by impersonating God and Jesus. By descending into the hell of leaving the Legion and facing the nothingness and fear of a lonely and uncertain future, I began to be born again and gradually to really trust God and Jesus. Despite my misgivings, on my journey of recovery I had to open up to a priest (a Jesuit!), a happily married ex-Marist brother, and a pastoral counselor! I also owe a debt to many others for the "new" spirituality that was burgeoning in me and providing nurturance while still in the Legion: Jacques Loew, John Powell SJ, Henri Nouwen, Adrian Van Kaam, French Dominicans Père Carre, A.-M. Besnard and other Catholic, non-Catholic, and non-Christian authors.

This "secret" is known to many other survivors: while in the Legion, as I studied in Rome and later worked in Mexico, I found my own spiritual sustenance, based more on the Compassionate Love of God than on Fear. A far cry from the Letters of Nuestro Padre, harangues force-fed to all LCs and RCs as their daily spiritual bread from the moment they enter. That is why there are so many inside with empty stomachs, who just regurgitate the same stones they are fed, instead of real food. Thank God I never developed a taste for stones. I was fortunate to always be able, and increasingly with the relative freedom that came from an apostolate outside the Regnum Christi Movement, to forage for my own sustenance. Thus, while in the Legion, I began to cultivate my own parallel spirituality. This would later save me when I jettisoned all the cargo of Legion securities to find His Image again. This "new" spirituality was no longer fabricated from the outside (Legion apparatus), out of my head, full of precepts, shoulds and obligations; but rather a spirituality that flows joyfully from a heart living in gratitude and trusting in God, even while I continue to be an imperfect vessel, full of limitations and passions and even sins. Without my knowing it, God had been watching over me. In my 23-year-long desert He provided me with manna (Gospel of St John, chapter 6, especially verses 48-51).

As I trust in God I begin to experience wonderful blessings, "coincidences," Providential Happenings: Suzanne Baars, daughter of Dr. Conrad Baars, whose psychology of Affirmation I avidly read in Mexico City at the School of Faith 1975-82, twenty years later was the keynote speaker at the Dallas Conference without my planning it! Blessings like the airline "buddy passes" that despite our post-Legion poverty brought people from all over the country, or the unexpected generosity of so many; or of the two new surprise members, Alejandro and Rafael, from Mexico, of the new supporters in Dallas; of the new exLCs, exRCs, family members and friends who are finding each other and enjoying freedom, healing, and new life. That is why I say:

In God I trust.[33]

REGAIN'S MISSION STATEMENT

This diverse group of people adversely affected by the Legion and Regnum Christi loosely formulated their goals:

To inform and educate the public regarding the true nature of policies and practices of the LEGION OF CHRIST -a seemingly bona fide Catholic Religious Congregation- the REGNUM CHRISTI Movement, their SCHOOLS and all their WORKS, in an effort to:

PREVENT PREMATURE RECRUITING, MANIPULATIVE MEMBERSHIP/COLLABORATION & DECEPTIVE FUNDRAISING

PROMOTE COMMUNICATION with and between present and past members, their families and the outside world

PROVIDE NETWORKING, GUIDANCE & SUPPORT for exiting and exited members, their families and all others touched and adversely affected by the Movement's Methods & "Apostolates."

THE MATRIX AND REGAIN

One of the most encouraging affirmations REGAIN has received in its short history is to be compared to freedom fighters *Morpheus* and his crew in the science fiction movie series, *THE MATRIX*. We are flattered by the imaginary parallels that arise with REGAIN'mission

The year is estimated to be around 2199, and humanity is fighting a war against *intelligent machines* created in the early 21st century. The sky is covered in thick black clouds created by the humans in an attempt to cut off the machines' supply of solar power. The machines responded by using human beings as their energy source, growing countless people in pods and harvesting their bioelectrical energy and body heat. The world which Neo has inhabited since birth is the *Matrix*, an illusory simulated reality construct of the world of 1999, developed by the machines to keep the human population docile. *Morpheus* and his crew are a group of free humans who "unplug" others from the Matrix and recruit them to their resistance against the machines. Within the Matrix they are able to use their understanding of its nature to bend the laws of physics within the simulation, giving them superhuman abilities. Morpheus believes that *Neo* is "the One", a man prophesied to end the war through his limitless control over the Matrix.

Neo is trained to become a member of the group. A socket in the back of Neo's skull, formerly used to connect him to the Matrix, allows knowledge to be uploaded directly into his mind. He learns numerous martial arts disciplines, and demonstrates his kung fu skills by sparring with Morpheus in a virtual reality "construct" environment similar to the Matrix, impressing the crew with his speed. Further training introduces Neo to the key dangers in the Matrix itself. Injuries suffered there are reflected in the real world; if he is killed in the Matrix, his physical body will also die. He is warned of the presence of *Agents*, powerful and fast sentient programs with the ability to take over the virtual body of anyone still connected to the system, whose purpose is to seek out and eliminate any threats to the simulation. Yet Morpheus predicts that, once Neo fully understands his own abilities as "the One", they will be no match for him.

Possible parallels:

Intelligent machines...Father Maciel and his inner circle

The Matrix...The Catholic Church according to the Legion of Christ

Growing countless people in pods...Legion & Regnum recruits in LC formation system

Morpheus and his crew...REGAIN group

Agents...Legionaries

Neo...Anyone willing to pay the price

17
RESPONDING
TO THE BIG QUESTIONS

"What brought you into the army, Joe?" said Willie. "Ah, the usual", said Joe. "I'll tell you what it was, Willie. I was walking along by the river in Ballina minding my own business. My father had sent me in to see about the purchase of some bolts for the barn doors. And a girleen came along and in her hand like a bunch of flowers..."

Sebastian Barry, *A Long, Long Way*

WHY DID YOU LEAVE?

Short answer: *I grew up and out of the Legion.*

That is probably the best summary I can conjure up forty years after leaving the Legion. This whole book is the long answer.

But why did I leave the priesthood itself? I could brush aside frontal questions with a simple risposte: "Why do married people get separated or divorced?" The answers to such highly complex and intimate questions tend to be subjective and often full of self-justification and blame. The process of leaving a serious and committed relationship of whatever kind is usually long and painful. Leaving the priesthood is not undertaken lightly. Nor should the question be asked lightly. A serious study of why priests leave the ministry can be found in David Rice's *Shattered Vows, Priests who leave*[34].

Some kind of fundamental flaw?

I believe a deeper question is: Was there something in my Legion experience that cracked my vocation to the Catholic priesthood and irreparably damaged it? Other former Legionary religious have been able to transition to the diocesan priesthood successfully. Why not me? Short answer: I tried and it did not work out, or I couldn't hack it. Maybe it was just too difficult. I couldn't hold onto the back of the bus "scutting" any longer. It became too painful. Maybe I was terribly lonely and deprived of affection. Maybe I just needed to express and receive tenderness Maybe I needed to love and be loved by a woman. Had I fallen madly in love in Mexico? That would be another story. Sex and lust? God forbid! Maybe I was suffering from a prolonged Major Depressive Disorder and the Legion was not to blame—except in not getting me treatment for it. I am too jaded to try to justify my decision, but I can try to understand and explain.

There is the common misperception that being a priest is the cake and being a Legionary or a Jesuit, for example, is just the icing. The icing can melt but you still have your cake. This was basically my mother's take the day I told her I was leaving the Legion.

"You know, son, they never treated you very well there anyway. You are better off without Father Maciel and the bunch of them. Now that you are free of the Legion, you can carry on and be a good priest." I had a sinking feeling that explaining the fragility of my priestly vocation would be a long haul and that, perhaps, Mammy could never understand anyway. I did make the effort to show her that things were a little more complicated. But a lot of conventional Catholics think like Mrs. Lennon. How much my priestly calling was tied up or enmeshed with the Legion calling needs some examination.

Essentially, joining the Legion of Christ meant my training and vocation was not about being a religious brother or a priest as such but about being a consecrated religious and then priest *in the Legion of Christ.* Legionaries are not religious brothers plain and simple. Nor was I ever just a priest; I was a Legionary-priest. This specific bond, between the calling and the calling to this particular order, is often overlooked by Catholics, religion reporters and the general public: my "vocation to the priesthood" did not come in a vacuum, free standing, and chemically pure; it came wrapped in and entwined with a call to the Legion of Christ, constituting one reality: "called to the Catholic priesthood in the Legion of Christ." Were these two vocations joined at the hip? Perhaps the essential call to the priesthood, as a self-sufficient entity, was never properly discerned or tested in my case. Could it be that the vocation to the priesthood perished when the vocation to the Legion foundered? My story, however personal and idiosyncratic, may offer some insight into the peculiarity of joining, living in, and leaving the Legion of Christ, as a brother and as a priest.

The privilege of being co-founders with Father Maciel of this new religious order of priests weighed heavily. While the Founder is alive, all who join are co-founders, a positive stroke to the ego. Legionaries from my generation were greatly influenced by the personal charisma of Founder, Superior General and Spiritual Director Father Marcial Maciel; for better and for worse. Our "vocations," both as Legionaries and priests, were tightly bound up with our personal relationship with him. He was our holy leader, our guru. We were there, not only because of Jesus Christ, but because of charismatic Nuestro Padre.

My disenchantment with the flawless leader's many character defects, pettiness and narcissism, together with disagreements, clashes, and punishments, undercut my allegiance to the Legion, long before I had any inkling of sexual abuse. When the general's feet of clay began to crumble, some troops began to doubt. Today, when the Maciel faithful dismiss me as a "disgruntled ex-member," I consider myself a "disenchanted ex-member." They don't understand that anger comes from disappointment and opposition comes from wanting to spare others the same disappointment.

There seems to be one recurring theme that runs through my struggle in the Legion of Christ: my inability or unwillingness to be properly oriented by my Legionary spiritual directors-cum-superiors. Perhaps, unbeknownst to me, the wheels were starting to fall off my Legion vocation from day one: that fateful Salamanca day in September 1961 when I went to my Legionary confessor and spilled out my feelings and doubts. Most likely I was suffering from homesickness, fear and confusion. He told me in God's name to disregard my thoughts and feelings; they were the Devil's snares trying to steal my vocation—a vocation yet to be discerned. So the flip side to that recurring theme could be a deeply flawed system of Spiritual Guidance based on disregard for the true self, mixed with Blind Obedience, and a system intent on recruiting, incorporating and retaining members at all costs.

I will add a final thought that came to me as I sat at Christmas Mass on December 25, 2007 and watched the young priest pronounce his homily and perform the sacred rituals. Yes, it is hard not to be able to do that: to preach the Word of God, the word of consolation and healing for the people, and to offer the Person of Christ to his Father for the redemption of the world. Another misconception about the vocation comes to mind: that the priestly calling is given to us as a tangible, an already perfect talisman, or a recently minted precious coin. This way you would "lose your vocation" if it fell out of your pocket, or you could sell it or give it way. But what if the vocation were only a tiny seed that is dropped into the ground of one's soul? A seed that has to grow and take root, a seed that can die if not properly cultivated. What happened to the seed of my vocation? Did I neglect it, denying it sun and water?

Or did it not find fertile ground in the Legion? That is the dilemma.

***

What took you so long to leave?

The short answer: *Easy to enter and hard to leave.*

I find a bundle of reasons. It may be easier to stay in the Legion, or the priesthood, than to leave. Fear of the great unknown weighs heavily. Besides, in the Legion you are on the conveyer belt moving swiftly to heaven. Why get off?

Life in the Legion demands absolute docility to one's superiors as representatives of Christ in the here and now. This is subtly and skillfully instilled in the candidate from day one, slowly but fiercely pruning away critical thinking and autonomy. The superiors know best. They know whether you have a vocation or not. They are the ones who know whether you should leave or not. You stay if they say so, and you go if they say "go." Over the years my belief in my superiors had taken a series of body blows and I became more skeptical of their guidance

Another reason for hanging in could lie in the humbling reality of my Irish stubbornness, not wanting to give up, not admitting defeat, together with shame of losing and fear of failure. But this stubborn attitude of "if at first you don't succeed, try, try again" fell perfectly well into the Legion vocation framework or trap. Slipped into his Kool-Aid from the moment he is tapped by Legion recruiters, the mantra will later be drummed into him during his training:

I, your recruiter—or God-given superior—assure you that you have a vocation to the Legion from all eternity. All that is needed is your generous acceptance: "Let it be done unto me according to your word" (Blessed Virgin Mary to the Angel in Luke 1, 38). Your job is

to respond to the Grace of God. He will not be outdone in generosity. If you fail it is because of your lack of generosity.

There is a redeeming side to my long painful stay in the Legion: I was able to pay my debt. The Legion had invested in me, in my nine years of training. I did feel a responsibility to pay the Legion back in some way. I believe I did so with my fifteen years of priestly ministry in the organization, embodied in six years on the Missions and seven founding and launching the successful School of Faith. The Legion invested in me and I was a good investment; I did not want to owe the Legion anything. I am now glad I received no severance pay or financial help with my transition. This tranquil conviction would facilitate my psychological separation and independence from the Legion. From this free standpoint I critique the institution. I am not indebted. I am not afraid. The Legion cannot blackmail me. But they can try to bleed me to death financially with lawsuits.

My favorite image, the Connemara wicker lobster pot, may help to further explain why I stayed in for so long. As a boy I traveled to Connemara to learn the language. I went out in the black 35-foot Bád Mór with Páraic McDonough to lay the pots to catch those beautiful crustaceans. The lobster pot was spherical with a narrowing funnel at the top opening that lead inward. The bait was placed with another piece of wicker; a sharp T-shape, attached inside; close enough to the opening to entice the lobster in, and far enough away that the lobster fell inside when attempting to reach it. It's hard to get out of the Legion once you are inside.

Other images: going down the garbage chute from the top floor of a high-rise; strapped into the space capsule heading for the moon; quiet, imperceptible pruning of the young candidate until, like a bonsai, he grows only in the desired direction; cooking frogs in gradually warmer water so they never want to jump out of the pot until it is too late; control of the member's every word and action like a prisoner of war in a concentration camp; and, finally, the violent metaphor used by the Spanish father who despaired of getting his son back: "They castrated his mind so he can't think for himself!" A Dubliner might brutally express the Movement's praxis behind all the glitter: "Grab them by the balls; their minds and hearts will follow!"

As I left the Legion I had one recurring nightmare: being aboard a runaway train as it hurtles along a mountain pass; to one side sheer rock, to the other an abrupt chasm. How to get out? An express, it doesn't stop at the stations. I get more restless. There seems no way of getting off the fast-moving train. The more speed, the more scared I am of jumping; the harder will be the impact when I hit the ground. What is out there in the black of night? My companions prefer the safety of the carriage. Is this train ever going to slow down or stop?

If I hadn't jumped out the window that day in Cotija, I probably would still be aboard the Legion train, enjoying a relatively comfortable life, with material and spiritual security. But I would have remained a prisoner, bouncing off the walls of that compartment; declining into human and spiritual sclerosis, withering to death, or ending up in a padded cell.

I didn't study philosophy for naught. There is still one more radical question that a man such as I can ask myself.

***

Why did I join in the first place?

It is hard to explain to the relatively affluent, sophisticated, self-assured and self-sufficient generations of the 21st century the factors going into our decision to become missionaries in the late '50s and early '60s; a bit of everything, surely, like an Irish stew. Besides our ignorance, naïveté, lack of information and "informed consent," we had a tremendous amount of selflessness, generosity and idealism. We possessed, or were possessed by, a strong willingness to give, to serve humanity—particularly the less fortunate—and to commit to a great cause of some kind. This type of surrender of the self is essential to the Legion of Christ and Regnum Christi mystique—*la entrega, la entrega total*, total surrender of the self to the cause.

Here I am indebted to a stroke of genius from an Irish writer. Although he is referring to a couple of generations before ours, the anecdote is illustrative. All who lived in the first half of the 20th century belonged to a kind of primitive time, an age of innocence. I was stunned when I came upon this passage which points to something easily overlooked: the facility with which we and our forbearers surrendered our lives. How did I say "yes" so easily to Father James Coindreau that day in the winter of 1960 when he invited me to the Legion of Christ? A partial answer comes from the trenches during World War I, from Irish youth recruited for the British Army.

> "What brought you into the army, Joe?" said Willie.
> "Ah, the usual," said Joe. "I'll tell you what it was, Willie. I was walking along by the river in Ballina minding my own business. My father had sent me in to see about the purchase of some bolts for the barn doors. And a girleen came along and in her hand like a bunch of flowers she had a fist of white feathers, and she crosses over the road to me smiling and she hands me one. Now, I didn't

know what that was, and my mother kept bees back in Cuillonachtan and I thought she was an itinerant selling feathers, because, you see, Willie, you use a goose-wing for the bees, to be brushing a rogue hive into the carrier box, and I know it wasn't the full wing or the like, but. So I asked her, I said, 'Are you selling these or what?' and she said 'No.' 'Is it something for the bees?' I said. 'No,' she said, 'something for the war. I'm to give you that feather so you will be feeling bad about not going and go on with yourself to the war.' And I said, 'Go away, I never heard the like of that.' 'Oh, yes", she said, 'what do you think will you go?' And do you know she was so pretty and nice and all that, and I felt so awkward about it, I said, 'Yes, yes.' And of course I mightn't have gone out at all, but just bought the bolts and gone home to my mother and father, but you know, when you say you will do a thing to a person, you like to go and do it."

"And that's how you came to join up? I can hardly believe it," said Willie with the tone of a child.

"That's the Gospel truth now, Willie, and didn't my cousin, Joe McNulty, come in with me for the company," said Joe, and threw his head back in pleasing laughter, not ironical or anything like that, just amused himself by the daftness of it all, considering how he had found the war to be an all that.[35]

***

An ounce of human kindness, a pinch of spiritual wisdom, and a pound of prudent discernment would have gone a long way. But as I look back on those twenty-three years in the Legion there is more sadness than anger. And now, in the denouement, there is more Joy and Peace than sadness. On the one hand I totally acknowledge the old Irish saying: "You can't put an old head on young shoulders," and think "If I had known then what I know now…" But on the other hand, when leaving, I embraced the credo expressed in the title of a beautiful book by Père A.-M. Besnard, *Pour Dieu il n'est jamais trop tard:* It is never too late for God. In my interpretation: at any time in our lives, no matter what has gone before, no matter what we have done, God can reach out to love and accept us exactly where and as we are. We don't need to go back and fix it. No need to recover that pristine gullible innocence. New wine needs new wine-skins. We don't need to go back to that fork in the road where we think we went wrong. Who said we went wrong? God is Love. God is Here. God is Now.

EPILOGUE

The Legion of Christ, as described on its own website, is a Roman Catholic Congregation of Priests founded in 1941 (in Mexico) by Marcial Maciel (then a 20-year-old seminarian), active in 20 countries, on 4 Continents, North America, South America, Europe and Australia, with over 600 priests and over 2,500 seminarians.

Regnum Christi is an apostolic movement (official numbers around 50,000) at the service of mankind, the Church and the Legion. Founded by Father Marcial Maciel (the date is hazy), the Regnum Christi Movement includes lay men and women, as well as deacons and priests. It contributes to spreading Christ's message to humanity by undertaking personal and organized apostolic activity. (There are three degrees or levels of increasing dedication to this New Ecclesial Movement: from Commitments according to one's state in life, through a second level of greater Commitment, and finally to Promises of total consecration to the Movement through Poverty, Chastity and Obedience whereby members live as quasi nuns and brothers, similar to the Opus Dei's "numerarios".)

One of the particular characteristics of the Regnum Christi Movement is its bond with the Legionaries of Christ. The founder had the inspiration to found (sic!) a religious congregation as part of a broader movement encompassing laity and diocesan clergy. The Legion's governmental structure is that prescribed by (Catholic) Canon Law for religious congregations (i.e., brothers and sisters consecrated to God by vows of poverty, chastity and obedience).

Above information is from official Legion & Regnum Christi web pages; explanations (between parentheses) were written by the book author.

The Legion & Regnum Movement does not release or allow access to statistics on attrition and defections in any of its sections or divisions. Neither is there independent oversight of statistics sent annually by Legion administration to Vatican authorities. Independent oversight is new to the Catholic Church and unheard of in the Legion & Regnum Christi.

***

BREAKING THE CONSPIRACY OF SILENCE

On July 1, 1961, John Paul O'Connor-Lennon left his home in Dublin, Ireland, to "try out his vocation" with the Legion of Christ. This event radically and definitively changed his life. He would spend twenty-three years with the group, on a mental, emotional and spiritual roller-coaster, until finally catapulting out after a "showdown" with the charismatic founder, Marcial Maciel.

Attracted by the ideal, so common in the Ireland of the early sixties, of being a Catholic foreign missionary, i.e. a Catholic priest working in faraway lands to spread the faith, he swiftly found himself enrolled in one of the most mysterious and manipulative of present-day religious orders. The Legion of Christ is a militant, conservative, orthodox, perhaps even fundamentalist group. Public controversy has swirled around the Legion since its earliest days in Mexico, Spain and Ireland because of aggressive recruiting and fundraising strategies. In recent years, worldwide attention has been drawn to the order because of another problem dogging its steps from the beginning: formal accusations of pedophilia—brought to the Vatican's attention—against the founder. An ever-present veil of secrecy and alleged deceit, deep-rooted in its leaders, methods and system, together with a need to control the most intimate aspects of members' lives, has even led some critics to consider it a "cult-like" group or "intra-ecclesial sect," i.e., a sect inside the official Catholic Church. At the very least, the Legion of Christ and its Regnum Christ is a "High Demand and Controlling Group." This story has intended to pierce the veil.

Though systematically denying it, the Legion, in general term, does resemble the better known *Opus Dei,* which was born in Spain during the 1920s and prospered under Generalissimo Franco.

The Opus Dei has been forced to open up as a result of being criticized by ex-members and maligned by the book and movie *Da Vinci Code.* The Legion, meanwhile, continues to operate mostly in the shadows. The Legion may thus be, in some aspects, more subtle in its approach than the Opus, but its drive and single-mindedness are equally intense. Like the Opus, the Legion's stated goal is to imbue all strata of society—educational, financial, professional, social and political—with Christian, or rather, conservative Catholic, values, beginning from the top down.

Though its priestly branch has been "exposed" by now in Ireland, Spain, and Mexico, where it is under scrutiny by the Catholic hierarchies, in the United States the silent Legion, a veritable Catholic "Fifth Column," continues to skillfully penetrate private Catholic colleges, parishes, and schools. Under the flags of Orthodoxy, Saintly Priests, Fidelity to the Pope, and Conservatism the pirate Legion has sailed unhindered into many unwary families, parishes, diocese and institutions. The

Fearful Faithful, including many Catholic bishops, conservative millionaire businessmen, and the occasional undiscerning or unscrupulous politician, have been won over to the cause. Even good Pope John Paul II was conned into photo opportunities with Father Maciel, and dazzled by the Legion's amazing success, publicly declaring it a beacon of hope for the Church and the pedophile Founder a model for youth.

There are two ways to leave such secretive and controlling groups: one can either be a "walk-away" or a "throwaway". One of the leaders may suddenly ask you to leave for a myriad of reasons you are not allowed to question. And you are expected to go quietly into that dark night, accepting the how, the where and the when of your departure. Exiting is programmed by the leadership privately, individually, silently and stealthily. There is no announcement to the community, and members have been conditioned to keep news of leaving to themselves: companions suddenly disappear from the Legionary's life, usually under cover of darkness, without any forewarning, explanation, or farewells. These are "throwaways."

Because of the peculiar atmosphere created in and around the group, a member who "walks-away" feels intensely shamed and ostracized. Having been personally called by Jesus Christ, the Church and the Legion to transform society, he is prone to feel he has betrayed a sacred cause. The communal guilt projected onto him casts him as a traitor, a turncoat, and a renegade. On leaving, he experiences a defector's loss without the glamour, a sinner's guilt without the pleasure, and a rebel's risk without the support of followers. When he is "in," the member has no way to track members who leave, and so he ignores their fate, experiencing a climate of scary unpredictability.

When he said goodbye to fellow Legionaries, Paul was filled with a sensation of loss, rejection and trepidation. He knew that by the mere fact of stepping out, members would no longer have anything to do with him, in the best tradition of Captain Boycott. He would be effectively "excommunicated" from the Legion. Once you oppose, or refuse to obey, the leadership there is no turning back, no absolution and no pardon. Even though he continues to consider active rank-and-file Legionaries his "brothers," the faithful, "integrated" Legionaries will "have him for a heathen and a sinner". But that will not be said openly. The institution will keep up the appearances, "never speaking ill of one of our members." Nevertheless, among the active members an effective mantle of silence is cast over him, his work in the Legion and his memory. The only effective way for him to tell his side of the story is to write a memoir.

It is extremely important for ex-Legionaries to tell their stories. The world should know the modus operandi of the Legion and its lay counterpart, Regnum Christi; know its praxis, as opposed to its theory. The Legion-Regnum is governed by strict rules of secrecy, euphemistically called "discretion."

***

DISCRETION AND RESERVE

In a letter critiquing his Alma Mater, the late Fr. Peter Cronin wrote of the Legion's Mind Control, and "Discretion & Reserve":

"(...)

8. The secrecy of the order towards the outside world

is another sect-like trait: in the order this is referred to as prudence or discretion or spirit of reserve. Outsiders are seen as a threat; the members are actually forbidden to communicate with anybody outside the community without permission from the superior, and this includes family members. No information about the order, its practices, rules, customs, schedules, plans, constitutions, rulebooks can be given to the outside. Try asking them for a copy of the Constitution, for their rulebooks, the complete edition of the letters of Fr. Maciel the Manual of Regnum Christi, the Chapter documents...

9. There is total control of communications from the outside world and with the outside: all letters to and from the outside, including those of parents and family, are opened and read by the superiors. This is true for novices, religious, at all stages of formation, and for priests. All newspapers, magazines and books are read and censored by the Superiors. There is no possibility of having a confessor, spiritual director or advisor outside the order. This is forbidden.

10. The control of communication with the outside world is also exercised within the order and between members. Nobody can ever confide in another member in any way within the order, especially if he has a problem of any sort. He must discuss it with the superior and only the superior. There is a constant supervision, vigilance by the superior at all times. NO friendship is allowed between members.

11. Within the order there is a total lack of dialogue, discussion, disagreement or dissent within the order. There is no room for any disagreement with the Legion. The member has to accept everything the order says without

> question. The motivation? Every rule, every order, every idea of the Legion id divinely ordained, directly inspired by God and, therefore, unquestionable. The moment one questions a policy, a rule, a decision that person is punished and maybe even banished, sent to some out of the way place (like the missions in Quintana Roo, Mexico) where he can have no influence on others." [36]

Serious concerns about the Legion of Christ and Regnum Christ Movement are scientifically discussed in an introduction by Dr. Michael Langone to a presentation by two ex-Legionaries at the International Cultic Studies Association conference in Enfield, CT, October, 2003; that presentation contained a systematic critique of the Legion/Regnum as a cult-like organization.[37]

***

TRIBUTE

I want this story to be a tribute to the "silent majority" of once-young men who joined from Ireland, Mexico, Spain, the USA, and other countries during the past fifty years, who later left and were never heard from again. For whatever reasons, they "abandoned their vocation to the Legion." Returning to a modern world in which they were trained not to live, they faced re-entry in varying stages of mental and emotional disarray. Each individual has his tale to tell. I pay tribute to better men than me, and better writers, such as Alejandro Espinosa in his *El Legionario,* other Spanish language testimonies[38], and more still to come.

But many ex-members of the Legion and Regnum Christi are either too jaded to tell their tale, too busy getting their lives back, too angry, too frustrated, too disenchanted, or too...afraid to go public. Others may be grateful for the good training they received, still loyal to the Legion and to Nuestro Padre, and opposed to any form of questioning or criticism, especially in public. Yet another group chooses to sit on the fence, for a variety of reasons. Some will accuse me of "hating" Father Maciel, wanting to discredit the Catholic Priesthood, "attacking" the Pope and "wanting to destroy the Church". Are they projecting their own biases, unresolved conflicts, and a certain animus toward those of us who dare shatter the Legion's tinsel ball and smash the seal of secrecy?

Today, December 25, 2007, I will upload this manuscript for publishing. I find myself in the middle of an expensive and stressful lawsuit with the Legion. Christmas Day Mass was particularly poignant. I asked for the Light that shines in Darkness to enlighten me. (John 1, 6-9). Am I on the right path as I resist the Legion? The Legion just ordained 48 priests in Rome in late December, 2007. Am I being proud and naïve to even question this Legion that is supported so generously by so many Catholics and appears to be blessed by the Vatican? With what right do I criticize? Am I just being stubborn? Such thoughts flooded the mind as I communed with Jesus. The heart being too overwhelmed with confusion and sadness, only desire cried out: *How beautiful on the mountains are the feet of the herald, the bringer of good news, announcing deliverance,* (Isaiah 52, 7)

But let me not end on a note of sadness. Here's to encouraging and congratulating *all* former Legionaries and members of the Regnum Christi Movement who now enjoy a better life, the camaraderie of networking, support groups, and the love of new families and friends. I hope I have been able to show in my own limited way that we can honestly face and own our past, and that there is life after the Legion and the Regnum. A path of peace and fullness can open, perhaps a real encounter with that Jesus, Father, God we sought so long ago. Meanwhile, on our way, let us meditate…

The Pillar of the Cloud

Lead, Kindly Light, amid the encircling gloom,
Lead though me on!
The night is dark, and I am far from home-
Lead Thou me on!
Keep Thou my feet; I do not ask to see
The distant scene-one step enough for me.
I was not ever thus, nor pray'd that Thou
Shouldst lead me on.
I loved to choose and see my path, but now
Lead Thou me on!
I loved the garish day, and, spite of fear,
Pride ruled my will: remember not past years.
So long Thy power hath blest me, sure it still
Will lead me on,
O'er moor and fen, o'er crag and torrent, till
The night is gone;
And with the morn those angel faces smile
Which I have loved long since, and lost awhile.

At Sea.
June 16, 1833
J. H. Cardinal Newman, Parochial and Plain Sermons, VIII, 254-5

APPENDICES

I- VATICAN COMMUNIQUE CONCERNING FOUNDER OF LEGIONARIES OF CHRIST

VATICAN CITY, MAY 19, 2006 (VIS)—With reference to recent news concerning the person of Father Marcial Maciel Degollado, founder of the Legionaries of Christ, the Holy See Press Office released the following communiqué:

"Beginning in 1998, the Congregation for the Doctrine of the Faith received accusations, already partly made public, against Father Marcial Maciel Degollado, founder of the Congregation of the Legionaries of Christ, for crimes that fall under the exclusive competence of the congregation. In 2002, Father Maciel published a declaration denying the accusations and expressing his displeasure at the offence done him by certain former Legionaries of Christ. In 2005, by reason of his advanced age, Father Maciel retired from the office of superior general of the Congregation of the Legionaries of Christ.

All these elements have been subject to a mature examination by the Congregation for the Doctrine of the Faith and—in accordance with the Motu Proprio "Sacramentorum sanctitatis tutela," promulgated on April 30 2001 by Servant of God John Paul II—the then prefect of the Congregation for the Doctrine of the Faith, Cardinal Joseph Ratzinger, authorized an investigation into the accusations. In the meantime, Pope John Paul II died and Cardinal Ratzinger was elected as the new Pontiff.

After having attentively studied the results of the investigation, the Congregation for the Doctrine of the Faith, under the guidance of the new prefect, Cardinal William Joseph Levada, decided—bearing in mind Father Maciel's advanced age and his delicate health—to forgo a canonical hearing and to invite the father to a reserved life of penitence and prayer, relinquishing any form of public ministry. The Holy Father approved these decisions.

Independently of the person of the Founder, the worthy apostolate of the Legionaries of Christ and of the Association 'Regnum Christi' is gratefully recognized."

II
THE DAY THE POPE DIED
MY PARTICIPATION IN MACIEL SEX ABUSE INVESTIGATION

To Men and Women of Good Will and Open Mind

Friday, April 2, 2005
From approximately 2:45 to 4:15 pm,
John Paul Lennon, ex-Legionary of Christ {1961-1984} was interviewed by Monsignor Charles J. Scicluna, at a Church on Park Avenue in New York City regarding Father Marcial Maciel. The Vatican "promoter of justice" was accompanied by an Australian priest who acted as official notary.

DEPOSITION

I gave my personal biographical details which included my Legion curriculum.

An oath was administered that I would tell the truth in my deposition.

The content of the deposition involved my experience of and contacts with Fr Marcial Maciel: first meetings with MM, his interaction with the community; what was my relationship and dealings with MM? I remarked how he liked attention and special treatment. Had MM any special relationships with first

Irish seminarians? I was aware of some. I told him I had never been sexually abused in the Legion by MM or by anyone else.

"Can you give a character portrait of MM?" I told about my 'run-ins' with MM.

"Do you feel there is credence to the accusations that MM has sexually abused LCs?

Do you know Juan J. Vaca? Do you trust his story?

Do you know José Barba-Martín?

Do you know Arturo Jurado?" "I do."

The interview, which was sworn, notarized and signed, lasted about ninety minutes.

At one point Monsignor received a call on his cell phone. When he tried to pick it up he lost it. Later we realized that the call was from the Vatican telling him of the Pope's death. After the interview we became aware that Pope John Paul II had died; together Monsignor, the notary and I said an Our Father for the repose of his soul.

Why was I involved? It appears I was called to be a "character witness" for the three accusers, and to give personal testimony regarding the person and character of MM. It reminded me of the way the Church conducts an annulment, whereby at least one of the parties (the petitioner) has to request it and then this person must present two witnesses to vouch for the character of the petitioner. So it was like being a witness for three of the accusers.

PSALTER OF MY DAYS IN NEW YORK

In the shadow of one of our country's greatest natural disasters, September 11, the author remembers grieving for all Legionaries and Regnum Christi members

New York, April Fools Day, 2005

Walking from Penn Station to 3rd Avenue and 40th Street

City of smells,
Dogs sniffing each other on corners,
Labrador and Yorkshire;
Taxis chopping your toes,
Citizens fast off the mark at traffic signals,
And tough-looking cops;
Talkative strangers immediately intimate,
Crowded grungy elevators,
Stub-stained carpets,
Newspaper stands,
Flowers, fresh vegetables and fruit,
Tobacconists, boutiques, lobbies and
Little parks among skyscrapers.

I have come to Gotham to make a deposition before a Vatican representative.

Lament for the Abused

At 9:30pm on the night of April 2nd in my hotel room a great wave of pain swept over me,

A tsunami of sorrow for my Legionary brothers and for myself.

I cried unabashedly for them,

- For the sexually abused by Father Maciel,

For all those abused in and by the Legion of Christ and the Regnum Christi Movement in any way, shape or form.-

Maybe because I was not allowed to be a brother to them when I was in:

The floodgates of compassion opened and

Great groans of grief
Broke from my spirit,
From my very soul.
I wept for the men I had vouched for:
"Do you vouch for the integrity and truthfulness of
Juan Jose Vaca?" Yes, I do
"Jose de Jesus Barba?" Yes, I do
"Arturo Jurado?" Yes, I do

I had just said goodbye to Juan Jose, his dear wife and his precious daughter; suddenly breaking down unexpectedly:

Dear ex-Legionaries and ex-members of Regnum Christi,
We have been abused in multiple ways.
Let us treat each other with Love and Empathy.
In the name of Christ,
Let us not accuse or
Recriminate each other, or be
Judgmental, or Self-Righteous.
We, the survivors,
Some of whom have not yet been able to grieve properly,
Let us be supportive and gentle towards each other.

I grieve for the Legionaries and Regnum Christi members,
Especially for those who do not grieve;
For those in denial,
For those in avoidance,
For those stuck in Reaction Formation—'Who, me abused?
It was all so wonderful!'—
I grieve for you,
I, the disgruntled old man;

I, who have been able to take care of my mental and emotional health;
I, who have listened to the abused tell their stories;
I, who have believed and understood;
I, who have accepted their testimonies…

I, too, was a victim to some extent,
But I am no longer helpless, or hopeless;
Nor am I bitter.
I am a survivor;
Recovering from multiple wounds
To body, mind and soul.

I feel anger and wrath against
The perpetrator of this abuse.
I feel indignation because my confreres'
Innocence was betrayed and their
Human dignity was trampled on.

We the survivors
Have been tempted to strike back
Against the Church that has permitted this,
Covered it up, or took no action.
But delving into the spirituality of Jesus
Has led to restraint:
'…I am calm and quiet;
Like a weaned child clinging to its
Mother.'

We come like the Poor of Yahweh
To the temple of truth of our conscience
To plead for justice;

And our real Father who sees in secret
Will hear our plea

We, the 'disgruntled old men,'
Will insist like that old widow
Until Justice is done:
'Then will not God give
Justice to his chosen,
To whom he listens patiently,
While they cry out to him day and night?
I tell you he will give them justice soon enough.'

(Psalm 131, v.2; see Matthew 6, 6; Luke 18, 1-7)

III
ECHOES OF THE REGAIN 2004 ATLANTA CONFERENCE

(From my spiritual notes)

LEAVING ATLANTA
October 17, 2004; 6:27pm Airport

But Scripture says, 'I believed, and therefore I spoke out,' and we too, in the same spirit of faith, believe and therefore speak out." (2nd Letter of St. Paul to the Corinthians 4, 12)

The REGAIN Atlanta Conference is over. Thanks to all who helped to pick up the scattered materials: Diana, Cal, Keith, Mary...Thanks to A. for helping me unwind later and see a bit of Atlanta, revealing your youthful, bright, and brave heart...

Now, waiting at Gate 10, Concourse C, I heave a sigh of relief. But the battle is not over. Just as John Denver (Autograph) decries the destruction of Nature's endangered species, I continue to lament the ravages of the LC/RC's continuing advance, the havoc caused in bodies, minds, souls, families, schools, communities, parishes, and dioceses, endangering Humanity's most precious species: generous innocent Catholic youth.

Now you say that the battle is over
And you say that the war is all done.
Go tell it to those with the wind in their nose
Who run from the sound of the gun;
And write it on the sides of the great whaling ships,
And on ice-floes where conscience is tossed;
With the wild in their eyes, it is they who must die,
And we who must measure the loss.

Nevertheless, Gratitude and Trust prevail.

Thank you all for allowing me, during the past three Spirit-filled days, to be clown-leader, learner-teacher, mediator-lion tamer, team player-catalyst, brother-father, healer-prophet, and priest…

What a varied quorum! Old and new ex-LCs and ex-RCs, distressed relatives of members, parents betrayed in their trust, concerned diocesan workers, couples separated in the name of Christ's kingdom; men and women, ages twenty to seventy, from all walks of life, wounded in their Faith by contact with the Movement that says it saves…

Thanks to all the LC old guard, to my beloved Mexican brothers; to Jose and Arturo for taking the trouble and expense to accompany and work with the American "front"; for your great solidarity.

Thanks to Juan Jose for his testimony, and for being our AFF liaison and promoter, enriching us with the visit of Mary and her team.

Thanks to Kevin for his relevant and professional presentation, for his Canon Law and other initiatives, for his personal friendship.

Thanks, Keith, for your great smile, common sense and support.

Thank you, Cheese-head, for your wonderful testimony and focused collaboration.

Thanks to Lia and our A-L, new-born into Christ's Freedom, and brave apostles of truth.

Thanks to Diane and Pam for stretching our local and universal Church awareness, for joining in our cause.

Thank you, Giselle, for improvising a profound testimony and analysis, and for your generous offer to head the book project.

Thank you, Anne, for being one of the "surprise entries," for your honesty and good humor.

Thank you, parents and relatives, M&DD, S&CH, for your testimonies, tolerance, solidarity, for your initiatives and projects, and for allowing me to minister to you in your loss.

Thank you, Mrs. Scholar, for your chutzpah, humor, and knowledge.

Thanks, MC, for taking time out, for your courage under pressure, for paying the price of battling the Beast.

Thanks to those many others who do not want their names or initials mentioned for fear of reprisals from the Legion/Regnum Movement.

Last, but not least, thanks to Glenn without whom the conference would not have happened. Period. All, together, we pulled it off! But, as the Apostle says:

"It is not ourselves that we proclaim" (2 Corinthians 4,5a)

IV
REGAIN HIT WITH A LAWSUIT 2007

PRESS RELEASE, August 21, 2007

On August 22nd, the Legion of Christ will appear in the Circuit Court of Alexandria, VA to demand a pre-trial seizure of property of REGAIN members, including computers, files and emails referencing Legion documents. This is a transparent effort to silence a group that has effectively revealed damaging evidence about the Legion. The REGAIN organization, composed of former members of the Legion of Christ and Regnum Christi Lay Movement, has been forthrightly dedicated to helping others understand this controversial group and recover from the widely-documented psychological trauma associated with membership.

Stating the damage to the Legion of revealing these "proprietary materials, including letters and other documents compiled by Legion members intended only for internal dissemination and discussion," a bond of $1.5m has been offered for the defendants' files, and REGAIN is additionally charged to reveal all contacts with the Legion past and present, to reveal the true identity of anonymous posters on a discussion board, and for REGAIN to remove all references to the Legion's constitution, which the Legion doesn't want publicly accessible. Using techniques common to Watchtower Bible and Tract Society and Scientology, the Legion of Christ has for years harassed its detractors, undermined them professionally, and indicted their credibility as loyal members of the Catholic Church.

YOU TUBE UPDATE, September 8, 2007

I, Paul Lennon, appeared in court on August 22, 2007, without counsel but trusting in God's truth, and the judge did not give the Legion what it asked for; instead he ordered Mr. Lennon and REGAIN to hand over any Legion property in their possession by September 5th. REGAIN had until the 5th to respond through legal counsel to the original complaint.

On Saturday, September 1st a local lawyer called me from out of town offering to defend REGAIN for a reasonable fee. On Tuesday, September, 4th, I signed a contract with him, and immediately heaved a sigh of relief. Careful scrutiny of the judge's order allowed me until September 12 to return property, and the lawyer secured another week to write the legal response. So our next deadline is September 12. We have not handed over anything to the Legion as yet, and hope to be able to prevent that.

The lawyer has to be paid. Response from REGAIN members, friends and concerned Catholics and the general public has been encouraging, but we are still far from our immediate goal of 10, 000 dollars. If the Legion digs its heels in and finds more legal subterfuges we could be talking in the hundreds of thousands of dollars. Please God, that will not happen.

HEARING Legion of Christ VS REGAIN, INC. & J.P. Lennon

November 14th, 2007,

Today the attorneys for Defendants Paul Lennon and REGAIN, Inc. appeared before Judge Lisa Kemler of the

Alexandria, Virginia, Circuit Court to argue that the complaint filed by the Legion of Christ should be dismissed. The judge heard oral arguments for about thirty minutes by the attorneys for both sides. The attorneys for Mr. Lennon and REGAIN argued that because all allegedly stolen property had been returned, the complaint should be dismissed as moot. The attorneys also argued that the claim for civil conspiracy lacked sufficient detail under Virginia law.

The judge agreed that the civil conspiracy claim should be dismissed, but disagreed that the detinue claim should be dismissed. The judge stated that she would have to allow discovery to see what documents possessed by the Defendants contained "excerpts" of allegedly stolen Legion property and whether the excerpts should be returned in addition to the other documents previously returned. The judge ordered that discovery should now be conducted by the parties. The Defendants have been ordered to provide documents and answer interrogatories in 21 days, and then the Plaintiff will have to provide documents and answer interrogatories shortly thereafter.

Our attorneys will be working hard for Defendants Lennon and REGAIN in the next 21 days preparing proper document responses and interrogatory answers. We also expect that the attorneys for both sides will start negotiating dates and times to depose the relevant witnesses for both sides, including yours truly.

As some of you may know about lawsuits, the discovery part of a lawsuit is very expensive. While the judge agreed that part of the case should be dismissed, there remains a part still to be defended. We appreciate as much support as possible during this difficult part of the case.

Conclusion

I, Paul, feel it is very important for REGAIN right now to stress that we feel no animosity towards the Church, the Pope, the Holy See, the Catholic Hierarchy, or Catholics in general.

We are distressed that the lawsuit could be a source of scandal, suffering, embarrassment, or even ridicule, to many Catholics. But we must explain to Catholics, to the media, and to the public in general that the Legion of Christ represents only a minuscule portion of Catholics, a tiny cyst lodged in the Church body. This controversial order, rapidly growing in numbers, money and power in the United States, loudly proclaims its doctrinal orthodoxy and papal approval, while flaunting its friendship with certain people in high places. This can have the effect of dazzling the gullible aspiring elite, and at the same time intimidating anyone who dares criticize or even question. As if the Legion still wanted to impose its secret vow never to criticize superiors on former members and other inquiring Christians or thinkers. REGAIN's loyalty to the Church makes us want to believe the Legion's methods of intimidation are in contradiction with the policy and practice of real religious orders, the American bishops, and Vatican authorities.

V
REMEMBERING SILENT FRIENDS ALONG THE WAY

Some of the books read, consulted, studied, and meditated during Resistance and Recovery

During my years in the Legion I was accompanied by an array of authors, beacons of light and warmth along the way. In the Legion the Letters of Nuestro Padre, some of which are collected in the American edition "Envoy," are meant to be the Legionary's main source of Spiritual Reading and Meditation. I once read them dutifully but was never convinced, preferring other authors for "spiritual reading." During my exiting crisis I relied more than ever on these silent counselors. Reviewing the treasure chest of books that has survived shipwreck and resettlements I trace the tracks of my recovery.

AT THE SCHOOL OF FAITH, MEXICO CITY (1976-1982)

As director and teacher at the School of Faith I had greater freedom of reading. One of my licit pleasures was to visit La Librería Parroquial in Claveria where the owner, Father Basilio, held court. I also stocked books of healthy spirituality to sell to my students.

One of my students brought me a book one day that had an impact on me and on my students:

Powell S.J., J. (1967). *Why am I afraid to love?* Nile, IL: Argus Communications. Presently the book is published by Thomas More, Allen Texas.

I read it, taught it, and together with my students made a workshop out of it. The subtitle now says: *Overcoming Rejection and Indifference*—prophetic words that I took to heart? Anyone who has read Father Powell knows that what he teaches is spirituality with a psychological grounding. He walks the line between psychology and spirituality, as opposed to Legion/Regnum teaching, which tries to sublimate human needs and urges by rules and self-control, bypassing the emotional and psychological and thus losing the truly spiritual human. I soon was devouring *Why am I afraid to tell you who I, Insights on self-awareness, personal growth and interpersonal communication*, originally published in 1969. I became a Powell fan and promoter. Edging further along the treacherous path of psychology I bought myself

Kennedy, E. (1977), *On Becoming a Counselor, A Basic Guide for Non-professional Counselors (*New York: Continuum). And boy, was I non-professional! I did have some hard-earned Southern Connecticut State College credits under my belt from 1970, when Dr. Eisen, a hard-nosed Freudian, gave us clergy a hard time by harping on "penis envy" and other sexually charged concepts. But, just like all other Legionaries, I had no clinical training. Psychology, psychologists, and especially female psychologists, were taboo to Father Maciel and staff. The psychologist of female gender was allegedly the most serious threat to one's priesthood—meaning celibacy—and had to be avoided at all costs. I suppose my intellectual, psychological and spiritual demise must have started early on.

ON THE QUINTANA ROO MISSION (1982-84)

November, 1982:

Bloom, Metropolitan Anthony (1981). *School for Prayer.* London: Darton, Longman & Todd; "spiritual Retreat at the Poor Clares, Bacalar, Quintana Roo, Mexico"

December 20, 1982—April, 30, 1983:

Besnard, A.-M. (1978). *Il faut que j'aille demeurer chez Toi.* Paris, France: Editions du Cerf. "Besnard is so intelligent, so gentle, and so spiritual. I thought I should read and meditate him as a preparation for Christmas."

Moser, H. (1982). *Itinerario Evangélico de María.* Turin, Italy: Editrice Elle Di Ci

February 1, 1984:

Saint-Exupery, A. (1979). *El Principito.* Mexico City, Mexico: Editorial Época.

May 1984:

Hinnebusch OP, P. (1974). *Friendship in the Lord.* Notre Dame, IN: Notre Dame Press.

I purloined from the School of Faith in Mexico City, and took with me to Quintana Roo

May, 20, 1984:

Loew, J. (1978). Seréis mis Discípulos. Madrid: Narcea

June 1984:

Powell S.J., J. (1969). *Why am I afraid to tell you who I am?* Nile, IL: Argus Communications. A marginal note says: "June, July, August 1984; borrowed or stole from Ray (Father Raymund Cumiskey, LC). I needed it. It helped me during my 'last months' in the Legion."

As I research this memoir I find a dusty early edition of another book on the shelf at my condo in Virginia. How did I get that English-language book in Mexico? Perhaps it was a present from one of my English-speaking School of

Faith students which I took with me from Mexico City to the Missions in 1982. That was breaking the rule of poverty and obedience! And worse still, I kept it. I did not begin reading it until Saturday, September 8, 1984, in the middle of my final crisis in the Legion, as I coped with loneliness in Bacalar, Quintana Roo, my Mexican exile:

Kennedy, E. (1974). *The Pain of Being Human.* Garden City, New York: Doubleday, Image Books.

Yes, I am a firm believer in "bibliotherapy".

IN THE USA, 1985-Present

No date: Van Kaam, A. (1972). *On Being Yourself,* Reflections on Spirituality and Originality. Denville, NJ: Dimension Books. Inc

March 25, 1985:

Cosgrove, M., Bloomfield, H.H. & McWilliams, P. (1981). *How to Survive the Loss of a Love.* A different kind of guide to overcoming all your emotional hurts. New York: Bantham Books. A gift from Mary H-R.

April 1985:

Newman, M. & Berkowitz, B. (1984). *How to Be Your Own Best Friend.* New York: Ballantine Books.

Stearns, A.K. (1985). *Living Through Personal Crisis.* New York: Ballantine Books

I found the above two perusing the self-help section at my favorite "Yes, Books" at Dupont Circle, DC.

Tuesday, April 23, 1985:

Nouwen, H.J.M. (1983). *Out of Solitude.* Three Meditations on the Christian Life. Notre Dame, In: Ave Maria Press.

In an effort to do a Spiritual Retreat, I don't have Bloom, I left A-M Besnard, and I took Nouwen

April 27, 1985:

Hesse, Hermann. (1973).*Siddhartha*. London: Picador.

Bought January, 1985, at Eason's Bookstore, O'Connell's St., Dublin, Ireland. "Now it's April 30, 1985, first day of another stage. I start again at 3:30 p.m."

May 15, 1985, Visit to Merida, Yucatán,

Nouwen, H.J.M. (1985):

With Open Hands. New York: Ballantine Books

October, 1985:

Collins, V.P. (1982). *Me, Myself & You*. St. Meinrad, IN: Abbey Press.

December, 1985:

Newman, M. & Berkowitz, B. (1981). *How to Take Charge of Your Life*. New York: Ballantine Books.

Thank you, beautiful Susan, for your note that I've kept since then in this book: your comments on our conversation after class at CUA. You were young and so mature, capable of understanding my complex past.

For Susan friend,
Joy, Gentle, Concern;
To love myself
Who helped me learn.

February, 1986:

Prather, H. (1981). *Notes to Myself: My struggle to become a person*. New York: Ballantine Books.

February 18, 1986:

Goergen, D. (1979). *The Sexual Celibate*. New York: Image Books.

March-April, 1986:

Brewi, J. & Brennan, A. (1982). *Mid-Life. Psychological and Spiritual Perspectives*. New York: Crossroads.

May 2-4, 1986:

Raines, R.A. (1979). *Going Home. A Personal Story of Self-discovery, a Journey from Despair to Hope.* New York: Crossroad.

Thank you, Robert and Cindy, for how you helped me at Kirkridge Retreat Center, PA, on mid-life crisis, "Rivers in the Desert"

May 19, 1986:

McGann, D. (1985). *The Journeying Self. The Gospel of Mark from a Jungian Perspective.* New York: Paulist Press.

August 14, 1986:

Bloomfield, H., M.D. (1985). *Inner Joy. New Strategies for Adding Pleasure to your Life.* Signed by Harold at Humanistic Psychology Conference in San Diego, CA.

New York: Jove Books.

August 26, 1986:

Vaughan. F.E. (1979). *The Inward Arc. Healing & Wholeness in Psychotherapy & Spirituality.* New York: Anchor Press/ Doubleday.

Back from conference, San Diego, CA, and workshop with Frances V., a wise woman

October 9, 1986:

Johnson, R.A. (1986). *HE: Understanding Masculine Psychology.* New York: Harper Row.

October 15, 1986:

Miller, A. (1981). *The Drama of the Gifted Child. The Search for the True Self.* New York: Basic Books

November 26, 1986:

Keyes, K. (1985) *Handbook to Higher Consciousness.* Coos Bay, OR: Living Love Center.

May 1, 1987:

Vaughan. F.E. (1979). *Awakening Intuition.* New York: Anchor Press/Doubleday.

July, 1987:

Vaughan. D. (1987). Uncoupling, How Relationships Come Apart. New York: Vintage/Random House.

October, 1987:

Jampolsky, G.G. (1979). *Love is Letting Go of Fear.* Berkeley, CA: Celestial Arts.

Many other silent but eloquent friends have continued to accompany me on my way to wholeness.

***

BOOKS ABOUT FATHER MACIEL, THE LEGION OF CHRIST & REGNUM CHRISTI MOVEMENT

Berry, J. & Renner, G. (2004). *Vows of Silence.* New York: Free Press;

——- (2006). *El Legionario de Cristo.* Mexico City: Random House Mondadori.

Erdely, J., Escalante, P., González, F., Guerrero-Chiprés, S., Mascareñas, C. & Masferrer, E. (2004). *El Círculo del Poder y la Espiral del Silencio* [The Circle of Power and the Spiral of Silence]. Mexico City: Grijalbo.

Espinosa, A. (2003). *El Legionario* [The Legionary]. Mexico City: Grijalbo.

González, F. (2006). *Marcial Maciel. Los Legionarios de Cristo: testimonios y documentos inéditos* [Marcial Maciel, The Legion of Christ: New testimonies and documents]. Mexico: Tusquets Editores.

Martínez de Velasco, J. (2002). *Los Legionarios de Cristo, el nuevo ejército del Papa* [The Legionaries of the Christ, the Pope's New Army]. Madrid: La Esfera de los libros.

——- (2004). *Los Documentos Secretos de los Legionarios de Cristo* [The Secret Documents of the Legion of Christ]. Barcelona: Ediciones B.

Ruiz-Marcos, José Manuel. (2006). *La orden maldita. La historia oculta de los Legionarios de Cristo* [The Accursed Order, the Secret History of the Legion of Christ]. Mexico City: Editorial Planeta.

Torres, A. (2002). *La Prodigiosa Aventura de la Legión de Cristo* [The Marvelous Adventure of the Legion of Christ]. Madrid: La Esfera de los libros.

——- (2004). *No nos dejes caer en la Tentación,* Escándalos, dinero y guerras de poder en la Iglesia española [Let us not Fall into Temptation]. Madrid: La Esfera de los libros.

***

BOOKS I PERUSED

These interesting books describe growing up in Dublin and Ireland in the 40s, 50s and 60s. I did not read them thoroughly so as to avoid plagiarizing and imitating. They may strike the reader as more entertaining than the present enterprise. They can also give you a fuller picture of the context and environment of my early years.

Crossan, J.D. (2000). *A Long Way from Tipperary.* San Francisco: Harper San Francisco [former Irish monk-cum-famous Gospel scholar]

Doyle, P. (1989). *The GOD Squad.* London: Corgi Books [a boy multiply-abused in institutional Ireland of the 1950-60s]

Kenneally, C. (1996). *Maura's Boy, a Cork Childhood.* Cork: Mercier Press [growing up in Cork City]

Kerrigan, G. (1998). *Another Country, Growing up in the 50s Ireland.* Dublin: Colour Books [personal account of growing up on the North side]

McGahern, J. (2005). *All Will Be Well, A Memoir.* New York: Alfred A. Knopf [masterpiece about growing up in Co. Leitrim]

O'Carroll, B. (1996). *The Granny*. New York: Plume Penguin Putnam [humor]

Sheridan, P. (2000). *44 Dublin Made Me*. New York: Penguin Books [literary, witty]

Two masterful books about the sorrows of leaving religious life and the joys of positive recovery are:

Armstrong, K. (2005). *Through the Narrow Gate: A memoir of spiritual recovery*. 2nd Ed. New York: St Martin's Griffin.

——- (2005). *The Spiral Staircase: my climb out of darkness*. New York: Anchor Books.

ENDNOTES

[1] Hesse, H. (1973) *Siddhartha*. London: Picador, pages 3-4

[2] Miller, A. (1984). *For Your Own Good, hidden cruelty in ...child-rearing and the roots of violence.* New York: ...Farrar, Straus, Giroux.

[3] Hesse, H., id., pages 4-5

[4] Hesse, H., id., page 10

[5] Murphy, M. (1996). *Mike and Me, a memoir of Mike Murphy.* ...Dublin, Ireland: Town House and Country House. Mike ...tells the story of his, his brother Declan's, and ...other family members', involvement with Father Maciel ...& the Legion of Christ. pp.65ff

[6] Hesse, H., id., page 11

[7] Armstrong, K. (2001). *Holy War.* New York: Anchor Books, page 93.

[8] http://www.centeringprayer.com/OpenHeart/open03-2.htm

[9] Author's article at: http://REGAINnetwork.org/article.php?a=47245807

[10] Hesse, H., id., pages 31-32

[11] Google: Secret Constitution of the Legion of Christ

[12] Hesse, H., id, page 57

[13] Hesse, H., id, pages 15-16

[14] See "A Missing Photo" in: ...http://www.REGAINnetwork.org/article.php?a=47245931

[15] Hesse, H., id., pp 19-20

[16] See http://www.REGAINnetwork.org/article.php?a=47246004

[17] Bettelheim, B. (1989). *The Uses of Enchantment, the ...Meaning and Importance of Fairy Tales.* New York: ...Vintage Books, pages 191-2.

[18] *Leaving on a Jet Plane*, popular song:

All my bags are packed. I'm ready to go.
I'm standing here outside your door,
I hate to wake you up to say goodbye.
But the dawn is breaking, it's early morn.
The taxi's waiting, he's blowing his horn,
Already I'm so lonesome I could cry.
So kiss me and smile for me,
Tell me that you'll wait for me,
Hold me like you'll never let me go.
'Cause I'm leaving on a jet plane
Don't know when I'll be back again -
Oh Babe, I hate to go.

[19] Hesse, H., id, pp 33

[20] Duncan, W.J. (2006). I can't hear God anymore, life in a ...Dallas cult. Rowlett, TX: VM Life Resources.

[21] Hesse, H., id, , pp 47-48

[22] Google: Secret Constitution of the Legion of Christ,

23 González, F. (2006). *Marcial Maciel. Los Legionarios de ...Cristo: testimonios y documentos inéditos* [Marcial ...Maciel, The Legion of Christ: New testimonies and ...documents]. Mexico: Tusquets Editores

[24] Although pious Legion Tradition attributes this list to ...Father Maciel, others believe it is based on some ...famous French priest's writings.

[25] http://www.REGAINnetwork.org/article.php?a=47245824
Brief excerpt:
Arturo Jurado Guzman, 58, who taught at the U.S. Defense Department School of Linguistics in Monterey, Calif., entered the Legion at 11. He says he was 16 when Maciel summoned him to his bedside.

In a darkened room, he said, Maciel was moaning with pain he attributed to abdominal problems. "He told me to put my hand on his stomach and start massaging," urado said with a sigh. Maciel told him "to go lower and lower," coaxing the teenager to masturbate him, while the priest began fondling Jurado.

"He said that he had a personal dispensation from Pope Pius XII to do these sexual acts because of his pain," Jurado said. He submitted to Maciel's designs about 40 times, Jurado said, and when he resisted Maciel's attempts at anal penetration, Maciel summoned another boy.

[26] González, F. (2006). *Marcial Maciel. Los Legionarios de ...Cristo: testimonios y documentos* inéditos [Marcial ...Maciel, The Legion of Christ: New testimonies and ...documents]. Mexico: Tusquets Editores

[27] http://www.REGAINnetwork.org/vice/vice.html

[28] The Reasons for my Silence ...http://REGAINnetwork.org/article.php?a=47245749

[29] http://www.REGAINnetwork.org/article.php?a=47245926

[30] Hesse, H., id., pp 78-79

[31] http://REGAINnetwork.org/article.php?a=47245737

[32] http://www.REGAINnetwork.org/article.php?a=47245737

[33] http://www.REGAINnetwork.org/article.php?a=47245739

[34] Rice, D. (1992). *Shattered Vows, priests who leave.* ...Tarrytown, NY: Triumph Books

35 Barry, S. (2005). *A Long, Long Way*. London: Faber and Faber, page 202

[36] http://greenspun.com/bboard/q-and-a-fetch-msg.tcl?msg_id=00ACOa

[37] http://www.icsahome.com/infoserv_articles/lennon_paul_legion_en0502.htm

[38] http://www.exlcesp.com, http://REGAINnetwork.org

***

The author can be reached at irishmexican43@yahoo.com and through http://www.regainnetwork.org

Tax exempt DONATIONS:
REGAIN, INC,
Box 3213,
Alexandria, VA 22302, USA

Made in the USA